Home Front

Also by Peter Shergold

The War in Northern Oman (Helion & Co)

Home Front

A History of Britain at War

&

6th Warwickshire (Sutton) Battalion Home Guard

Text Copyright © 2022

The right of Peter Shergold to be identified as the Author of the work has been asserted by him in accordance with the Copyright, Designs and Patents Act 1988.

Published by Boldmere Press Limited

Apart from any use permitted under UK copyright law, this publication may only be reproduced, stored or transmitted, in any form, or by any means, with prior permission in writing of the publishers or, in the case of reprographic production, in accordance with the terms of licences issued by the Copyright Licencing Agency.

All picture credits © Boldmere Press Limited

Every effort has been made to fulfil requirements with regard to reproducing copyright material. The author and publisher will be glad to rectify any omissions at the earliest opportunity.

Printed and bound in Great Britain by Amazon

ISBN 97 9835 2073 4 21

BOLDMERE PRESS LIMITED
Boldmere
Royal Sutton Coldfield
B73 6NP

Contents

Acknowledgements	iii
Introduction	vii
Chapter 1 – The Defeat in France	1
Chapter 2 – The Civilian Defence	24
Chapter 3 – The Local Defence Volunteers	47
Chapter 4 – The Officers of the Battalion	69
Chapter 5 – The Company Officers	89
Chapter 6 – The Enlisted Men	110
Chapter 7 – The First Three Months	130
Chapter 8 – The Home Guard	150
Chapter 9 – The Blitz	176
Chapter 10 – Training	196
Chapter 11 – The Second Blitz	217
Chapter 12 – The Americans Arrive	237
Chapter 13 – Mobile Units and Maturity	257
Chapter 14 – 1944 and Closedown	280
Chapter 15 – Bibliography	294
Annex A – Battalion Strength over time	298
Annex B – List of unit locations	300
Annex C – OKW Directive No. 16	307
Annex D – Raids on Sutton Coldfield	312

Available in Part II

Annex E – List of Officers

Annex F – List of WOs and NCOs

Annex G – List of Junior NCOs

Annex H – List of Civilian Support

Annex I – Full List of all Raid Locations

Annex J – List of other ranks

List of Maps

Map 1: Britain May 1940   xi

Map 2: Britain September 1940   xiii

List of Tables

Table 1: Home Forces Structure 1940	13
Table 2: Formation Locations 1940	18
Table 3: Western Command Structure 1940	21
Table 4: Zone and Subarea Staff	58
Table 5: Chain of Command 1940	61
Table 6: 6th Battalion Structure 1940	71
Table 7: Battalion Headquarters and Staff	73
Table 8: Aircraft Markings for Home Guard 1940	125
Table 9: Birmingham Factories of note	156
Table 10: Home Guard Courses	208
Table 11: Casualties Goosemore Lane 9th / 10th April 1941	223
Table 12: 6th Battalion Structure 1942	241
Table 13: 6th Battalion Structure 1943	260
Table 14: Ammunition Holdings 1943	272
Table 15: Battalion strength over time	298
Table 16: Company strength by year	299
Table 17: Unit locations	300

List of Images

Image 1: B Company (Sutton News 1942) — 170

Image 2: The Commanding Officer (Sutton News 1943) — 170

Image 3: Gunner Edward Ruston (Eddie Knight) — 171

Image 4: No.14 Platoon, D Company (Phil Doulgas) — 171

Image 5: Sgt E Douglas and LCpl P Douglas (Phil Doulgas) — 172

Image 6: Royal visit 1942 (Philip Butler) — 172

Image 7: Mounted patrol (Sutton News 1943) — 173

Image 8: Female Section, Mounted Patrol (Sutton News 1943) — 173

Image 9: The Mounted Patrol on exercise (Sutton News 1942) — 174

Image 10: Howard (Philip Butler) — 174

Image 11: Lieutenant John Alfred Ollis (Steve Woodward) — 175

Image 12: Arthur Crutchley (Leigh Crutchley) — 175

In memory of the unsung residents of Sutton Coldfield
who died serving their town in
The Second World War

Killed in Action

Volunteer George Alfred Webster 6th Warwickshire (Sutton) Home Guard
Volunteer Sydney Barley 6th Warwickshire (Sutton) Home Guard
Private W/14376 Clarice May Thorne Auxiliary Territorial Service
Gunner Edward Ruston 378 Battery 45th (Royal Warwickshire Regiment) Searchlight Regiment TA

Killed in the Blitz

Ruby Maureen Bunford, aged 7
William Ralph Philip Haywood, aged 35
William Frederick Holcroft, aged 62
Arthur Briant
Charles Edmund Brown, age 41 – Fire Watcher
And four unknown civilians

Acknowledgements

This book would not have been possible without access to the public archives in Sutton Coldfield Library, Warwickshire County Archives, and the National Archives. Thank you to all the staff that keep these fantastic resources available to the public and for the support of Zoe Toft and the Friends of Libraries in our Sutton Coldfield (Folio), who supported me at a number of community events. I would like to thank all those who took the time to be interviewed by me during the course of this book; Eddie Knight, Steve Woodward, Philip Butler, Leigh Crutchley and Phil Doulgas to name a few. Thank you to Chris Woffenden for the fantastic images and maps he has produced, these really bring the book alive.

Thank you to Isabella Hickman who took the time to proofread this work, a painstaking task, which she did with huge enthusiasm. Finally, and most importantly, thank you to my long-suffering wife Laura for giving me the time to do this work. She is simply perfect.

I have often wondered however what would have happened if two hundred thousand German storm troops had actually established themselves ashore. The massacre would have been on both sides grim and great. There would have been neither mercy nor quarter. They would have used Terror, and we were prepared to go all lengths. I intended to use the slogan: You can always take one with you.

Winston Churchill, *Their Finest Hour*

Introduction

During the second world war over three and a half thousand men, women and children served in the 6th Warwickshire (Sutton) Battalion Home Guard. The scale of the battalion was such that on most roads in Sutton Coldfield almost a third of homes had a member of the Home Guard living there. The battalion was part of the life and fabric of war time Sutton Coldfield, which stretched from the border with Birmingham at New Oscott and Boldmere, through the Royal Town, to the villages to the east of the town on the River Tame, at Kingsbury, Wilnecote and Coleshill. The battalion was in reality a very large infantry formation, almost a brigade in scale, which as it grew, became part of E Sector, covering as far east as Nuneaton. The role of the battalion, as the war went on, saw Home Guard soldiers being called up via conscription into the battalion, manning anti-aircraft defences over the second city, and operating in mobile columns ready to respond to an enemy attack by air, land, or sea.

The life of the Home Guard was one of training, guard duties, patrols, and marksmanship, but it also grew to be one of the community hubs in wartime, providing support to those who had been bombed during the Birmingham Blitz, aiding the emergency services, and providing support to the local population. The Home Guard ran musical events from their band, football competitions, sporting galas and other fun occasions. They were made up of many soldiers who served in the First World War, but also of young men who would go off and fight in the second. They had a mobile cavalry platoon, with a women's section, boy scout runners and support staff from Bishop Vesey Grammar School. They had platoons based at local businesses, such as Boldmere Garage, and were very much part of the community. Most of all they were people of Sutton Coldfield and the surrounding area, who wanted to serve their country at its time of need. In 1940 they were willing to fight and die for it no matter what the odds.

During the war, two soldiers were known to be killed in action, both killed by a German bomb whilst manning anti-aircraft defences on Sutton Park. Others died in training accidents or were severely wounded. One Sutton resident, who was in the Auxiliary Territorial Service, died in action during an air raid; she was a mother of two.

The battalion was never tested in war, as the invasion never came, but the soldiers' spirit and determination were tested during the Blitz and during long nights on guard and patrol. In 1940 over half of the battalion was made up of soldiers who had fought in the First World War and knew what it was like to be in battle. They were on average in their 40s and had a thorough understanding of what the dangers were. There was no doubt in their mind that they would fight and die if required; they knew their job.

The misnomer of an unprofessional 'Dad's Army' is exactly that. This was a force of soldiers who were veterans in the truest sense, well led and ready to defend their homes. You do not need to be 21 to man a defensive position, you need to be able to know your job, stand your ground and fight hard. These men could do this and would have been able to hold firm.

I hope this book brings to life an important part of the history of Royal Sutton Coldfield and its people. The recent pandemic brought the people of this town together in such a way to see a huge sense of community; eighty years after the events in this book, a different challenge was faced and overcome. This book is here to inspire future generations on what can be achieved by teamwork, friendship, and community.

Peter Shergold
September 2022
Sutton Coldfield

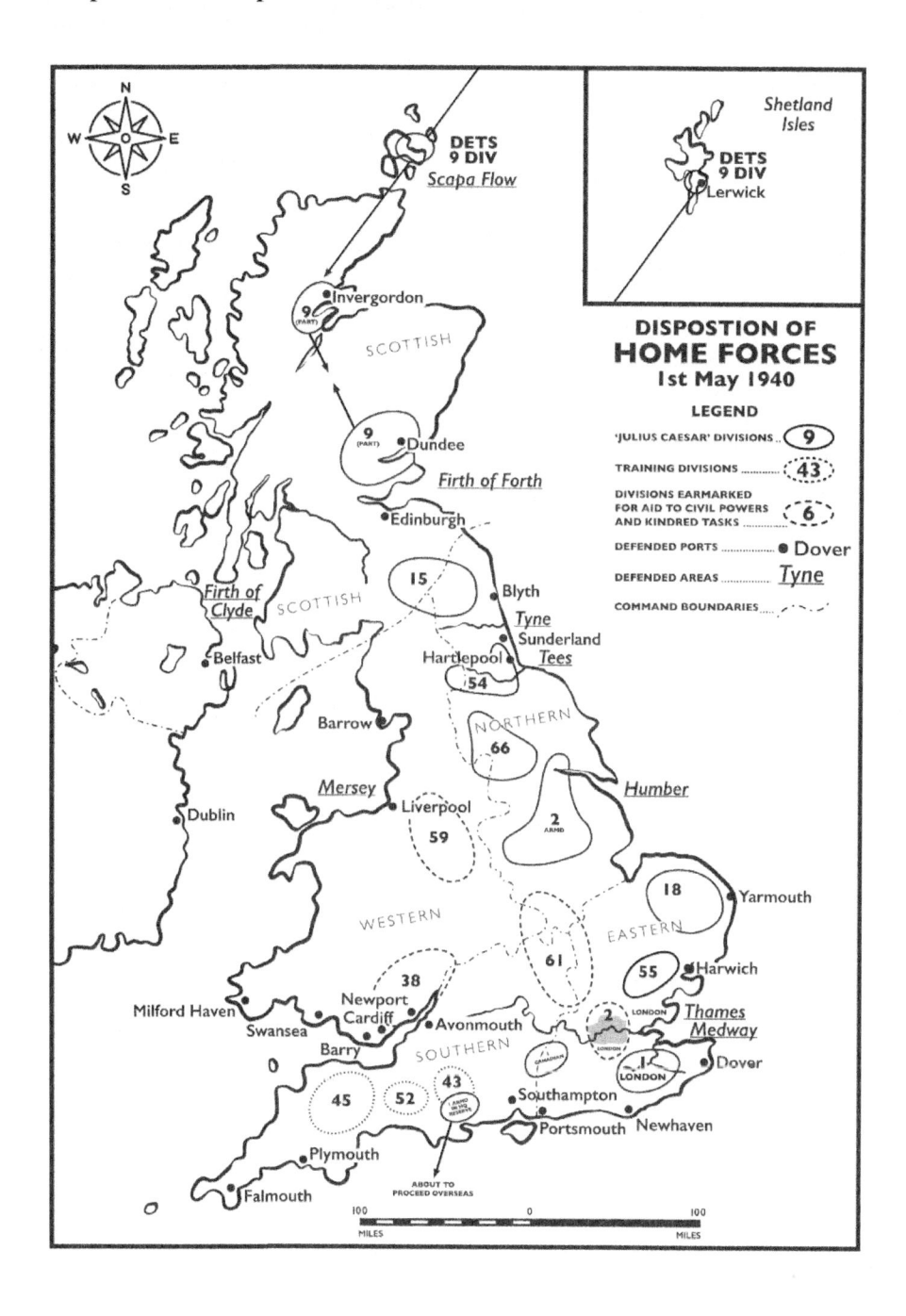

Map 1: Britain September 1940

Map 2: Britain September 1940

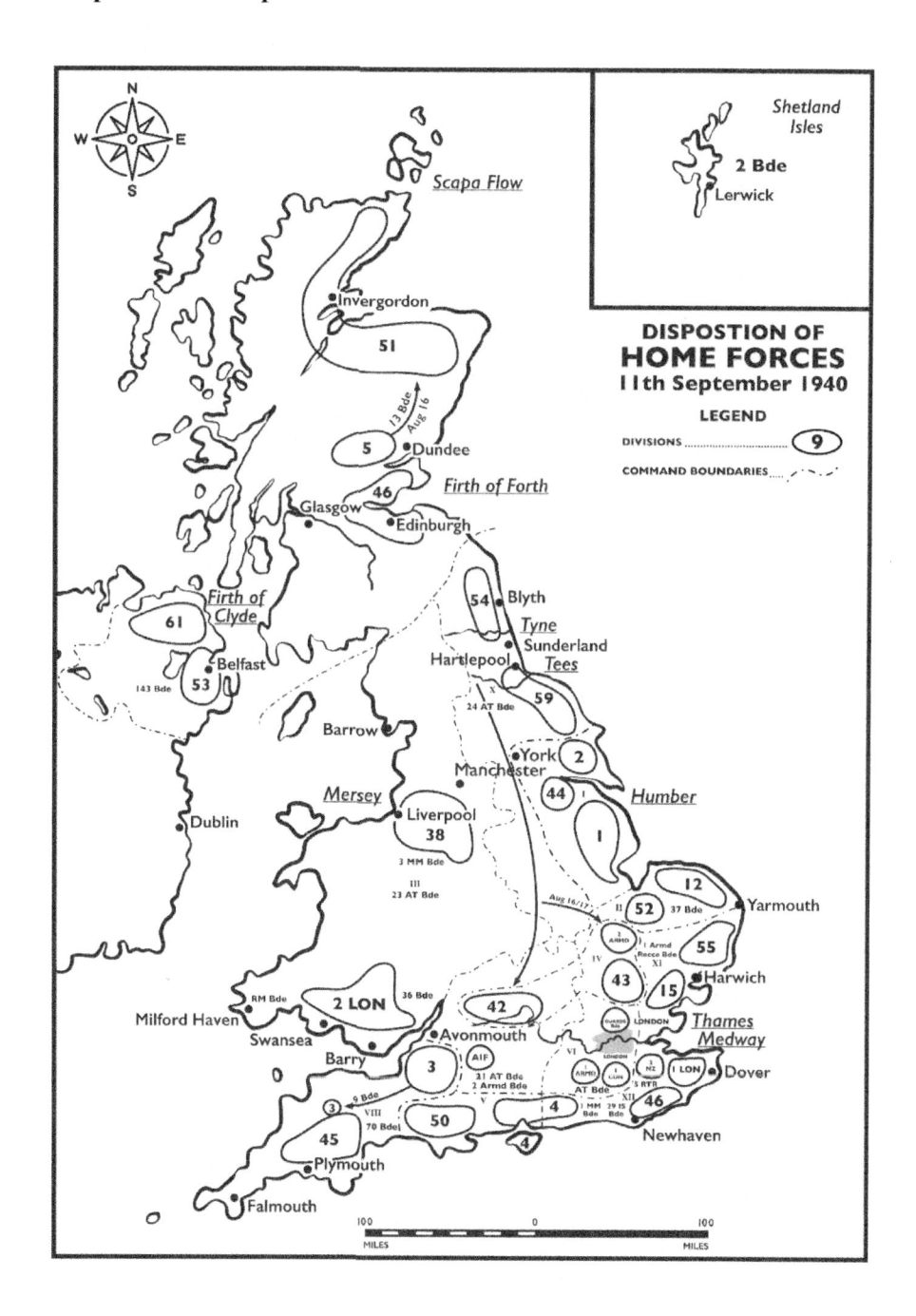

Chapter 1

The Defeat in France

To say that Britain was in a difficult position in late spring 1940 would be an understatement. Poland had fallen in Autumn 1939, and despite a period of relative quiet in the phoney war period, the spring had led to Britain's key allies being defeated one by one. Denmark and Norway were invaded and defeated, the Low Countries were overwhelmed and then finally France was defeated. Italy entered the war, and this led to the invasion of Egypt and war in Eastern Africa. U-Boats were having a considerable

1

impact and drawing on the resources of the Royal Navy. Britain and her Empire stood alone with all her allies defeated. It is not the purpose of this book to give a comprehensive history of what led to the formation of the Local Defence Volunteers in 1940, but details of the circumstances of the time, both internationally and within the United Kingdom are important in order to understand the reasons for the formation.

The 14th May 1940 was a difficult day for the United Kingdom. The British Army was being pushed into a small pocket on the French coast at Dunkirk, and although many would make it back to England through the now famous efforts of the Royal Navy, most of the weapons, vehicles and equipment were left behind with the last day of the evacuation scheduled to take place on the 4th June 1940. As the battle of France was fought, the new Prime Minster, Winston Churchill, promised that Britain could have only 'blood, toil tears and sweat' and he prepared for a general defence of the British Isles.

The British Army in the home islands, even after Dunkirk, consisted of only 15 Infantry Divisions and one under strength Armoured Division. All of these Divisions had less than half their manpower, and about one in six of their artillery and anti-tank weapons. The British Army had only 213 tanks of any real worth at this point. This force would have to defend against the huge German army if they made it across the channel. The Germans had an enormous air force and much of the Royal Navy was committed to the Mediterranean and defending trade, so a concentrated German operation could in theory cross the channel. The threat of a German assault of the home islands was clouded in a lack of intelligence and a perception of its invincibility after a series of rapid victories.

Therefore, the balance of perception and reality are not always aligned. That said, it was clear that there was a German intent to invade the British Isles, and this was articulated in Fuhrer Directive Number 16, where it was stated that "The Fuhrer and supreme commander has decided that a landing in England is possible, provided that air superiority can be attained, and certain other necessary conditions fulfilled." This directive issued on the 16th July 1940 stated that "The landing will be in the form of a surprise crossing on a wide front from about Ramsgate to the area west of the Isle of Wight. Units of the Air Force will act as artillery, and units of the Navy as engineers."

Directive 16 stated further that "The Army will lay down the methods by which the invasion is to be carried out and the individual forces to be employed, and will determine points of embarkation and disembarkation in conjunction with the Navy". But what were the forces which would complete such a task? The German Army at this point was overwhelming all opposition which they faced. In the public mind, these were largely through two new types of weapons, armour, and paratroopers. There was no shortage of land based German Army forces to land in the United Kingdom and although they were limited in amphibious warfare, they had some experience from landings in Norway. The Operation Sea Lion plan of 25th July 1940 showed a force of nineteen infantry divisions and eight Panzer and Motorised Divisions. Such a force, if landed would have not only outnumbered the British forces but would also have had a greater amount of modern equipment and mobility.

In the spring of 1940, the German Army had 7000 fully trained paratroopers, however, losses in the Poland Campaign had already reduced these to a single regiment of 4500[i] men. The invasion of Holland, particularly the assault on the border forts and the 'Battle for the Hague', caused further losses, noticeably among transport aircraft, with 213 of the 475 *Junkers 52* transports being damaged or destroyed[ii]. These losses meant that the *Fallschirmjeger* could deploy only 3000 men during an invasion of the British Isles. However, the number of available aircraft for Operation Sealion did increase as the losses from initial campaigns were made up over time. By the 11th July there were available for the *Fallschirmjeger* 100 gliders and 400 *Junkers 52*. On 16th July 1000 *Junkers 52* and 75 gliders were available. By late August, 270 of these aircraft were moved to Romania, but despite this, the lift capacity had increased to a likely attack force of 15,000 men.[iii]

Despite this loss of equipment and manpower, the intelligence to inform British defences of these losses was not present, therefore there was a fear that the English Channel, which has held off many invaders, would not be able to do so against this force. "The threat of invasion had suddenly become real, and if one single factor seized the public imagination, it was the German use of parachute troops. This innovation seemed to render the Royal Navy, England's traditional bulwark against invasion, impotent."[iv] This view was captured very much in the public mind with the press dubbing the Home Guard when formed as 'parashots'[v] showing the reaction was from the threat from the skies above. This was the first threat of invasion to middle England, where traditionally such threats would have been handled along the coastline and this danger was really a twin threat in the mind of the population of parachutists and traitors.

The *Fallschirmjeger* landings would have been supported by the special forces of Special Brigade 800 which included three battalions of special forces, first amongst these the Brandenburg Regiment. This unit had conducted a number of infiltration and assault operations during Operation Yellow, (the invasion of Holland). This new method of attack seemed to render the Royal Navy, England's traditional bulwark against invasion, impotent. Such uses of special forces were, in the minds of the British population, a key threat, and rumours of enemy spies and saboteurs landing as nuns, and other such methods were rife. During 1940 very few enemy agents landed, and all were captured and imprisoned, many being turned into double agents, but the perception of the threat was high in the minds of the population, which was heightened as the secret services did not advertise their success.

The armoured units of the German Army were a potent force, and considerably outnumbered the British equivalents. In 1940 the German Wehrmacht had five active Panzer Divisions, mainly armed with Panzer I and II light tanks formed into four battalions, split into two regiments, in total over 300 tanks in each division. In addition, there were four Light Divisions, which contained a mixture of combined arms units, including each containing a battalion of 60 armoured cars, and a battalion of 39 Light Panzer II Tanks. Both of these units contained motorised artillery, anti-tank and motorised reconnaissance forces. In comparison the British 1st and 2nd Armoured Divisions were the only remaining intact formations in Britain and contained a total of 395 Light Tanks, 72 Infantry Tanks and 33 Cruiser Tanks.[vi] At the same time, there were only 37 Armoured Cars and 54 two pound Anti-Tank Guns available to the British. The German forces in France had well over two thousand tanks at this point, compared to the few hundred in the British arsenal. If the Germans were able to successfully cross the channel with armoured forces intact, they would vastly outnumber and outgun the defenders, as well as having much more experience from recent campaigns of mechanised warfare.

But how would these forces cross the channel? Directive 16 was clear that it was the role of "the Navy [to] procure the means for invasion and [to] take them [to England], in accordance with the wishes of the Army, but with due regard to navigational considerations." The *Kriegsmarine*, the Navy of Germany, was much smaller than the Royal Navy, however its ships were concentrated in Europe, whereas the majority of the Royal Navy were deployed across the world defending trade and the Mediterranean. The Germans did not need to achieve a defeat of the Royal Navy but had to be able to dominate the channel and allow the transportation of fighting troops across a narrow straight. The support of the *Luftwaffe* would be needed to do this, combined with the mass use of mines and other equipment. The Kriegsmarine could field a force of around four battle ships, two heavy cruisers and six light cruisers, supported by a large number of destroyers and torpedo boats, although some had been lost in Norway. Such a force, as used in the Norway campaign, could hold off the Royal Navy, and block their entrance to the channel to allow the movement of the Wehrmacht forces.

Despite the local *Kriegsmarine* forces they could bring into action, there was a reality that to sustain any force landed, the channel would have to be held for a number of weeks, if not months. The Germans were reliant on mines, and coastal artillery to do this, over the use of their ships, which in turn meant that the frontage of any assault would have to be a lot less that the Army would have wished. Directive 16 stated that "It is also the task of the Navy to co-ordinate the setting up of coastal artillery i.e. all artillery, both naval and military, intended to engage targets at sea-and generally to direct its fire. The largest possible number of extra-heavy guns will be brought into position as soon as possible in order to cover the crossing and to shield the flanks against enemy action at sea." The use of artillery against ships was not entirely appropriate in this case, as such guns were not trained or designed to fire at a moving sea target, except in a small number of cases with coastal artillery. In addition, the statement of using the navy like engineers and artillery, treated the channel crossing as a river crossing in terms of the army, which was a considerable underestimate of the challenges involved, which would be shown later in the war. There was also a lack of amphibious shipping, which meant that only a limited number of troops could be moved across the channel and in the calmest of conditions.

Key also to the invasion plans was the domination of the sky above the channel and southern England by the *Luftwaffe*. Directive 16 was clear with this, stating that "the task of the Air Force will be: To prevent interference by the enemy Air Force, to destroy coastal fortresses which might operate against our disembarkation points, to break the first resistance of enemy land forces, and to disperse reserves on their way to the front." The tactical use of the *Luftwaffe* in this way was tried and tested throughout the campaigns in Poland and the Low Countries. It would be critical to the defence of Britain that the Royal Airforce should prevent the *Luftwaffe* from achieving this domination.

Another important aspect of the invasion plan was the closest cooperation of the three services in their plans. Directive 16 talked about the movement of headquarters to facilitate this, "from 1st August the operations staffs of Commander-in-Chief Army, Commander-in-Chief Navy, and Commander-in-Chief Air Force are to be located at a distance of not more than 50 kilometres from my [Hitlers *Oberkommando Der Wehrmacht*] Headquarters (Ziegenberg)". This collaboration was in reality limited, with the difficult interservice rivalries actively encouraged by Hitler. That said, despite these issues, the Wehrmacht has seen huge successes over the last year, and Hitler was at his peak of respectability, therefore the invasion plans were seen as credible and were started to be planned in detail as the summer moved on.

The Wehrmacht had the equipment and morale to conduct an invasion, it was only the reticence of Hitler to commit to the invasion which meant it was not launched earlier, and then the defeat of the *Luftwaffe* by day, and the focus on strategic bombing which would lead to indefinite cancellation. During the nights of the of 1st and 2nd August a large number of leaflets were dropped on the United Kingdom, as a last appeal to reason. This was a copy of the Reichstag 'peace offer', but although most British people saw this as a joke, Hitler had not given up on the British throwing in the towel. Again, on the 30th August Von Brauchitsch (Commander in Chief of the German Army) gave orders for Operation Sea Lion that stated that "execution depends on political situation". Despite these delays, the plan became more credible over time before its cancellation, with the increased collaboration of the services, and the increase in availability of shipping and aircraft.

There was much political argument in Britain after the defeats in the Low Countries, and the battle of France, but what opposition there was to Britain continuing the fight was defeated by the new Prime Minster, Winston Churchill. The main dissenter, Lord Halifax had turned to follow Churchill's lead, on the 22nd July, stating publicly "We shall not fighting until freedom is secured", but stating defiance and being able to win were two different things. To counter such a threat, "Total Defence, as it became known, transformed the political, military, social and physical landscape of Britain"[vii] The mobilisation of the population of the United Kingdom in defence of these islands became a huge task, which involved not only people's willingness to learn to fight, but also a huge bureaucratic effort to mobilise and organise those willing people into a force which had utility. The Home Guard would be a critical and by far the largest element of this mass mobilisation.

> *Sometimes on a Tuesday or a Thursday winter's evening in years to come, we shall surely be sitting at home, by the fireside, listening to the rain beating upon the window pane and the wind howling, and we shall think of those four winters when we used to turn out for Parade at the Drill Hall. Perhaps a friend will be there to share our thoughts and we shall start yarning about those Home Guard days and nights...*[viii]

The Royal Navy started to concentrate its forces of the Home Fleet, distributing Destroyers to the ports on both the eastern and southern coast. This tactical use was controversial, as it reduced flexibility, but would allow an immediate response in case of invasion, before the majority of the Home Fleet could move down the east coast. Fighter Command also reduced its commitment to the last days of the battle of France, allowing a considerable build up of forces ready for the enemy to attack. Throughout that long summer, and before the main German assault would start in late August, both the Royal Airforce and Royal Navy enhanced their preparations for defence.

The role of defeating the enemy when they arrived would fall to the British Army. By mid-June the reconstituted British Expeditionary Force (52nd Division, 1st Armoured Division and 1 Canadian Division) had been brought back from Cherbourg, St Malo and Brest. 368,491 British, 25,000 Polish and 5000 Czechs were included in these numbers; they would form the basis of formations which would now be established. Alongside the troops, 300 artillery pieces and 3000 vehicles returned, all of which were urgently needed. In view of his exceptional responsibilities, the Commander-in-Chief, Home Forces, was given direct access to the Government, and set up an Advanced Headquarters close to the Cabinet War Room, where he and his senior officers would be available for consultation by ministers and the Chiefs of Staff if invasion came.

The structure of the British Army was complex and divided across the three services. Even within the army, elements sat within the Air Ministry, such as Anti-Aircraft Command, and under the Navy with local Navy Defences and fortifications. With the small size of the British Army there was a need to provide a mechanism for mass defence across the United Kingdom. The size of the defence of the United Kingdom was to build to an impressive scale in both its scope and detail especially as it was formed in such a rapid period of time. This speed of mobilisation was largely because the defence was based up on the existing Regional Commands which sat under General Headquarters Home Forces. The 'Command' was originally an administrative formation, designed to ensure that all army units within, (regular, territorial, and reserve), were trained and administrated effectively. They were commanded by a Lieutenant General who had a relatively small administrative staff.

Throughout the war, the Regional Commands were updated to allow for effective defence, and for better coordination between the various districts and sub districts. Sutton Coldfield in the northeast of Birmingham was in the centre of the United Kingdom and therefore played a critical part of the boundary of these Regional Commands. Initially as war broke out the areas of Sutton Coldfield and Birmingham were under the geographical area covered by Southern Command, it found itself low on the priority list in this command over those counties on the south coast who faced invasion. However, the introduction of the General Headquarters Plan saw poorer quality units being based on the coast, and the more powerful units inland ready to strike post invasion and in the most effective way. In addition, at this time the main threat from invasion was seen to be through East Anglia, and therefore the Eastern Command was also on the front line.

The Territorial Army was based across the United Kingdom and formed into a series of Infantry Divisions. In April 1939, each first line Territorial Army Division was ordered to form a second line Divisions. The first line units were mobilised on the outbreak of war and the majority deployed to defend France. With the expansion of the Territorial Army, the divisions of Southern Command differed in their approach. The 43rd (Wessex) Division split geographically with a new 45th Infantry Division taking on the north and east of the region. However, the 48th (South Midland) Division, to which most of the Territorial Army units in North Birmingham and Warwickshire belonged, formed the 61st Infantry Division which covered its entire recruiting area. The 61st Division was deployed for Home Duties in Northern Ireland from 1940 to 1943.

The Territorial units within these areas were largely administered through a parallel structure, the local Territorial Army Association. These associations were charged with ensuring that reserve units were fully administered; this was conducted separately to ensure there was not an excessive burden on regular forces. The responsibilities of the Territorial Army Association included accommodation, allowances and expenses, clothing equipment and stores, finance and accounts, records of personnel and transport. Once a unit was mobilised, the responsibility moved to the regular forces in the 'Command' in which the mobilised unit found itself, however, any training and depots remained under the charge of their home association.

The first significant change to the Commands came on the 19th June, with a redrawing of the boundaries to move much of the Midlands into Western and Northern Commands, allowing a greater focus on the coastal areas for Southern and Eastern Commands. Southern Command now only stretched as far as Gloucester and Oxfordshire, with Birmingham and Buckinghamshire working with them to form the South Midlands Area. In the Midlands itself a new Central Midlands Area was formed within Western Command, containing Birmingham Garrison, and three Subareas, Birmingham and South Staffordshire; Warwickshire and Coventry; and Worcestershire. The boundary for Birmingham and South Staffordshire was the A5 main road, leaving the majority of rural Staffordshire in the West Lancashire area, but bringing the urban midlands into one command.

Northamptonshire moved into East Midlands Area, part of Northern Command, therefore leaving the River Tame running up to the Peak District as the eastern boundary of Western Command. This consolidation left Warwickshire Subarea, as part of Central Midland Area as a fortified block in the centre of the country, able to react to the south or east dependent upon the enemy threat. To that end it was central to any invasion counterattack plans.

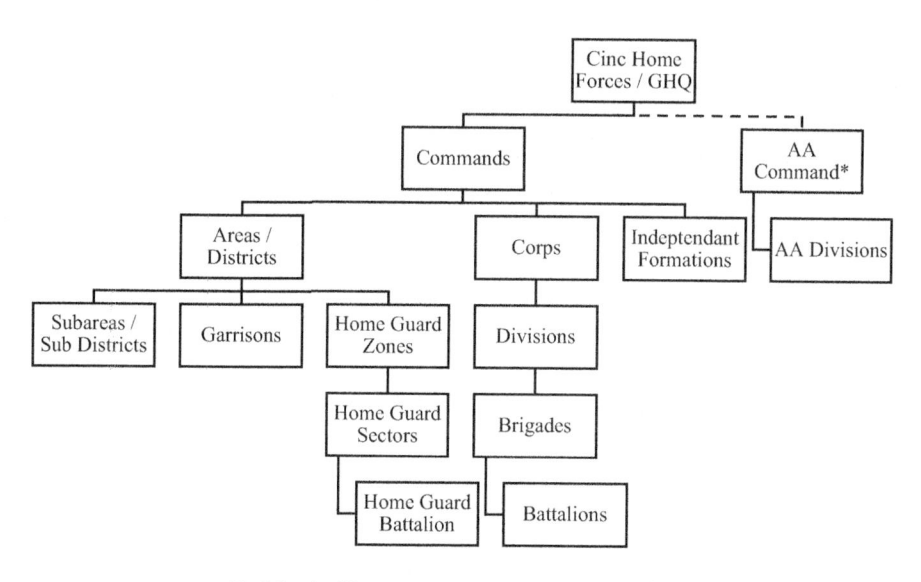

Table 1: Home Forces Structure 1940

In June 1940, a new series of corps headquarters were formed with the evacuation of the British Expeditionary Force from France. They were numbered V Corps to XII Corps (minus IX Corps which was not formed until April 1941). These Corps were allocated to the regional commands to allow a Corps level tactical command structure of the divisions which remained in the United Kingdom for homeland defence. They also allowed a separate regular chain of command for the army in addition to the Local Defence Volunteer (Home Guard) forces within the commands.

By the end of the summer there were 26 Divisions across 11 Corps in five Commands. Two additional Division, 61st (2nd South Midlands) and 53rd (Welsh), were based in Northern Ireland District under VI Corps. Working from Scotland south, Scottish Command did not have a Corps, but directly commanded three infantry Divisions, these were 51 (Highland), 5th and 46th Divisions. Northern Command which covered from the Scottish Boarders in the northeast, down the east of the Pennines until the Wash and the East Midlands had two Corps Headquarters, I and X. I Corps had returned from France as part of the British Expeditionary Force, and was based in Hickleton Hall, South Yorkshire. It contained 1st, 2nd and 44th (Home Counties) Divisions and was seen as a mobile defensive force with its Regular Divisions at its corps. X Corps was a new Corps formed in June 1940 and was based at Scotch Corner near Darlington largely on anti-invasion duties with 54th (East Anglian) and 59th (Staffordshire) Divisions.

Eastern Command was on the front line of anti-invasion duties, covering both East Anglia and also the southeast of the United Kingdom. Although later in 1940 a new South East Command would be formed to take over the responsibilities at the straits of Dover, it was initially Eastern Command where the brunt of the defences were to be formed. This was especially the case as it was perceived that the main German threat was to be against East Anglia. Within Eastern Command there were four Corps Headquarters, II, VII, XI and XII. At Lower Hare Park near Newmarket II Corps had its headquarters. It consisted of the 4th, 43rd (Wessex) and 52nd (Lowland) Divisions. Again, it was a regular force which had been part of the British Expeditionary Force and seen as a mobile defensive corps. VII Corps, based at Headley Court in Surrey, consisted of 1st Canadian Infantry Division, 1st Armoured Division, and 2nd New Zealand Expeditionary Force. The Corps was placed under the command of Lieutenant-General Andrew McNaughton, a Canadian Army officer who had been tasked to counterattack and destroy any enemy forces invading the counties of Surrey, Kent, Sussex and Hampshire. XI Corps based at Bishop's Stortford in Hertfordshire (containing the 15th (Scottish) and 55th (West Lancashire) Divisions), and XII Corps based at Royal Tunbridge Wells in Kent, (containing the 1st London Infantry Division (renamed 56th (London) Infantry Division 18 November 1940)) and 45th Infantry Division both had static defensive roles along the coast.

Southern Command covered from Hampshire across to Cornwall but also up to Bristol and the approaches to the Midlands, it had three Corps Headquarters, IV, V and VIII. IV Corps, based at Guilsborough House near Northampton. It commanded most of the armoured reserves of the British Army and was envisaged as a counter-attack force under its commander Lieutenant-General Sir Francis Nosworthy. It contained 2nd Armoured Division (which after Dunkirk became the main priority for armoured reinforcement), 42nd (East Lancashire), 43rd (Wessex) Division and 31st Independent Brigade Group. V Corps was based at Bhurtpore Barracks in Tidworth Camp and contained 4th Infantry Division, and 50th (Northumbrian) Infantry Division. It was largely tasked with static defence of the south coast. VIII Corps was based at Pyrland Hall near Cheddon Fitzpaine in Somerset and it commanded the 3rd and 48th (South Midland)

Divisions largely on static defences of Somerset, Devon, Cornwall and Bristol.

Finally, Western Command, which spread from Gloucester to the Scottish Borders, and also covering Wales, had only III Corps under Command, based at the Old Rectory in Whitchurch, Shropshire, which contained 35th Division and 38th Welsh Division. The 38th Welsh was replaced by 2nd London in June 1940. To build up the manpower of the surviving formations of the British Expeditionary Force, four second line Divisions were disbanded on the 23rd June 1940. This included the 23rd (Northumbrian), 66th Division, 12th (Eastern) and the improvised Beauman Division.

The command structure was complicated further as it was these regular forces which were drawn upon for much of the administrative structure in the Districts, Areas and Zones across the country, as well as to provide a training system for the huge number of forces that needed mobilising at this time. In addition to this structure, there was also the overlapping Anti-Aircraft Command, which had seven Anti-Aircraft Divisions across the Commands, moving to face new threats over time. As threats changed, and new formations joined the order of battle, the Divisions within Corps and Commands also changed, causing new relationships and liaisons to take place.

Despite the concept of Britain standing alone, the Imperial contribution was considerable even in the summer of 1940. This contribution meant that even the limited 15 Divisions that were available to the British Army were backed up by forces from across the globe. Not only that, Imperial troops were able to take over garrisons and allow British regiments and formations to return home. Directly in support of the United Kingdom, and based in the Home Islands by the summer, were 1st Canadian Infantry Division, and by September, the 2nd Canadian Infantry Division, both with attached artillery units. The 6th Australian Division arrived in the United Kingdom that summer, and two New Zealand Infantry Brigades also landed. The Indian Army largely took over responsibilities in the sub-continent and in Africa and the Far East, however some mule transport companies arrived that summer. In addition, an artillery regiment, (1000 men strong) arrived from Newfoundland, along with several well trained Pioneer Companies. These contributions were not insignificant and helped Britain in its time of need.

By late 1940 the command boundaries had been changed, and Sutton Coldfield and Warwickshire would find itself, for the remainder of the war, under Western Command. Throughout the war, the county was on the boundary of the four main geographical commands and therefore was a key area of liaison and defence. In 1940 Southern Command was under Lieutenant General Sir Bertie Fisher. The Command was broken down into a series of Areas, some of which had Subareas, or Garrisons. Warwickshire was in the South Midlands Area, but within this was the Birmingham Subarea (also referred to as Birmingham Garrison).

The South Midlands Area was commanded by Colonel H T MacMullen MC, and Birmingham Garrison by Colonel P Docker TD TA. The Area level of command was a subdivision of the 'Command' and in terms of its logistical and administrative responsibilities, it has a very small staff to perform these. The Subarea even less so, with Colonel Docker having only one member of staff, his Garrison Adjutant. The South Midlands Area covered a large amount of territory, including Worcestershire, Warwickshire, Northamptonshire, Buckinghamshire, Berkshire, Oxfordshire and Gloucestershire. This vast area of land included Birmingham Garrison in its very north. Warwickshire was on the boundary with Western Command and the West Lancashire Area and Northern Command, through North Midlands Area.

Command	Scotland Command	Northern Command	Western Command	Eastern Command	Southern Command
Corps		I / X	III	II / VII / XI / XII	IV / V / VIII
Divisions	51 / 5 / 46	54 / 59 / 44 / 1 / 2	35 / 2 Lon	43 / 1 Armd / 4 / 45 / 15 / 1 CAN / 2 NZ / 1 Lond / 55 / 52	3 / 50 / 48 / 2 Armd / 42

Table 2: Formation Locations 1940

The Command structure of the United Kingdom went through a series of changes during the war, however on the outbreak, the operational chain of command was through Commander in Chief Home Forces, to the Regional Commands. As previously stated, within these Regional Commands sat Districts, which at various times these were also referred to as Areas. The Central Midland Area was made up of Worcestershire, Warwickshire and Herefordshire. The Area Commander was Brigadier J Blakiston-Houston CB DSO and to command his staff there was a General Staff Officer 1st

Grade responsible for the Home Guard; this was in 1940 Brigadier (The Honourable) Cuthbert Audrey Lionel Graham DSO. Supporting the 'Area' were a number of staff functions; there were two majors and five captains in various general staff roles. The Adjutant General's and Quartermaster General's Staff consisted of the Assistant Adjutant and Quartermaster General Lieutenant Colonel RHM Lee of the Worcestershire Regiment, supported by three majors and two captains. These staff dealt with the personnel administration and logistical issues in the district. In addition, there were specific medical staff under the Assistant Director of Medical Services, Lieutenant Colonel G Petit MC, with two Majors in support, including a hygiene specialist. Overall, the staff contained the following functions in 1941:

- Assistant Director of Medical Services
- Deputy Assistant Director of Medical Services
- Deputy Assistant Director of Hygiene
- Assistant Director of Ordinance Services
- Deputy Assistant Director of Ordinance Services
- Deputy Assistant Provost Marshall
- Staff Officer Air Defence
- Intelligence Officer
- Area Cipher Officer
- Area Education Officer
- Area Catering Officer
- Assistant Inspector of Messing By-Products
- Entertainment Officer
- Agricultural Officer

Prior to 1941 the Regimental Depots took responsibility for the training of recruits, but in August of 1941 the responsibility was given to the Regional Commands. New Infantry Training Centres were opened, with No.22 ITC opening in Warwick for the Royal Warwickshire Regiment. By seeing these function, there can be a wider understanding of the logistical functions of the Area structure. However, as the war continued the responsibilities of the Subarea and Zone rapidly increased and staff functions grew to reflect this.

Therefore, within Western Command were a huge number of organisations and units from the Army, not to forget that on top of this were a layer of Airforce, Naval Coastal Defence and Anti-Aircraft units of all types. III Corps was very much independent of the defensive Areas, and Independent Units also maintained a separation by their specific tasks. Territorial Units were still mobilising troops into their units through depots, and regular unit depots were trying to bring in recruits on top of this. Huge logistical organisations were being formed to support the massive expansion of the Army, and all of this activity was supported by a considerable civil servant and industrial mobilisation never before seen.

Within the Area (or District) were a series of Subareas. Warwickshire Subarea (again sometimes referred to as a District) comprised of the County of Warwickshire but also the addition of Dudley from Worcestershire. The Subarea sat on the boundary of the Central Midland Area with the North Midland and used Watling Street as its boundary. Warwickshire Subarea was commanded in 1941 by Colonel NV Blacker DSO MC. Colonel Blacker was of the East Yorkshire Regiment (Regular Army Reserve of Officers) and had commanded 210 Independent Infantry

Brigade from 10th October until 4th November 1940. He then moved to Warwick Subarea as the independent Brigades were no longer required, and a larger established structure based on Regional Commands was needed. In support was a General Staff Officer Grade 3 Captain JEM Maw MBE who was in 1941 a Staff Captain, Captain CE Stearns OBE an Intelligence Officer and in 1941 Lieutenant LG Tredwell as Territorial Army Reserve officer.

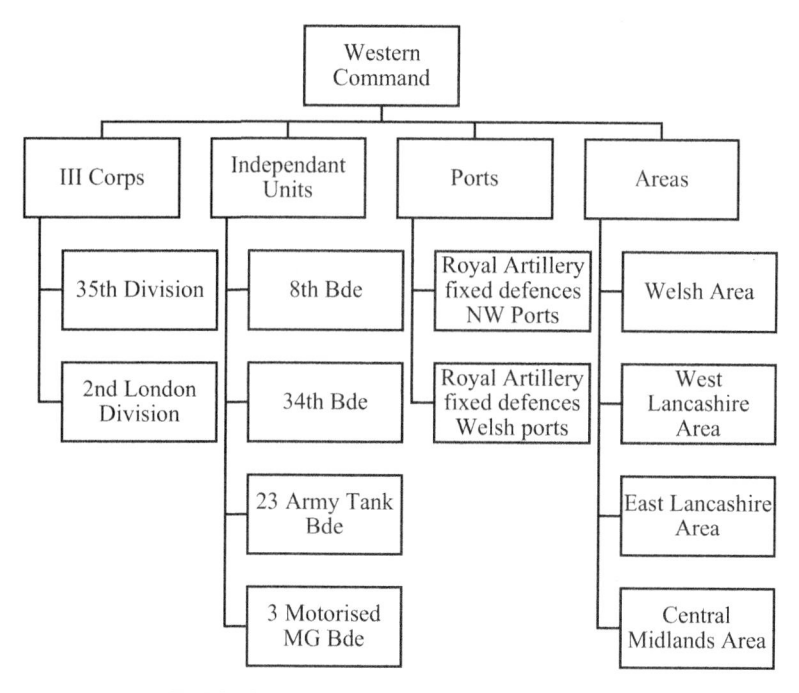

```
                        Western
                        Command
    ┌──────────────┬────────────────┬──────────────┐
 III Corps     Independant        Ports          Areas
                  Units
    │              │                │              │
 35th Division   8th Bde      Royal Artillery   Welsh Area
                              fixed defences
                                NW Ports
    │              │                │              │
 2nd London     34th Bde     Royal Artillery     West
  Division                   fixed defences   Lancashire
                              Welsh ports        Area
                   │                              │
                23 Army Tank                 East Lancashire
                    Bde                          Area
                   │                              │
                3 Motorised                    Central
                  MG Bde                    Midlands Area
```

Table 3: Western Command Structure 1940

It was in the context of this complex structure, where a fighting force of 15 Divisions was administrated and commanded, that the concept of the Local Defence Volunteers, and later the Home Guard, was generated and administrated. Against the might of the *Wehrmacht* was a military hierarchy which was able to grow at scale very quickly, and when the call came to generate a force of over a million men in a rapid period, it was able to support this, and utilise it to good effect. Fundamentally, it allowed a new volunteer force to take over a large number of static guards and administrative tasks to allow the regular forces to be available to fight

[i] A *Fallschirmjeger* Regiment was the equivalent of a British Brigade, with three battalions and association support weapons companies.
[ii] These figures can be found in Robinson, D. (2006) *Invasion 1940: Did the Battle of Britain Alone Stop Hitler*. Robinson Publishing
[iii] Of note 22,000 *Fallschirmjeger* of the 7th *Flieger Division* landed on Crete in 1941, supported by a follow up force of the same scale.
[iv] A detailed appraisal of British defences of all types can be found in Clarke D. M. (2011). *Arming The British Home Guard 1940 – 1944*. Cranfield University
[v] This view of the early Local Defence Volunteers is brought to life in, Flemming, P. (1958). *Invasion 1940*. Hamish Hamilton
[vi] As of 8th June, but details of forces in the United Kingdom and France at this type are difficult to fully interpret due to the changing situation and flow of French troops rescued from Dunkirk back to the mainland.
[vii] This total defence and the speed of the build-up is very well articulated in Clarke D. M. (2011). *Arming The British Home Guard 1940 – 1944*. Cranfield University
[viii] Quote from Brown, P. (1944). *1940-44 Being a diary of D Company 20th Battalion (Kent) Home Guard*. Published by Kent Home Guard.

Chapter 2
The Civilian Defence

With the onset of war, plans were already in place for the coordination of civil defence across the United Kingdom. These defences were complex in nature and covered a multitude of activities. However, first and foremost, with the evidence of the mass aerial bombing of the Spanish Civil War, was the role of the Air Raid Precautions Department. This department would include both the immediate response to attack by air, but also the support needed to maintain the morale of the civilian population. There were plans being put in place to coordinate the activities within government to this new threat, but also to link it to the complex military structure across the United Kingdom. To ensure that in the case of mass bombing, or worse invasion, plans were being made so that parts of parts of the United Kingdom could operate in isolation from central government if required. All of these factors were considered as part of a civilian defence programme which grew over the late 1930s into the war period.

In 1936 Whitehall, The Lord Privy Seal, Sir John Anderson, was the responsible minister for the coordination of policy between departments for civil defence. He was the chairman of the civil defence (policy) sub-committee which was in turn part of the committee of imperial defence. This committee was responsible for the reviewing of the planning and organisations of all departments concerned with civil defence measures and their coordination. The first of these departments was the Air Raid Precautions Department which operationally fell under the Home Office. This was the first department where a president was set in terms of civil defence activity and these procedures were laid down in statute in 1937 by the Air Raid Precautions Act. The Lord Privy Seal also coordinated the war plans of the Fire and Police Divisions of the Home Office. Procedure stated that "On the outbreak of war the Lord Privy Seal becomes charged with the responsibility of ensuring that the plans of departments responsible for civil defence and of the local authorities are correctly coordinated."[i] At this time, the Regional War Rooms would be activated and in this role, he would ensure departments were coordinated and did not conflict with each other in terms of plans. When Sir John Anderson became Home Secretary and Minister of Home Security on the outbreak of war in September 1939, he became directly in control of the Air Raid Precautions Department, Police and Fire Divisions and chaired the Civil Defence Sub Committee of the cabinet which did the same work. This continued until October 1940, when Herbert Morrison would take over this role.

The Regional Commissioners Act became law on 1st September 1939. Appointments were announced in Parliament on 18th April 1939 and the appointed persons took up paid appointments, of up to £2500 per annum, on 25th August 1939. The 12 Regional Commissioners were not invested with any specific powers, but were expected to use their influence to coordinate the civil defence plans of local authorities and the Government departments, which also operated with regional appointees. The idea of Regional Commissioners had its roots in Great War planning and today the Regions are still the administrative Regions of the United Kingdom as used by Central Government planning. "The commissioners had no legal powers, but did have the power of 'influence and prestige' and have been asked to do things, have done them and have therefore acquired the power of precedent."[ii] Commissioners could be declared an 'authorised person' in Defence Regulations Chapter 27, which gave specific powers, such as creation of a hospital in an emergency.

The situation of home defence became so serious in 1939 that London was activated as a region nine months before the outbreak of war. In the other regions the set up was not as complete, with regional and deputy regional commissioners nominated but warrants not issued by the king until September 1939. Many Whitehall departments did not have staff at a regional level, such as the casualty department of the Ministry of Health, so struggled to coordinate with the new regional commissioners who were now tasked to bring together the activities of civil defence. Clarity was given by a Cabinet paper on the 11th December 1939, which gave specific direction that Commissioners were empowered to issue instructions (prerogative) on the model of Indian Governors, decide if an emergency decision was needed (in a state of emergency or if the government was not functioning), power to arbitrate all disputes (where there was no time to refer to courts or proper authority) and power to the king in council to declare state of emergency locally or generally. Importantly, this paper gave clarity that throughout these powers Regional Commissioners were to safeguard rights of subjects and had no power to override courts decisions.

There was much discussion about liability for such a decision by the Commissioners and their staff, and examples of this were very much historical in their context. For example, the bulldozing of houses during the great fire and liability being held with the person who ordered the bulldozing, if compensation was not given to scale that is needed. The summary of such discussions were that if an officer acted in good faith and within their powers, then they would be acting as the government. In true Civil Service parlance, Whitehall declared that "only an average catastrophe will require the commissioners". This split direction was largely because Whitehall would not write into policy, or admit publicly, that any attack on Britain could not be defeated, and there may be a change that these Regional Commissioners were needed.

It was expected that if the Central Government ceased to exist, or communications with London were broken, control would pass entirely into the hands of a Regional Commissioner, a person of Cabinet rank, who would wield absolute power in his region and would become 'the whole government'[iii]. Written authority of delegation for the Commissioners were provided on the outbreak of war by the Home Secretary, the Secretary of

State for Scotland, the Minister of Health and the Minister of Home Security. Their staff would replicate all parts of Central Government. Each of the Regional Commissioners would assess his region's situation, send out people to survey the local area, contact other command bunkers subordinate to his and prepare to run the region he controlled as best he could, by whatever means he could, in the hope that something could be salvaged from the post partial or total Nazi occupation of the United Kingdom. If needs be, the United Kingdom could be controlled with an invasion ongoing in one part, with functioning government in another under the Commissioner. A key issue with such planning was that the twelve commissioners did not match the seven Military Commands, (later eight), and such overlaps did not aid clarity in defence.

The Regional Commissioners were provided with a regional staff, led by a Principal Officer, very much like a Principle Assistant Secretary to a department, and an Assistant Principal Officer. The duties of the Regional Officers were listed to be to maintain and further good relations with Air Raid Precautions Department and the public (including public bodies) both prior to any emergency but also in case of an emergency. They had a key coordinating function, providing the public advice and working with departmental officers with details of their schemes (such as health, the regional surveyor and chief constable) across the various regional Whitehall departments. They would also have a monitoring function, being tasked to watch the performance of local authorities under the act and an information function in that they would stimulate public interest, particularly in the Air Raid Precautions Department. Finally, these Principal Officers had the bureaucratic function of approving expenditure for the wider team.

Within this Regional team were also Home Office Fire Brigade Inspectors, Police Staff Officers, the Senior Regional Officer of Air Raid Precautions Department and the General Inspector of Ministry of Health which worked with Regional Commissioner on evacuation and casualty services. In addition, a General Inspector, who was a high grade civil servant with no portfolio, was provided, so that with the outbreak of war, health functions could be transferred to regions.[iv] This staff grew over time with a Finance Officer joining from the treasury, (who quickly authorised the administration of free travel for regional officers) and Liaison Officers were appointed with other departments who joined at the weekly conferences. In addition, Technical Staff, started being appointed which included a Technical Advisor who advised on public air raid shelter construction.

A key appointment in the regions were the Regional Information Officer,[v] who had three key functions. Firstly, to operate an emergency information service, which allowed the flow of information from the Ministry of Home Security War Room to the local level. Secondly, to counter alarm and rumour through local information committees, finally to assess morale considerations of local population, including the general will of people for war, the efficiency of mobilisation and the condition of public mind as a result of enemy action. These roles were critical in assessing the impact of enemy bombing and other attacks and were used to make assessments on the morale of the general population.

Below regional level were the County boroughs, consisting of 98 County Units and 134 County Boroughs, in addition to 16 Local Authorities.

Therefore, there were 249 local units, with 10 to 20 per region. These local units were responsible to the Regions for all civil defence matters, and where these geographic areas were particularly complex, a Joint Controller was appointed, who helped with the pooling of resources and mutual support. Therefore, the civil defence of a local area went down a civilian chain of command running parallel to other systems, most notably the military at this time. In the most complex of cases this ran from the Ministry of Home Security War Room to the War Room in the Region, to a Group Headquarters (Joint Controller) to a Local Authority, to a Report Centre (for bigger local Authorities). The purpose of this chain was principally to collate information on air raid damage and casualties, but also could be used in case of invasion, for civil defence.

On the 1st April 1940, a new appointment of the Chief of The Operations Staff, General Sir Hugh was made to assist and guide policy on training and operations for the Civil Defence Staff. The military being appointed to such a role concerned many within this civil service based structure, with comments around its voluntary nature being impacted upon by the military. "It should never be overlooked that Air Raid Procurations are, essentially, dependent upon voluntary effort and goodwill of the people."[vi] However, improvements were made with the system over the summer as the first German Bombs fell and simple improvements with procedure were agreed, such as the principle that for casualties in air raids, the Civil Defence will get them 'to the door' of the hospital, a point of clarity which was needed in times of complementary systems in place.

The Regional Commissioners for the Midlands Region (Region 9) was William Humble Eric Ward MC TD, 3rd Earl of Dudley with the Deputy

Commissioner being Mr. S. J. Grey. William Ward, who was born in 1894 and educated at Eton and Christchurch, Oxford. He enlisted in the Worcestershire Yeomanry in 1912 and in 1914 transferred to the 10th Hussars. He served in France from 1915 to 1918 and was awarded the Military Cross in action. After the war, he served in the Staffordshire Yeomanry and reached the rank of Major and in 1933 he was made Honorary Colonel of the 51st (Midland) Medium Brigade Royal Artillery. His military experience gave him the knowledge of the role, but also his political and social connections were also very strong, as he was formerly Viscount Ednam until July 1932 when he became 3rd Earl of Dudley and he was the Conservative Member of Parliament for Hornsey 1921 - 1924 and Wednesbury 1931 - 1932. He inherited Round Oak Steelworks and Baggeridge Colliery and set up Dudley Zoo in 1937. The Headquarters of Region 9 were split across a number of locations, with an administrative headquarters in Worcester, and Regional Communication headquarters at both the Drakelow Tunnels, near Kidderminster, and also at the ammunition store at Swynnerton, Staffordshire. Most of the public information about the Regional Commissioners shows a role which was very public and ceremonial, including inspections of Home Guard troops, rather than these more behind the scenes functions which were unknown to the public at the time.

Long before the creation of the Regional Commissioners, the first elements of civil defence were generated as the Spanish Civil War waged, and the impact of arial bombing on urban areas was seen for the first time. In 1935 the Air Raid Precaution Service (later known as Civil Defence) was set up. During its history, over 1.9 million people served in this organisation, of which 2400 were killed. This body was delegated to local authorities to organise, which in the case of Sutton Coldfield became the responsibility of Warwickshire County Council, but also elements to local authorities in Birmingham and Sutton itself. In November 1937 Councillor Bigwood, then the mayor appealed for the recruitment of Air Raid Precautions staff. "Everyone can help in some capacity and in allotting volunteers to their posts, in will be the endeavour to choose situations convenient to their residences or place of business." He ended with "knowing the patriotism and public spirit of the people of Sutton Coldfield, I am certain that the full number of volunteers will quickly be forthcoming."

The structure of this volunteer force was made up of many key roles. Wardens were the bread and butter of the organisation, and recruited in wards across the country, with preventative roles, but also actions to occur in terms of coordination on the declaration of an incident. Supporting these wardens were Fire Watchers who stood as a key part of the infrastructure, and ensured that fires did not spread or get out of hand, as well as assisting in rescue. A central Report and Control Function had many signalling and staff roles at all levels, supported by messengers who were often young school boys or boy scouts. If an incident occurred there were three key teams who were trained and equipped to respond; these were the Rescue Parties, the First Aid and Stretcher Parties and the Gas Decontamination Teams. The latter, with the threat of poisoned gas, were thankfully never tested to their full extent. Finally, to help these teams were the Welfare Support, who provided an important service both for the staff in the Air Raid Precaution Service, but also for the civilians impacted by the incident.

The force was the statutory authority in case of emergency and general conflict, and the foresight in generating such an organisation allowed for an effective civil response to the outbreak of war and the impact of the

Blitz which was to follow. However, as with all voluntary forces, recruitment prior to the outbreak of hostilities was an issue and on the 29th August 1939 another campaign was started by Birmingham Council to employ additional staff for the war effort. It announced that 15,662 Air Raid Precaution Wardens were needed, 2000 Civil Nursing Reserve, 10,338 Auxiliary Fire Brigade, 15,263 Casualty Service and 8090 General Services. Apart from the Auxiliary Fire Brigade none of these units were up to strength. As the nation's second city, a Civil Defence of 50,000 people would be needed. At this time, elements of this organisation in Sutton Coldfield were controlled through the Warwickshire County Council, but locals, as they were on the boundary with Birmingham and often worked there, volunteered across these administrative lines. As the war started many of these roles were taken on by women, including key roles, such as Volunteer Fire Fighters. The Frederick Road Fire Fighters were all mothers, and all fully trained. Not only that, but they used their skills in the raids of the Blitz. In 1938, the Women's Volunteer Service for Air Raid Precautions was formed and became the largest voluntary organisation in history. The service was formed to recruit woman into the Air Raid Precaution Service, to assist civilians during and after air raids by providing rest centres, food, first aid and the evacuation and billeting of children.

The Air Raid Precaution staff were given a large amount of training on many areas of air raids, including recent lessons from the Spanish Civil War. They also signed off as competent local fire watchers and fire guards, who would work at local factory units and prevent fires from breaking out during air raids. This training for Fire Guards, consisted of incendiary bomb control, training in smoke, team training and the conducting of a tactical exercises. These unsung heroes of the Blitz had considerable impact at a local level, knowing what action to take when an incendiary landed, often in sticks by the score.

Air Raid Precaution staff were trained primarily in three areas; for bombs and shelters, for incendiaries and fire, and for poison gas. Thankfully the latter was never used in the war, but the wide range issuing of gas masks, and the intense training people received showed how real the risk was perceived to be. Areas of training such as decontamination, first aid relating to chemicals and detection were learned by line and guided by visual aid cards. The police issued a chemical reminder showing the nine most common poison gasses and their first aid treatment which could fit into a pocket. These ranges from commonly known Mustard and Chlorine Gas to the lesser known blister agent Lewisite, and the mass used Tear Gas.

In 1937 the population of Sutton Coldfield was 37,000 people over an area of 22 Square Miles, with 113 miles of roads. 60 miles of this roadway was built up on both sides, and 20 on one side, only 33 miles of road was not built up. A risk assessment was conducted in April 1937 for Sutton Coldfield by the Air Raid Precautions team. It assessed that to protect the population the town had five full time firemen and 14 retained firemen, these maintained a continuous duty and were funded by the town council. The local authority had agreements to give mutual assistance to Lichfield, Aldridge, Solihull and Meriden; however not Birmingham. The central fire station had two self-propelled motor pumps, one heavy and one medium with escape, and two motor tenders with escape. They contained 8,900 feet of 2.5 inch unlined hose, of which 6,400 was on the appliances. The brigade dealt with 137 calls per year, of which 21 were chimney fires and five percent outside of district.

There were five water pumps across the borough, (two steam, one oil and one electric). Pumping stations were located at Pipe Hill, Shenstone, Sandhills, Little Hay and Bournevale, and three major trunk mains connected this water supply to the borough, two of these were within 20 feet of each other on the Lichfield Road. There were supplementary water supplies, including the seven pools in Sutton Park, along the Plants Brooks and eight pools outside the park. There was also the Birmingham Canal at Minworth. There was no phone line between police and fire brigade, which needed to be rectified.

In order to prepare for the expected war and mass bombing which had been seen in Spain, the Town Council ordered on the results of the risk assessment a plan to recruit 200 Auxiliary Firemen to man an additional thirty medium pumps, these pumps would be towed by local haulage firms. In case of war the fire units would be dispersed to move one appliance to the builder's yard on Jockey Road, and another to the Electricity Sub Station on Green Lanes. These would be manned by the auxiliary firemen. 20 motorcycle patrols were to be recruited also for despatch riders and communication. This recruitment was successful with all posts filled prior to the outbreak of war, and there is no doubt that these fire fighters, supported by the 6,600 volunteer fire guards in Sutton Coldfield, saved many lives. This means that one in six people in town were trained as volunteer fire guards, able to give basic first aid, and extinguish basic fires.

Like the fire service, the ambulances for the town were funded by the local authority. There were two ambulances, one in Boldmere and one in Four Oaks. There was a central rescue party at the Sutton Police Station, with links to repair units for railway, water, gas, canals, General Post Office phones and to the police. The plan for war would be that all ambulances would move under the command of the Air Raid Precautions Services.

There was often competition for space, and this would later get worse as the Home Guard competed for many venues too. A note from Observation section, Area number 3 of the Air Raid Precaution Service to the Local Defence Volunteers with a key from vicar of Walmley allowing the use of the parish church for training in May 1940 showed the early stages of these competing priorities. The official Civil Defence was backed up by a large number of voluntary organisations such as St John Ambulance, British Red Cross, Church Army, Young Men's Christian Association, and Friends Ambulance. During the war, all of these organisations played a vital role in supporting the Civil Defence, giving much comfort to those in need. The Women's Voluntary Service were a considerable supporting element during the war. In Sutton Coldfield 130 women made dressings for all the wardens and all first aid points in the town, this was over 100,000 dressings. In addition 30,000 socks were repaired by Sutton Laundry, and Women's Voluntary Service provided regular catering at the fire station and supported the citizens advice bureau. The Regional Commissioner stated that "Whenever a dirty, uncomfortable, hazardous, annoying job of work has cropped up that is nobody's particular business, the first thing anyone says is lets get the WVS to do it. And done it always is, quickly, efficiently and willingly." During the war 241 members of the Women's Voluntary Service were killed on the home front.

A key part of the defence preparations was the construction of air raid shelters for the public. In 1938, Sir John Anderson was placed in charge of the efforts to ensure effective air raid precautions. From February 1939, over 1.5 million of these shelters were constructed prior to the outbreak of war. Those who earned less than £250 a year were given a shelter; those above this income paid £7. The shelters were simple to construct, made of corrugated iron and split into six panels. The shelters held a family of six and captured people's imagination, being built across the city. In addition to these individual shelters, a large number of public shelters were constructed, especially in large urban areas. The use of public shelters were popular, often because Anderson shelters half buried in the garden were quite difficult to make comfortable as they filled with water and were dark and cold. In Sutton Coldfield, Safa Constructions, a local business offered for sale concrete, concrete and brick and gas proof shelters for more than the £7 Anderson shelters. Streathers Limited of Four Oaks provided £30 shelters with considerable additional protection. Some of these shelters have been found since across the borough. One such 'Stanton Shelter' from a Nottingham based company was found on Rosemary Hill Road.

Another available shelter was the Morrison shelter, officially termed 'Table (Morrison) Indoor Shelter'. It was in the shape of a table and had a cage like construction beneath it. Designed by John Baker and named after Herbert Morrison, the Minster of Home Security at the time, it was the result of the realisation that due to the lack of house cellars, or a garden to build an Anderson shelter, it was necessary to develop an effective type of indoor shelter. The shelters came as kits and needed to be bolted together inside the home. The shelter was provided free to households whose combined income was less than £400 per year (equivalent to £25,000 now). Half a million Morrison shelters had been distributed by the end of 1941, with a further 100,000 being added in 1943. In one examination of 44 severely damaged houses, it was found that three people had been killed, 13 seriously injured, and 16 slightly injured out of a total of 136 people who had occupied Morrison shelters; thus 120 out of 136 escaped from severely bomb-damaged houses without serious injury.

In 1939, to aid civil defence, the Police formed a reserve service, bringing back those who had recently retired, this was known as the First Police Reserve, and was later known as the Police War Reserve Constables. There was a real challenge of maintaining Police numbers with many officers joining the army to fight, and in addition to these retired police, Female Police were recruited and their duties increased as the war continued. War Reserve Constables were armed with rifles to assist with protection from enemy action, enemy sabotage and to assist with the armed forces. Their duties included all the normal duties of police, but with additional roles of enforcing blackouts, combating black market activity, helping in evacuations and air raids and capturing deserting soldiers. Another role was the Police Auxiliary Messenger Service, which involved scouts between age 14 and 18. In 1939, the police changed this to be 16 plus in age and gave pay for a 16 year old to 23s,[vii] not a small sum for a young boy on messenger duties. Many of the volunteers in the Warwickshire, Sutton Coldfield Division came from Bishop Vesey Grammar School.

To defend the city and surrounding areas from low flying aircraft, the Royal Airforce set up a number of barrage balloon units across the Midlands. No.5 Centre Royal Air Force (Balloon Barrage) and 31st Barrage Balloon Group were guarded by Royal Air Force personnel and with a mobile force of 100 men, it was located at what is now St Georges Barracks. 1466 balloons were deployed around Britain to prevent low level bombing. At Grange Road Erdington, there was a small force of mobile Royal Air Force to support these sites with maintenance. The actual Balloon units were spread across the north of Birmingham to defend the city from what was to become 'Heinkel Alley' as German bomber moved across the undefended skies of Wales into the Midlands to flank air defences. In the area of Sutton Coldfield, No.911 and No.912 (County of Warwick) Squadrons Royal Air Force were based at Flying Field No.1 at Whitehouse Common, and No.913 Squadron was based in Erdington and Sutton Park with 40 Balloons. The first house in the in the local area damaged in the war was hit by a barrage balloon cable. A balloon escaped from Pype Hayes Park not long after war was declared in 1939 with the steel cable hitting and damaged a house before coming down over Sutton Coldfield.

In defence of the area around north Birmingham and Sutton Coldfield was the 4th Anti-Aircraft Division. This organisation would expand rapidly as the war started, with a second formation, the 11th Anti-Aircraft Division, formed in 1940. Initially, the 4th Anti-Aircraft Division had 71 Anti-Aircraft Guns defending Birmingham largely drawn from 34th Anti-Aircraft Brigade which was made up of six regiments. The defences grew from 31 sites at the outbreak of war to 61 by 1942. Key locations in Sutton Coldfield were 'H5' Heavy Anti-Aircraft site in Sutton Park, 'H63' in Walmley golf course and 'H54' in Walmley Ash. Supporting these anti-aircraft units were large search lights commanded by Territorial Army. 54th Anti-Aircraft Brigade were made up into defence islands, each with light anti-aircraft guns, and large search lights to track enemy aircraft. The 45th and 59th (Royal Warwickshire) Regiments manned the key locations across north Birmingham, including a major defensive island of made from 378th Battery of the 45th Regiment, located on the dominating high ground of Sutton Park to the north of Birmingham.

To support the defence from the air, the observer Corps was originally set up by the Police in 1938. Two observation posts were set up in Birmingham, one at Erdington Reservoir, the other at Selly Oak. Each had 12 special constables attached to the post, but in 1939 these were transferred to the command of the Royal Air Force.[viii] In 1939, 25 sirens were installed around the city, and 55 operators were appointed to man these in case of a raid. This system was tested throughout the winter of 1939 and these became increasingly more organised and frequent as the invasion of France started. On the night of the 9th and 10th May 1939, a practise blackout was held across 28 counties of the United Kingdom, to test that the systems were working. The Royal Air Force also conducted dummy attacks across the area to test the defences. On the outbreak of war, No.5 Group of Royal Observer Corps was commanded from their Coventry Control Centre and consisted of 30 sites with ten clusters. Sutton Coldfield Cluster was covered by F1 Erdington, F3 Hartley, and F2 Meriden. These volunteer observers provided a critical service to the air defence of the United Kingdom and to give warning to the Civil Defence forces.

Additional preparations were made in case of chemical attack, with gas masks issued across the midlands by the 40 depots across the city. At this time, it was still a likelihood that Germany may use poison gas, and Britain's expected use in its defence meant that it was doubly important for these distributions to take place. Numerous First Aid Points were put in place across the city by the Air Raid Precaution Services, with equipment set up ready for any need. The three main First Aid locations in Sutton Coldfield were at St Nicholas School on Jockey Road, Boldmere Garage and at 11 Drake Street. The main rest centre was at Britwell Hall. As the phoney war continued, much of this equipment was placed into storage, as the needs for the 'village halls' were more for training. However, as the first raids occurred, a new focus was given to public health, such as at First Aid Post No. 13 in Walmley, where competing training needs of the Local Defence Volunteers, Air Raid Precautions staff and other organisations led to much correspondence on this issue with the trustees of the village hall.

The Air Raid Precaution posts were placed across Sutton Coldfield, with seven major locations (listed A to G) with each having a number of wardens posts working to them. For example, Warden Post E2 was manned by Senior Warden J Harford, and Wrden Post G1 by Mr W H Cozens. These were coordinated at the main Air Raid Precautions post at the Police Station, where the plotting officer, borough surveyor worked with the divisional controller, who was the town clerk, Mr R Walsh.

Some public shelters were tested, for example two buildings, number five and six Gloucester Street blew up by royal engineers to test the strength of the shelters to bombing.[ix] Sutton Coldfield itself is a town to the northeast of Birmingham, but even though at this time it was not part of the city, it was geographically close, and many people in the town commuted daily into the city for work. It was also linked by the historical connection of being in Warwickshire, and therefore the efforts were very much joined. The Home Guard Birmingham and within the county of Warwickshire were both within Warwickshire Subarea although Birmingham Garrison due to its scale had some autonomy of command and administration.

Although there was a clear focus on defence and training, there were wider preparations for civil support for when the air raids continued in the spring. A detailed emergency plan was issued, particularly around the feeding of the population in case of widespread destruction of homes. This was particularly important in Sutton Coldfield due to the proximity of the town to the main targets of the night raiders. However, it was not until the Blitz started in earnest, that on the 24th of February 1941 a plan was issued for the feeding of ten percent of the population in case of emergency. 4500 meals were ordered to be provided daily through twelve first line centres. These centres were located at schools, public buildings, and assembly halls. The Town Clerk was empowered through the Divisional Food Officer to do this. The Borough has been divided into four groups each having a group officer and deputy. These group commanders were largely school headmistresses who were seen to have a clear authority amongst the local population.

Food was listed as biscuits, tea, margarine, soup, sugar, beef hash, meat roll, condensed milk, baked beans and cocoa. Each was securely locked away. The Midlands Divisional Food Officer responsible for replenishment. Each centre had eight water bins with ten gallons capacity. Emergency lighting was fitted, which could work independently of gas and electric supply. £20 was allocated to each centre to purchase equipment for feeding, and a very prescriptive list was produced of what could be purchased, down to one medium broom and 12 packets of dry soap. The centres would each have a Centre Leader from the Women's Voluntary Services and the Local Education Authority.

Meals were authorised to be issued once per day at lunch time, with no charge for the first 48 hours, but contributions would be asked for. Bread and milk would be provided fresh, but biscuits were saved 'just in case'. Additional food was allowed to be purchased, but only if sold at cost price. Records would be maintained of any given for free. Nine-month-old children to school age would be provided with rice pudding and tinned soup. No provision had been made by the ministry for those under nine months.

The Emergency Feeding Officer at the Ministry of Education, for the local authority was Mr Harvey Freeman. The Mayor was granted powers to grant emergency feeding in Sutton Coldfield. Food facilities in Group I under Mrs Stansfield covered the area of Boldmere, Wylde Green and New Oscott. There were feeding centres in Green Lanes, New Oscott and Boldmere Schools, as well as at the Baptist Church on Chester Road, Princess Alice Orphanage and St Michaels Youth Hall. Second Line Centres were at the Boldmere Hotel, Parson & Clark Hotel, Horse & Jockey Hotel and Pavilion Cinema. In total there was capacity to feed up to 4000 people at these centres.

Group II under Mr Gurney, the headteacher at Minworth School, covered Minworth School, Walmley School and the Shrubbery School and only 500 people in these areas could be fed. However, the reality was that the schools had greater capacity if needed, but this was not funded. Mrs Antrobus from Sutton Coldfield Grammar School for Girls commanded

Group III, and this had a capacity of 3000 people. Centres were at the Girls's Grammar School, Victoria Road Boys' School, Bishop Vesey Grammar School, and the Town Hall. In addition, there were second line centres at the British Restaurant on South Parade, the House of Friendship on Anchorage Road and the Masonic Hall on Mill Street. Finally, Group IV was under command of Councillor Bodley but only had capacity for 500 people in Four Oaks, and was at Hill Schools and Moor Hall Gold Club.

The totality of this feeding programme was impressive in scale and would allow feeding of those bombed out of their home, or, if needed, to support soldiers in time of crisis. Teachers taking on these roles, in support of the Women's Voluntary Service is another forgotten war time role, for an already stretched profession. Further emergency response training also took place, working in partnership with the Air Raid Precaution wardens and other civil contingency organisations.

The civil defence mechanisms in place, from Regional Commissioners appointed by the King at the highest level, to Mr Gurney the headteacher at Minworth School covering Group II feeding unit, to the Fredderick Road Volunteer Fire Unit, were all part of a detailed and integrated plan for defence. In Birmingham alone 50,000 volunteers were part of the Civil Defence forces, with many more involved in other volunteer organisations such as St John Ambulance, and in existing public sector roles. It was in the context of this huge volunteer sector demand that the Local Defence Volunteers were formed, meaning another role was needed within society. This of course was all in addition to the critical war work that would take place across the factories of the Midlands, where over half of Britain's weapons were manufactured.

[i] TNA HO 199/15 – Notes of a lecture by D J Lidbury, civil servant at The Home Office, on Regional Commissioners dated April 1940. These notes give a comprehensive view of the role of Regional Commissioners and how this evolved with the outbreak of war. It also gives context of their perceived role in case of invasion.

[ii] *Ibid*

[iii] *Ibid*

[iv] TNA HO 199/15 – Taken from document HIS/0/100 regarding Civil Defence regional organisation procedures. This document includes the original signed formed of delegation form the Ministers to the Regional Commissioners, giving clear authority if needed. The Home Office delegation opens several further questions considering the various security elements under their authority.

[v] TNA HO 199/15 – This paper on Regional Information Officer roles gives insight into the potential and actual roles of the Regional Commissioners with regards to morale, propaganda and the role of the Ministry of Information.

[vi] TNA HO 11862/3/39 – The Code of Instructions for Regional Commissioners written in March 1939 by the ARP Department gives clear recognition to the role of volunteers within the Civil Defence structure, and therefore the alignment to the maintenance of morale. Prior to the Blitz there was a real concern that mass bombing could destroy the morale of civilians and therefore Civil Defence could be ineffective. In reality this was not the case.

[vii] Brazier, C. & Rice, S. (2018) *Condition Red.* (West Midlands Police) give excellent background information on the role of the Police in the Second World War in Birmingham, with incredible stories of bravery and dedication by this often unsung organisation.

[viii] *Ibid*

[ix] *Ibid*

Chapter 3
The Local Defence Volunteers

The battle for France started on the 10th May, with the Germans again making rapid advances. On the 14th May, Secretary of State for War, Sir Anthony Eden announced the formation of the Local Defence Volunteers.

> *In his broadcast, the Secretary of State for War outlined the new threat posed by German parachute troops, and asked for volunteers to report to their local police stations: Since the war began the Government have received countless enquiries from all over the Kingdom from men of all ages who are for one reason or*

another not at present engaged in military service, and who wish to do something for the defence of the country. Now is your opportunity. We want large numbers of such men in Great Britain who are British subjects, between the ages of 17 and 65, to come forward and offer their services in order to make assurance doubly sure. The name of the new force which is now to be raise will be the 'Local Defence Volunteers.' This name, Local Defence Volunteers, describes its duties in three words.[i]

Following the initial announcement many people drove straight to their local Police Station to register their interest to serve. There was little organisation at this point, and the Police were cautious in their application of these volunteers. They generally accepted those with former service backgrounds and known good conduct. The first person to come forward and volunteer, and therefore issued Regimental Number '1', was railway worker J B Dodd, who joined the Railway Section, later part of D Company. He was a Lance Corporal from the First World War. In real terms the selection criteria were simply to be 'capable of free movement' and to be between the ages of 17 and 65,[ii] this allowed many who had not previously found a role, and the huge number of veterans of the First World War, a role to play in defence.

A week after the announcement on the 20th May, a secret memorandum was issued from the War Office regarding the Volunteer Defence Force[iii]. This stated that the Local Defence Volunteers would follow the organisation of the civilian police, on the bases of a county organisation (called Subareas), within which would be companies, platoons and sections, corresponding to Police Divisions, Sections and Stations. A section should be around 7 or 8 men. Note that above Company (Military) or Division (Police), the arrangement got more complex due to scale, inserting both battalions and zones, as the county became more than the envisioned battalion, to actually a military division in scale, containing many thousands of men.

On the 22nd May 1940, the Warwickshire battalion formed, at this point under the name of the 'Warwickshire Home Guard Area'. The local Territorial Army Association were asked to select officers, and therefore as the chair of the local association, it became the responsibility of the Lord Lieutenant to appoint the commander. In addition, the Regional Commissioner was asked to provide assistance to this task.[iv] The Lord Lieutenant of Warwickshire was John Verney, 20th Baron Willoughby de Broke. Baron Varney at least had a military background and therefore some judgement in these issues. In the First World War he was awarded a Military Cross in 1918, and after the war was an aide de camp to the Governor of Bombay, before becoming the Adjutant of the Warwickshire Yeomanry and later the Commanding Officer of the County of Warwickshire Squadron from 1936 to 1939. After his appointment as Lord Lieutenant, he continued his military service during the war, becoming a Duty Controller for No.11 Group RAF Operations Room in Uxbridge (where he received a mention in despatches) and then became Deputy Director, then Director of Public Relations at the Air Ministry.

The initial Area Commander to be selected by Baron Varney was Colonel Reginald John Cash. Reginald Cash was born in 1892 and came from a middle class background, where his father Sidney was a manufacturer of ribbon from Coventry. He was an only son and lived in a house as a child with four servants. Reginald studied at Oxford and, after working for his father, joined the 8th Battalion the Loyal North Lancashire Regiment as a 2nd Lieutenant on the outbreak of First World War. What followed was an impressive career where he served on the staff, including in France from September 1915. Moving from staff appointments back to his battalion as Adjutant, he was wounded in September 1916 with a gunshot wound to his left thigh. With his injury, he was moved through No. 3 West Riding Field Ambulance to No. 25 Ambulance Train, and then was transfer to 77th Field Ambulance, 25th Division. Despite his wounds he returned to front line service, and in December 1917 he was awarded the Military Cross for distinguished service in the field. In January 1918, he was awarded a Mention in Despatches, and promoted to temporary major, given the role of Brigade Major. He was cited for bravery twice more in 1918, being awarded a further mention in despatches and a Criox de Guerre for his services as Brigade Major.

After the end of hostilities, Reginald Cash continued his service, as a Captain in the 7th Battalion the Warwickshire Regiment and then Major in 1940. This role in the Territorial Army would have seen him as a close friend of the future Lord Lieutenant who was serving over the road with the Yeomanry. Promoted to Colonel in 1934 and commanding the 7th Battalion of the Royal Warwickshire Regiment, he would have been commanding at the same time as Baron Verney commanded the County Yeomanry. As war approached, Reginald was promoted to Colonel in 1938, and was given the rank of temporary Brigadier in August 1939, commanding of the 182nd Infantry Brigade. This was the second line Brigade formed as part of 61 Division, and contained the 2/7 Warwicks, 9th Warwicks and 9th Worcesters. As the Brigade became operational and moved with 61 Division to Northern Ireland, it was given a substantive Brigadier in command, with Reginald reverting to Colonel, although he was awarded an OBE for his efforts. The timing of this move allowed Colonel Cash to be appointed as the Zone Commander by the Lord Lieutenant, and in turn make arrangements for the appointment of sub zone commanders. [v] The selection of sub zone commanders were initially designed to be the companies within the Home Guard battalion, however the scale of recruiting led to Colonel Cash's role being much more substantial, with over fifty battalions under command, across the six sectors, in real times the size of a peace time corps formation.

Within the memorandum of the 20th May, it was made clear that although structured on Police lines, the Home Guard would come under military command. Their action would be rapid action against the enemy by any means. They would not leave their local area unless ordered to by a military commander. On this order it suggested the ringing of church bells as a method of sounding alarm. It made clear local liaison was key with neighbouring military units. It was noticeable that it stated than you could not already be a member of the Air Raid Precaution Service, Fire Service or Police Auxiliary, which led to many resigning from the Air Raid Precaution Service. In the first instance, knowledge of firearms was made to be a key selection criteria, however this was ignored by many. Orders initially stated that you could wear old uniform (if an officer) with an 'VDF' band (note VDF not Local Defence Volunteers) and all Officer Training Corps over 17 years would be automatically enrolled in the Home Guard. The first badges of rank consisted of two or three chevrons on the sleeve of non-commissioned officers.[vi]

Some initial local civilian defence units had been formed prior to the Home Guard. One example of this was by Edith Summerskill MP, who eventually founded the Women's Home Defence Corps, an illegal private army in effect. John Langdon Davies, the famous journalist and author of the time, also called for the Women's Home Guard Auxiliary.[vii] This pressure to allow women to join was resisted by Whitehall and General Headquarters, and it was only in 1943 that 'Nominated Women' were allowed in the Home Guard. They were only supposed to take on non-combat roles, but the reality was often different. In Sutton Coldfield, these regulations were ignored almost immediately with the formation of a Women's Cavalry Section from the riding school; many stories of the riding across the park in the early days of the summer of 1940 are remembered by those who were there.

Much of the information of the early days of the Local Defence Volunteers is surrounded in rumour and legend with little factual data to back it up. There is very little correspondence of these first days of the Local Defence Volunteers in Warwickshire. On the 17th May, Mr Gwilym Griffith of Goldeslie Road enrolled in the Sutton Local Defence Volunteers at the local police station, and later recorded in his diary that his first duty was on 4th June; this had been spent conducting three hours of stopping traffic to check identity papers and driving licences, followed by two hours of rifle drill. Most of the time was spent on guard duty.

The first official paperwork mentioning the Warwickshire Local Defence Volunteers was sent on the 18th May 1940 by the County Surveyor addressed to Local Defence Volunteer Commanders, asking them to keep an eye out on bridges, due to them being key infrastructure[viii] This was followed by further correspondence on the 15th June asking for the protection of vital water supply points also.[ix] However, the first firm direction came on the 20th May 1940 from the Chief Constable of Warwickshire Police who sent a letter ORDER 1940/18 to the County Police Division and Sub Division Commanders outlining the procedures for signing up to the Local Defence Volunteers. There were 80 forms sent to each Sub-Division, and there was outlined a clear priority of commanders and experienced men to be signed up first. Also, there were clear instructions for the local police to vet those who applied. All forms were then to be returned to Divisional Headquarters. The original structure of the Home Guard was based upon these Police boundaries to ensure that order was maintained, as well as weapon ownership.

There is a myth of speed and efficiency of this enrolment across historical sources which claim that "Within a few hours they had duplicated the form setting out the questions which applicants were required to answer. These forms were checked by the police on the security side and then passed to the Home Guard commanders who selected recruits."[x] The reality was somewhat different, with many Police Stations running out of forms, and therefore simple lists being made of names and addresses. It took time to appoint commanders, and to organise structure to this mass of men. The chaos and confusion of those late May days were outlined by the plethora of correspondence from the Chief Constable's Office to try and bring order. HRB Keeble was the Chief Constable of Warwickshire, and he worked hard at trying to give clarity on what was expected. In many cases this was around calming excitement and confirming intelligence.

Initial set up instructions for tactical positions were sent out from Colonel Cash on the 24th May 1940 and these included establishing observation posts across the county to cover possible enemy landing grounds. This was the first directive issued, and also mentioned the sewing of armlets.[xi] At this point, there was an embryonic structure based around a headquarters of the Warwickshire Local Defence Volunteers, co-located with the Chief Constable in Warwick, communicating with sub-zone commanders across the county, where he had appointed company officers. These in turn were appointing their own section and platoon leaders in various locations. Slowly order was being generated from the chaos.

A letter of the 27th May 1940 to Divisional (Company) Commanders shows some structure was present at this point, but not a formed battalion. This was written by Colonel Cash who had assumed the duties in Command of the County / Subarea (later Zone). The terms for this geographical area changing over time, cause much confusion in our understanding, but is typical of the military 'love of a restructure'. Those Divisional (Company) Commanders would quickly become battalions in their own right, with huge number of soldiers under their command. Clarity was given through orders on three areas: storage of weapons outside of villages, (where owners would be able to keep them, but must store the bolt in a separate room), orders for all Local Defence Volunteers to attend one night of guard per week minimum, and interestingly that church bells should not be rung in emergency, as this was an unsuitable response.

Another instruction was issued by the Chief Constable on the 27th May 1940 giving further direction[xii] to the Local Defence Volunteers, largely about the use of firearms, and their storage and training requirements. At this point, the police were still concerned regarding the proliferation of firearms and therefore items such as fire arms certificates were still needed. The letter also reiterated the need for further arms and requested these went via the police and not directly to units in the Local Defence Volunteers. At this point Colonel Cash was directly talking the Divisional (Company) Commanders, rather than any sub-structure. Also the future subunits to the east of Sutton Coldfield were seen as a separate company. On the 29th May 1940, Colonel Cash again wrote to all his men informing them of refined methods of communicating across headquarters in case of phone lines being jammed in an emergency.

On the same day, (the 29th May 1940) the King sent a stirring message to the British Expeditionary Force: "All your countrymen have been following with pride and admiration the courageous resistance of the British Expeditionary Force during the continuous fighting of the last fortnight… The hearts of everyone of us at home are with you and your magnificent troops in this hour of peril."[xiii]

The memorandum sent from the Chief Constables office on the 30th May 1940 makes clear about the vetting process for those joining the Local Defence Volunteers.[xiv] "No fasoists [Sic] or Communists are to be allowed to enrol in the Local Defence Volunteers. Any such persons already enrolled are to be discharged forthwith." It makes it clear than anyone with a foreign father cannot be enrolled. Those and other 'undesirables' will be told numbers exceed requirements, rather than the cause of non-acceptance. As the days went by, the more haphazard recruitment was being reduced, and more deliberate screening was taking place.

Despite this improvement in recruiting, there was still a chaotic approach to the reaction to enemy activity, as shown by this letter from Colonel RJ Cash (Zone Commander) to Battalion Commander Local Defence Volunteers Sutton Coldfield:

> *Many reports have reached this HQ in regard to enemy parachute landings and air defence. Every endeavour is made to establish confirmation of such reports and parties of regular troops and LDV have been despatched for this purpose. At present, in almost every case it is impossible to establish the identity of the original informer or get positive confirmation.*
>
> *It must be understood therefore, that all such reports must be closely investigated at their origin, and wherever possible the name and address of the informer obtained, not only for clarifying the situation but also to enable the necessary action to be taken in case of ill disposed persons starting bogus scares.*
>
> *It is in no wise the purpose of this letter to deprecate or discourage the reporting of these instances. All such information is eagerly sought and appreciated, but the identification of the originator must be stressed as the important factor.*
>
> *It is requested that the contents of this letter be circulated down to the smallest formation.*

The headquarters of the Home Guard Zone was located at 23 Jury Street in Warwick. Here Colonel Cash could talk to the Subarea Commander, which was the administrative military command for the same geography worked from. Both of these reported to the Central Midland Area which was located at 35 – 39 Kenilworth Road, Leamington. This structure meant that parallel to the Subarea was a Home Guard Zone; these zones were for tactical defence, rather than administration, and therefore created a two-tier structure. In theory, units within the Subarea were under administrative command of the sub area but operational command of the zone. In addition, they had the local Territorial Army Association providing logistical home base support. This could become quite confusing.

Colonel R J Cash commanded the Warwickshire Zone Home Guard Units. He had quite a small team but by 1941 this would grow to include his second-in-command, two staff officers, and four transport officers. The regulations of the Home Guard termed the structure as follows: "Each military district or area may include one or more Home Guard zones or groups under a commander.[xv] Each zone (or group) will comprise of two or more battalions. The battalion is the basic unit of the Home Guard. Size of battalion will depend on local requirements." This structure was hugely increased in scale with the complexities of the West Midlands conurbation, with Districts having Areas, Subareas (and Zones) and then within these sectors. A much larger scale than in the rural areas of the United Kingdom. In June 1940, Colonel Cash was referred to as Subarea Commander, but by July as Zone Commander, with Colonel Blacker taking over the role of Subarea Commander in its wider administrative sense.

The overlapping responsibilities of Zone and Subarea can be understood by the following table breaking down the responsibilities by staff function. It can be seen that the sub area responsibilities were based upon the tactical delivery of local units, whereas the Zone responsibilities were much wider. Layered upon these were the wider District responsibilities for air defence and civil protection. This was quite a complex structure which many outside of the chain of command struggled to understand.

Warwickshire (Home Guard) Zone		Warwickshire Subarea	
Commander	Col R J Cash	Commander	Col N V Blacker
2IC	Maj W Flack Later Col Worrall	Birmingham Garrison	Lt D A Col Bullock
Staff Officer	Maj G W Moore Capt G L Wells Capt D A Williamson	Staff Officer	Capt J E Maw Capt C E Sterns
Intelligence Officer	Capt H G Vallance 2Lt J D Warmington	Intelligence Officer	Lt Treadwell
Liaison Officers	Lt W H Perkins Lt W T Williams		
Fielf Engr	Capt A K Richards		
Sig	Capt J F Holt Lt J B MacColl		
Motor Contact	2Lt H K Crawford 2Lt R S Burn 2Lt J Jequier		
Subarea	2Lt W D Thursfield 2Lt S F Snape		

Sector	2Lt H J J Dormer		
	Lt G C W Large 2Lt A McL Smith 2Lt A McK Forsyth		
Pigeon	Capt T J Casey Lt P W Walker		
Medical Advisor	Lt Col H Gibbons Ward		

Table 4: Zone and Subarea Staff

In 1942 Colonel Cash continued to command the Warwickshire Zone, with a second-in-command of Lieutenant Colonel P R Warrall CBE DSO MC. There were a large number of staff officers at this point in the war including three general staff officers, two intelligence officers, a field engineer, signals officer, then a number of logistics, including a transport officer, eight motorised transport officers, a pigeon officer and medical advisor. By 1943 Major Flack was promoted to the second-in-command, there were at this point ten staff officers and eleven logistics officers, two pigeon and a medical advisor. A considerable increase in support

Warwickshire Subarea was further divided into a series of sectors, each of these were commanded by a senior officer with a small staff; they were designed specifically for local defence and became a key areas for Home Guard defence. Each sector contained a number of battalions of Home Guard. F Sector was also known as Birmingham Garrison and contained 31 battalions of Home Guard divided into 5 Groups (A to E). Birmingham Garrison was commanded by Lieutenant Colonel DA Bullock of the Royal Devonshire Regiment, who was brought in from retirement from the reserve of officers. The wider structure of the Warwickshire Subarea contained 46 battalions of Home Guard and was structured as follows:

A Sector – Rugby – 2 & 7 Warwickshire Home Guard

B Sector – Coventry – 11 to 19 Warwickshire Home Guard

C Sector – Solihull – 5 Warwickshire Home Guard

D Sector – Warwick – 1 & 4 Warwickshire Home Guard

E Sector – Sutton and Nuneaton – 3 & 6 Warwickshire Home Guard

F Sector – Birmingham Garrison – 21 to 52 Warwickshire Home Guard

E Sector was commanded in 1940 by a commandant, Major Pollock, and was headquartered at Packington Old Hall, Meriden, with a battle headquarters at Coleshill Police Station. E Sector grew in terms of scale as the war continued and over time it was commanded by a Colonel and divided between the two battalions within it, just east of the River Tame. To the west was the Central Midland Area boundary with the Staffordshire Home Guard, and to the southwest was the boundary with Birmingham Garrison, with 46, 23, 36 and 33 Warwickshire Home Guard running west to east.

As the threat changed, there were adaptations to the boundaries of the Regional Commands, with the biggest being the movement of the Central Midland Area into Western Command in autumn 1940. In addition, within the Warwickshire Subarea, Birmingham Garrison and South Staffordshire Subarea were created as sperate entities. The command of the Central Midland Area remained with Colonel Blakiston-Houston, but under the new General Officer Command Western Command General Sir Robert Gordon-Finlayson.

Military Operational	Military Administrative	Other Military	Civilian
Commander in Chief Home Forces / General Headquarters			National Government
Western Command			Regional Commissioner
Central Midland Area		4th Anti-Aircraft Division	Civil Defence Group
Warwickshire Zone	Warwickshire Subarea	Warwickshire Territorial Army Association	Warwickshire County Council (Local Units)
E Sector (Group)			Report Centres
6th Battalion			

Table 5: Chain of Command 1940

Therefore, the chain of command for the 6th Battalion, which was complex to many, could be described in its mature form as follows:

- Commander in Chief Home Force (Commanded by General Sir Alan Brooke)
- Western Command (Commanded 28th May 1940 – 9th June 1940 (Temporary) General Sir Henry Cholmondeley Jackson) 10th June 1940 – 24th November 1941 General Sir Robert Gordon-Finlayson)

- Central Midland Area (Commanded by Brigadier J Blackiston-Houston). Within Central Midland Area the Home Guard Commander was Colonel Osborne. [xvi]
- Warwickshire Zone (Commanded by Colonel R J Cash) for Home Guard Units / Administrative Chain of Command Warwickshire Subarea (Commanded by Colonel N V Blacker)
- E Sector (Group) (Commanded by Major Pollock in 1940 and Lieutenant Colonel W Bigwood from 1942)
- 6th Warwickshire (Sutton) Home Guard Battalion (Commanded by Lieutenant Colonel W Bigwood)

The chaotic start of local groups started to form into structures which would be formalised by the end of the summer. All those under the age of 65 were able to join, and 40 percent of those who signed up initially were veterans. Across the country over 100,000 Officer Training Corps graduates were signed up in the guise of Local Defence Volunteers which boosted the number further.

For many units, the first operations which took place were road blocks. Volunteer Order 1940/3 on the 3rd June from Warwickshire Zone under Colonel Cash, established road blocks at Company (Division) level, including in Sutton Coldfield. Private Gwilym Griffith[xvii] kept a diary of his time in the Home Guard in 4 Platoon A Company (later Platoon Sergeant of 13 Platoon D Company) and commented on his first duty:

> *"5th June 1940. Yesterday I did my first few hours' duty with the LDV. It was the kind of duty which I should choose as last of all possible choices – stopping the unending stream of traffic on a*

> *busy road to examine ID Cards and drivers' licences; doing this encumbered with a Lee Enfield loaded with ball cartridge, and without my spectacles. Three hours of this and two hours of rifle drill and target practise."*

An order on the 3rd June 1940, titled 'Road Block in 'Division' of Local Defence Volunteers' named the setting up of road blocks on the junction of Lichfield Road and Anchorage Road, Sutton Coldfield, as well as the Chester Road and Collage road junction in Sutton Coldfield. These would, over time, become permanent features of the defence of the town, but this initial exercise prioritised the major junctions which dominated the area, and to some extent focused activity on just getting troops on the ground. The need for such road blocks was on the basis of a perceived 5th column in the United Kingdom of German sympathisers or agents. In reality, these agents were all captured on arrival, so many have seen these road blocks, with retrospect, as more of a hinderance. However, at the time, with the Germans still advancing in France, the need was seen as real, and not only this but by the Local Defence Volunteers taking on these roles, regular and reserve forces could mobilise and prepare for the invasion proper. This relief of regular troops was much needed across the variety of static defences. It did not matter in reality if the Local Defence Volunteers were armed for these duties, they were not there to have a fire fight, but to alert and protect.

> *"It was the LDV's great delight ... to pull up all policemen and ask for their identity cards, especially inspectors. One squad even tried to detain a constable, who refused to comply, while he in turn threatened to arrest them for carrying arms without a licence.'*

Amusing as such anecdotes are, it should be born in mind that the police played a vital role in establishing the LDV as a properly constituted and armed force.[xviii]

On the 30th May, the Home Guard were handed over to the War Office, as General Headquarters and the regular army prioritised the decisive battle, it would fight against the coming invasion. Although the Home Guard would be commanded at the tactical level by the Zones, the Territorial Army Associations and the wider War Office administration would administer the new force, leaving the priority for arms and equipment to the regular forces. To support this county association, on the 3rd August Home Guard units were given county badges, but this was all to come. In some respect, the Local Defence Volunteers were formed due to the threat of widespread parachute drops, which could not be defended against. To that end, the new force was rapidly gaining utility by taking over vast number of static guard roles, including over 5000 miles of coast and thousands of vulnerable points, all of which took troops which could be used as a mobile force to counter attack the enemy. In addition, many administrative roles, including escorts, stretcher bearers and fire piquets were being taken on by the Local Defence Volunteers. It would be in this local static defence that the Home Guard made an immediate impact.

The Permanent Under Secretary for the Secretary of State for War, Sir Frederick Bovenschen called the whole idea of the Local Defence Volunteers 'slap dash' and most irregular. He claimed it was illegal as the fighters would be *Franc-tireur*[xix] in international law, and therefore shot out of hand when captured by the Germans. This was reinforced by the one million shotguns which were issued with single large lead ball lethal shot, this were seen by the Germans also to be illegal in combat. It is very likely that the Germans would have shot out of hand those armed with them, as they did in the First World War, this only exacerbated by the concept of the firer being a *Franc-tireur*. Despite these reservations, the Local Defence Volunteers were placed under the defence regulations and made subject to military law, to make them a formal fighting force, but in reality this would likely not have been recognised until uniform arrived. Writing shortly after the Second World War, Churchill was candid: "The massacre would have been on both sides grim and great. There would have been neither mercy nor quarter. They would have used Terror, and we were prepared to go to all lengths. I intended to use the slogan "You can always take one with you". I even calculated that the horrors of such a scene would in the last resort turn the scale in the United States."[xx]

As May became June, evidence of the first Home Guard operations appear in records, with patrols and observation posts causing a number of false reports. This is also the first piece of correspondence which refers to the 'Battalion Commander' of Local Defence Volunteers Sutton Coldfield. Two weeks after the first announcement of the formation of the Local Defence Volunteers, Warwickshire has restructured its defence from what was initially a single battalion of Home Guard, to a multi battalion formation, which would grow to be over 50,000 men, of which over 6,500 would be based in Sutton Coldfield. The operations of the Home Guard increased in their frequency, and rapidly platoons and companies were formed. The Sutton Coldfield Local Defence Volunteers was no exception, with vast number of volunteers turning up to duties across the town. As commanders who had experience of the military took command, local rotas were formed, with those weapons which were available being used on a rotational basis to ensure guards could be posted. At this time, the threat of invasion was rapidly becoming a real likelihood. On the French coastline at Dunkirk, a huge operation was underway to evacuate the British Army from France. The evacuation was being conducted by 222 British Naval vessels and 665 other craft; the King himself stated that "so difficult an operation was only made possible by brilliant leadership and an indomitable spirit among all ranks of the Force." By the 4th June, Operation Dynamo was complete with 338,226 men evacuated, including 112,000 French troops, many of whom would return to fight as the campaign continued on the continent.

[i] 'Mr Eden's Appeal', as written in Cambridgeshire and
Isle of Ely Territorial Association (1944) *We Also Served*. Local Publishing. p100.
[ii] This view of the criterial is given much analysis in, Flemming, P. (1958).
Invasion 1940. Hamish Hamilton.
[iii] LDV/600/1 SECRET 20 May 1940, a copy of which can be found in the Warwickshire Archive under CR 301/32
[iv] The section is outlined in Longmate, Norman. (1974) The Real Dad's Army: The Story of the Home Guard. Arrow Books, London. However, in addition to this, there is a reality of personal association, such as the fact that Wilfred Bigwood was the commander of the Special Constables and therefore a very close work colleague if not friend of the Chief Constable.
[v] As Zone Commander, Colonel Cash still had time for many other roles in the establishment. He became the TA Association Military Member at Horse Guards in 1942, Honorary Colonel of the Royal Warwick's in 1943, and a member of the Air Force Association in 1944 as well as being appointed as a Deputy Lieutenant. After the war he became the Vice-Chairman Territorial and Auxiliary Forces Associations and High Sherrif of Warwickshire in 1950. He again was Honorary Colonel of the Royal Warwick's in 1953.
[vi] The records of rank are very mixed, with some units referring to soldiers by traditional ranks rather than those listed in official rules. An explanation of this confusion can be found in Longmate, Norman. (1974) The Real Dad's Army: The Story of the Home Guard. Arrow Books, London.
[vii] I highly recommend Atkin, M. (2015) *Fighting Nazi Occupation (British Resistance 1939 – 1945)*. Pen and Sword. For those who would like to find out more about the more mysterious Home Guard and defence organisations.
[viii] This letter dated 18th May 1940 from the Warwickshire County Surveyor and other correspondence can be found in the Warwickshire Archive under file CR 301/32.
[ix] *Ibid*.
[x] The pamphlet provided by Cambridgeshire and
Isle of Ely Territorial Association (1944) *We Also Served*. Local Publishing. p16. Provides a account from near to the time which gives an honest appraisal of the challenges involved.
[xi] The correspondence to the Local Defence Volunteers in Warwickshire is spread amongst a large number of files in the Warwickshire Archive, but Colonel Cash was prolific in his memorandum in these early days.
[xii] As well as Colonel Cash, the Chief Constable's Office Warwickshire added to the correspondence at this time, these can also be found in the Warwickshire Archive in various files.
[xiii] Churchill, W. (1955) *Finest Hour*. Houghton Mifflin Harcourt
[xiv] Warwickshire Archive Ref: Z/5813/Duty A. Volunteer Memorandum 1940/6 Dated 30 May 1940
[xv] The codifying of these complex arrangements were finally written in the Regulations of the Home Guard 1942. Prior to this (and post) there was

considerable variation and in some cases confusion.

[xvi] Technically a District

[xvii] A fantastic diary can be found in Sutton Coldfield Library under, War Time Sutton: Extracts from the diaries of Gwilym O Griffith 1940-40. Sutton Historical Society.

[xviii] Longmate, Norman. (1974) The Real Dad's Army: The Story of the Home Guard. Arrow Books, London.

[xix] There is much discussion of *Franc-tireur* in many documents during the war. This term defined in international law, was originally used to define irregular military formations deployed by France during the early stages of the Franco-Prussian War. The actions of these *Franc-tireur* from this date could be deemed illegal and therefore they were subject to summary execution.

[xx] Churchill, W. (1955) *Finest Hour*. Houghton Mifflin Harcourt

Chapter 4

The Officers of the Battalion

What were these men like who volunteered at the country's time of need? Each had a story to tell, from widely different backgrounds, but all made the commitment to serve at this difficult and demanding time in British history. Although records do exist, there is no comprehensive list of Home Guard members prior to this book, and the details can be found in Part II of this book of all known members who served in the battalion.

There are known to be 6542 people who served in the 6th Warwickshire (Sutton) Home Guard Battalion during its period of existence. Of these, 203 were officers, at the most senior rank they served, these can be broken down into 43 2nd Lieutenants, 107 Lieutenants, 31 Captains, 15 Majors, three Lieutenant Colonels and two Colonels. There were eight Doctors and two Padres amongst them. 82 of these officers served in the First World War (of which records have been found) and 45 of these were in the infantry. Nine had been awarded the Military Cross or Military Media for bravery and five had the Distinguished Service Order for leadership. Some decided that Platoon Command was the best job for them despite more senior experience; 2nd Lieutenant James Irwin, who commanded No. 4 Platoon, was a Captain from the First World War, but also had been awarded the Distinguish Conduct Medal twice for leadership. Likewise, Lieutenant Charles Wetton who commanded No. 11 Platoon C Company, served in the Machine Gun Corps as a Major and company commander in the First World War.

Leadership is not easy, especially with the real threat of invasion, and many of the records show both officers and senior non-commissioned officers who 'reverted to the ranks at their own request'. The challenge of leadership is to inspire, to look after your men, and to give clear direction. It is noticeable that after the first few months, considerable changes in junior leadership took place, with young sergeants and lieutenants replacing some of those who presumed appointments in May 1940. The appointment of company officers by the battalion commander was always going to have an element of nepotism, but it is interesting how 'captains of industry' moved into key roles and led men in work and in the Home Guard in many cases.

There was not a shortage of experienced officers and soldiers in Sutton Coldfield. It was an affluent town, which although in Warwickshire, was in a sense a suburb of Birmingham, with many captains of industry and retired officers living in the town, with its big Victorian houses, and one of the largest parks in Europe. The selection of officers for the companies, and the structure of the battalion itself was made very quickly. The main defence of the town was structured on the basis of a normal infantry battalion, with three rifle companies (A, B and C) and a Headquarters Company (D). Each company would have four platoons, and the Headquarters company the specialist and support components.

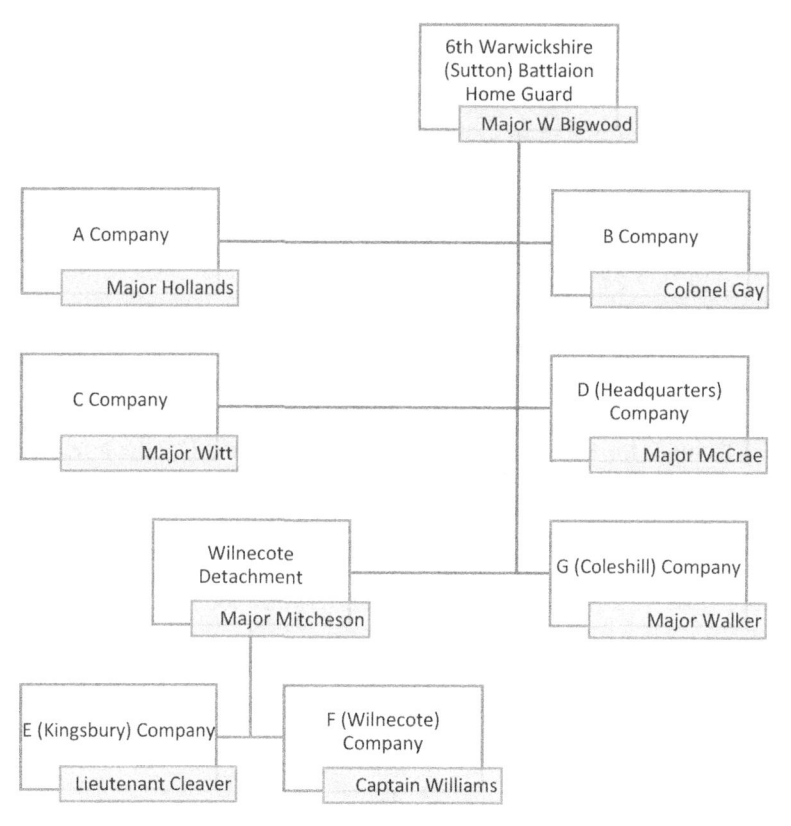

```
                    6th Warwickshire
                    (Sutton) Battlaion
                       Home Guard
                     Major W Bigwood

    A Company                              B Company
    Major Hollands                         Colonel Gay

    C Company                              D (Headquarters)
                                              Company
     Major Witt                            Major McCrae

              Wilnecote
              Detachment                   G (Coleshill) Company
            Major Mitcheson                   Major Walker

  E (Kingsbury) Company    F (Wilnecote)
                              Company
    Lieutenant Cleaver     Captain Williams
```

Table 6: 6th Battalion Structure 1940

However, due to the large area of responsibility within the battalion area of operations, there was a need for a larger structure to the east of the town. The rural area covered all of the small villages to the east, spread along the river Tame at Kingsbury, from the villages surrounding Wilnecote just to the southeast of Tamworth, moving south through Kingsbury itself and down to Coleshill. This line of villages was structured to be amongst three additional companies. In the north there would be the Wilnecote Detachment, made up of E (Kingsbury) Company and F (Wilnecote) Company. This detachment would be commanded by a senior officer and the companies would be based upon the individual villages running down the river tame. In the south, G (Coleshill) Company would be based around the large village of Coleshill and the six other small villages surrounding this. This complex arrangement meant that the battalion was in effect a small brigade[i], with a battalion size force in Sutton Coldfield itself, and a smaller half battalion in Wilnecote Detachment and an isolated company at Coleshill.

To command these units, men came forward who either were senior in rank, some more so than the now Major Bigwood, or those who knew Wilfred through his various connections. The command of the companies, therefore, ended in a wide variety of officers, some with more field experience than others. The rural companies (E and F) were commanded by junior officers at first, as their structure was refined over time, but in comparison, B Company was commanded by a Colonel. The rank system at first was not fully established, and it was not until July when normal military rank structures were put in place. Rapid promotion was the order of the day, as units required commanders and NCOs to bring them structure. It was down to local commanders to decide who was most appropriate. In some cases senior managers in civilian occupations were placed above those in senior ranks in the military, as they were more used to managing large numbers of people from their current occupations.

In battalion headquarters there were many experienced officers who would make the battalion work in an efficient way. The role of these officers were to administrate the battalion, mainly under the direction of the battalion second-in-command. However, the battalion administrative assistant was in place to ensure that a full-time paid member of staff was present to oversee the day-to-day running of the battalion when those in appointment were at their daytime employment. The key officers in the headquarters were the adjutant, (in charge of discipline and administration), the intelligence officer and the training officer. In addition, there were the support services under the lieutenant quartermaster, who ensured the battalion were equipped, fed and moved on time and in the right place. His team of an ammunition officer, transport officer and catering officer, as well as a pioneer officer to set up defences were key to the logistics and running of the battalion. The following table shows the key staff officer known to be in the battalion in the early part of the war.

Rank	Name	First Name	Appointment
Lieutenant Colonel	Bigwood MC	Wilfrid	Commanding Officer
Lieutenant Colonel	Strevens DSO MC	Harry	Administrative Assistant
Major	Dingley MC	Philip	Second-in-Command
Major Doctor	MacFarlane	William Mair	Senior Medical Officer
Captain	Freeley	F B R	Adjutant
Captain	Freeman	Harvey	Intelligence Officer
Chaplain	Harvey	George L H	Chaplain

Captain	Pitchford	Albert Clarance	Transport Officer
Lieutenant	Howard	John	Quartermaster
Lieutenant	Collins	Walter Edmund	Battalionn Ammunition Officer
Captain	Rymond	Arthur Earnest	Transport and Food Officer
Lieutenant	Pattison	George Raymond	Battalion Catering Officer
Captain	Turner	Horace Henry	Pioneer Officer
Lieutenant	Crich DCM Bar	Joseph William	Pioneer Officer
Captain	Ross	Joseph Harrearon	Training Officer
Lieutenant	Powell	John Hirst	Weapons Training Officer
Captain	Sampson	Frederick Harrold	Liaison Officer
Captain	Sharpe	Charles Harvey	Regimental Signals Officer
Lieutenant	Walker	P W	Pigeon Officer

Table 7: Battalion Headquarters and Staff

As the war continued, officers promoted, retired or even sadly died, and new specialities and requirement emerged. Like all organisations structures changed, as did the structures in those organisations above the battalion. These are the stories of some of the officers who served in headquarters of the 6th Battalion, there stories are interesting to understand the nature of the men who served.

The Commanding Officer

The deep red cliffs had pale dust travelling slowly down the steep re-entrant settling on to the parapet of the trench. Wilfred crouched low next to the young soldier who had just taken over guard duty on this stretch of the line. He was tired, but he was the duty senior non-commissioned officer, and he had to check the corporals had posted all the sentries correctly. Above them, Dead Man's Ridge had a dominating view of their trench, and it was likely that the Turks would counterattack this morning, so he had to make sure the men were ready despite the testing times. They would be relieved tonight and move into the reserve trenches to the rear, still dangerous, but less chance of snipers. As Wilfred, Sergeant Wilfred Bigwood, move slowly along the trench at a crouch to the next sentry position, an eruption of rocks and red dust shot up behind him. He heard the shouts of 'man down' and breathed a deep sigh as he worked his way towards the site to deal with what he found.

That night, on the 9th June 1915 the 1st Battalion of the Auckland Infantry Regiment moved into reserve in Monash Valley Gallipoli. During the day they had lost one killed and three wounded by artillery fire, giving the total losses of the battalion for the campaign of 12 officers and 83 soldiers killed, 23 officers and 527 soldiers wounded, and one officer and 77 other ranks missing.[ii] For a small battalion raised from settlers who were only in the second generation after the province was founded in the 1860s, this has been a huge loss. Despite this large numbers of replacements from the small towns and villages back home were joining them after the intense recruitment campaign to serve the British Empire at its time of need.

Sergeant Wilfred Bigwood had served in the battalion since December 1914, although he was from Bromsgrove in Birmingham, England, has was working on business in New Zealand as a young man after attending boarding school at Kings Norton Birmingham. On the outbreak of war he was living in the Victoria Hotel, Auckland and he immediately signed up for the local regiment.

After the hard fighting and rapid promotion to Sergeant, Wilfred was recommended for commission. In January 1916, the Regiment landed in Egypt to refit and train after the end of the Campaign. In the same Army which had landed in Gallipoli and were now refitting, were the 4th Battalion Worcestershire Regiment, a Battalion of the Regiment from Wilfred's home in England south of Birmingham. Wilfred was given a commission as a temporary 2nd Lieutenant in this battalion, taking command of soldiers from England and now he was an officer in the British Army, all be it only temporary for the duration of the war.

After two months of training, re-equipping and inducting the replacements, on the 15th of March 1916, the 4th Battalion embarked on the merchant ship 'Merchant Vessel Transylvania'[iii] at Alexandria and sailed for Marseilles on the 20th. The battalion, with their new platoon commander, now 'Mr Bigwood' as subalterns were termed, arrived in France and moved through the towns and villages to the northwest, where they joined the huge industrial machine which was in place on the western front, stretching from the Swiss boarder to the sea. The British Army had grown beyond all recognition, and the New Army had just taken part in the opening days of the disastrous Somme campaign. The battalion joined the line, in much different circumstances to the Mediterranean climate they were used to and took part in the attack on Beaumont Hamel on the Somme briefly. For the soldiers this was their first experience of combat in this theatre, no longer against Turks, but fighting Germans. Wilfred took this time to gain experience of command, and how to be an officer: useful experience for the challenges ahead.

On the 31st of August 1916, the battalion was pulled back from the front and into the town of Ypres. After a brief period of rest in a tented reserve area, on September 8th they marched up the Menin Road through a very damp and misty night to the *Bellewaerde* trenches, to relieve the Newfoundland Regiment on the front line[iv]. The battalion posted sentries and got into the routine of life on the front line. Wilfred took turns as duty officer inspecting the positions, checking on the men, and doing his turn in the command dug out awaiting any orders form company or battalion headquarters. As things were at the time, offensive action was often called for, and the battalion planned a series of raids into the opposing German trenches to capture prisoners and disrupt their routine.

The raiding part would be commanded by Lieutenant Wyatt and consisted of three officers and 30 men. It was supported by a preliminary bombardment from artillery to keep the Germans' heads down while the men moved across no man's land. It was planned to enter the enemy trenches on a small salient which protruded south of Rouler's Railway. The raid was carried out on the night of September 15th. The raiding party moved across no man's land, but in the darkness and shellfire the party split up, with only a small force under Lieutenant Wyatt and Lieutenant Bigwood making it into the enemy trench. As they entered the trench, a fierce fight started, where bombs were thrown, rifles were fired and then bayonets, and entrenching tools were used. The enemy were driven into their dugouts and the trench way gained.

Lieutenant Wyatt was shot in the stomach during the fight and was in a bad way, which left Wilfred in command, however during the fight he had fallen and broken his ankle and also received a bullet wound. Despite his injuries, he commanded the platoon and sent men forward to bomb the dugouts. One dugout surrendered and four German prisoners were gained, which was the main purpose of the raid. There were no non-commissioned officers, so Wilfred ordered Private Edkins and Private Dean to get a litter and corral the prisoners. The privates led the men back over no man's land towards the British lines. Once the last man was accounted for, Private Dean helped Wilfred move back over the parapet and from shell hole to shell hole towards the British lines held by the 2nd Hampshire's. They were fired upon heavily the whole way back and four of the prisoners were killed. However, Wilfred commanded the platoon into safety, and managed to bring their own casualties back as well as successfully completing their mission.

On the 16th of November, as Wilfred was in a field hospital in northern France, the London Gazette announced that both Lieutenant Bigwood and Lieutenant Wyatt were awarded the Military Cross and Privates Edkins and Private Dean were awarded the Military Medal. The citation for Wilfred read:

> *"2nd Lt. Wilfrid Bigwood, For conspicuous gallantry in action. He carried out a daring raid with great determination. Though wounded, and, with his ankle broken he would not leave the enemy trench until he had collected his party."*[v]

Wilfred's wounds were non-life threatening, but required time to recover from. He returned to England, received some leave, and spend a lot of time gaining his strength again. Wilfred was now 27 and had not lost his thirst for adventure or being part of the colonial army. He missed the wildness and fun of his New Zealand soldiers, less formal that the ridged structures of the British Army of the western front, where he would always be a 'Temporary Officer'. Wilfred looked at options and decided to join the Indian Army, which was very short of officers at this time, and he applied and was accepted for a commission in the 16th (Indian) Cavalry.

Wilfred joined the 16th Cavalry on the 19 January 1917. The 16th Cavalry were the successor Regiment of the Robilkhand Horse, later called the 16th Bengal Lancers. They were made up of two squadrons of Sikhs, one of Dogras (from Bengal) and one of Addl (Muslim soldiers from Bengal), Wilfred would be a troop officer to start, which meant he would be one of the pool of british officers in the troop, responsible for the local (or native) soldiers. The 16th Cavalry were part of 6th (Indian) Cavalry Brigade, 7th (Meerut) Division, and had served firstly on the Western Front, but from 1915, in the Mesopotamian campaign ending in Baghdad in March 1917. Wilfred joined the Regiment in the last stages of the campaign, as they moved west to Palestine, where the sieges of Jerusalem against the Turks had taken place, and the army was becoming a garrison force.

Life became more of a routine for the Regiment as patrols took place into the mountains and deserts in holy land. As a cavalry officer, stable parades, inspections and musters became the order of the day. Then training to be ready for whatever challenge came next, with one eye on the Regiment returning to India, where they would again be used as part of the British Indian Army in the constant garrison duties and border wars there. In January 1918 Wilfred became a squadron officer, formally part of the Regiment and no longer attached. He was now a troop leader, with 40 soldiers and mounts under his command, leading independent patrols into the interior often against local Arab fighters, who were demanding their own state from the British and French protectorates in the region.

In August 1918, the Regiment sailed back to India and to become part of the garrison forces of the British Indian Army. The Regiment moved initially to be part of the Burma Army in the Far East of the sub-continent, at that time a very undeveloped region, with only some local rubber plantations. Some of the soldiers who had fought in Europe and Mesopotamia were released back to their homes, other locals joined as new soldiers. As always, patrols and training followed, with new mounts purchased locally to strengthen the size of the troops and squadrons into a larger more effective cavalry force. Life in the British Indian Army was a joy for Wilfred, with many privileges, such as a smart officers' mess, servants and even some local events with the rubber plantation owners and other ex-patriots in the region.

On the 13th of May 1919, the situation changed again when the Afghan Army under King Amanullah invaded Northern India, taking advantage of the lack of troops due to the war in Europe. In response, the 16th Cavalry moved rapidly by train to the Northwest Frontier and joined 10th Cavalry Brigade in the offensive against Jalalabad. The rapid campaign was very familiar to Wilfred due to the fighting he had done in Mesopotamia, with long patrols, rapid charges and dealing with local fighters. The campaign came to a swift conclusion, but the 16th Cavalry then immediately moved to Waziristan where a rebellion had taken hold, again to be quelled by the soldiers of the 16th Cavalry and their very much experienced troops leader Temporary Captain Wilfred Bigwood MC.

It had been a long five years of constant fighting and garrison duty. The Indian Army was starting its demobilisation process, and as more British Indian Army units moved back to the sub-continent there was talk of reductions in Regiment and moving to a peacetime establishment with less sub-units and therefore officers. It was time for Wilfred to decide on what was next for him, and although he loved the colonial life, he did not yet have a family and understood maybe it was time to go home. On the 10th of November 1919, Wilfred resigned his commission and returned to England. Wilfred was entitled to many medals for his service but at the time he had not applied for them. It was not until 1926 when he decided the time was right to get them from the War Office.

On his return to Birmingham, he re-joined his parents and as his father was in the auctioneer business focusing on house sales, he got a job as an insurance broker. A year later he had met Stephanie Gertrude Lindner and whilst he was living at the Grand Hotel in Birmingham, he married her on the 30th of September 1920, over the road at Birmingham Cathedral. With his new wife, he moved back to Sutton Coldfield where he became a director of numerous businesses and moved into the Corner House on Four Oaks Road.

After an adventurous youth, Wilfred threw himself into his work as he did his military service. His family grew with children, and he became successful in his various business, including in the insurance world. A decade later, he entered public life from 1932 to 1936 he was a Magistrate in the town, then a town councillor, and from 1938 to 1939 he become mayor of Sutton Coldfield. In 1937, he was granted the George VI Coronation Medal as the local recipient. In 1939, he opened a road called Bigwood Drive off Vesey Gardens, in his honour. He took over as commander of the Warwickshire Special Constabulary in

November 1939. Wilfred was a war hero, a businessman and a trusted pillar of the community, just the kind of man people look to when there is a time of need. With the announcement of the formation of the Home Guard, Wilfred volunteered to command the local unit in Sutton Coldfield. He knew the local political players, and spoke to the chief constable, the Regional Commissioner and the Lord Lieutenant to make sure he was able to take up the role. The dashing cavalry officer, with medals and experience in war was just the man to lead the town's defenders in its time of need.

Battalion Second in Command
Philip Dinley served in the 6th Battalion the Worcestershire Regiment in the First World War, but also in the Royal Tank Regiment. In February 1918 he was awarded the military cross for conspicuous gallantry and devotion to duty. When his own tank was put out of action and the officer of another was wounded, he took charge of the other tank led it to the objective and kept it in action for seven hours. He set a splendid example of initiative and devotion to duty.

Battalion Administrative Assistant
Lieutenant Colonel Harry Strevens DSO MC was 61 years old on the formation of the Local Defence Volunteers in Sutton Coldfield in May 1940. He had served in the Army for 44 of those years from the age of 17. Born on 25th October 1879 in Oxfordshire, Harry joined the Royal Warwickshire Regiment in October 1897 and never looked back. On joining the 2nd Battalion, he deployed to fight in the Second Boer War, then afterwards moved to garrison duty in Bermuda to guard Boer prisoners. In 1903, Harry returned home with the Battalion and started a period of home duty, training, guards and exercises. Harry was promoted

through the ranks, becoming a platoon sergeant then a company quartermaster. Harry continued to be promoted and by 1914 was a warrant officer, a Company Sergeant Major.

On the outbreak of the First World War Harry as company sergeant major moved with the battalion to France from their Garrison posting in Malta. With the rapid need for more officers, with the expansion of the army to its wartime establishment, Harry was commissioned and made a second lieutenant during the first action of the battalion as contact was made with the Germans near Mons. The battalion formed part of 22nd Brigade, 7th Division, with which they saw a huge amount of fighting over the next two years. Everywhere the battalion fought, Harry was at the forefront, being awarded the Mention in Despatches twice, and then, in November 1916, the Military Cross for distinguished service in the field. On 2nd January 1915 Harry was promoted to Captain and was serving alongside a Bernard Law Montgomery, a fellow Captain in the Regiment.

In September 1917, Harry was posted to Italy where he was promoted to Major and served with the 9th Service Battalion of the Devonshire Regiment. He commanded the support company of the battalion and ensured that all the logistical and transport arrangements were in place, and assisted the battalion headquarters with planning. On the 15th April 1918, he was awarded the *Croix de Guerre* for bravery in the face of the enemy, working with the Devonshire Regiment. In May 1918, he was Mentioned in Dispatches for a fourth time during the war. In June 1916, he was awarded the Distinguished Service Order for his work with the battalion, a significant honour and reflection of his command ability.

Harry worked extremely efficiently with the battalion and was given a staff appointment as an acting Lieutenant Colonel from September to December 1918 with the Commander in Chief of British Forces Italy, General Cavan. The forces in Italy were small but Harry gained a huge amount of experience in the headquarters. In June 1916, he was awarded a fifth Mention in Despatches for his work in the headquarters.

As the war reached its end, Harry continued as a regular officer and reverted to his substantive rank of Captain. As the army moved to a peacetime establishment, he was appointed as Adjutant of the 6th Battalion The Royal Warwickshire Regiment, in charge of administration of the territorial battalion. Harry's career continued after the war in the smaller army, moving through the ranks quickly, becoming a substantive Lieutenant Colonel in the territorial force by 1923. His career was not without hiccups, with a Courts Martial in 1923 leading to the withdrawal of his good conduct medal for conduct unbecoming an officer. Harry was stationed at Thorpe Street Barracks throughout the 1920s, home of the 5th and 6th (TA) Battalions of the Warwickshire Regiment.

Married to Edith Dickenson, he had achieved the incredible journey from Private to Lieutenant Colonel over his career. When war broke out and the call came for volunteers for the Home Guard, Harry stepped up without hesitation. Too old to take command, he decided to support Wilfred by being an administrative assistant to the battalion. With the scale of the battalion and the challenge of the formation, this was much needed and gave Wilfred considerable assistance.

Senior Medical Officer

William Mair MacFarlane was born in 1897 to Thomas, a boot warehouse foreman and his wife Janet. William and his sister grew up in Birmingham and the family were wealthy enough to have a domestic servant living with them. During the First World War, William signed up to serve with the Cameronian Highlanders and was commissioned as a second lieutenant. He was shot at the Somme in 1916 and because of this was moved to London Garrison where he served until 1918.

Post-war he signed up to study medicine at the University of Glasgow. William had an interesting career in medicine, being the Medical Officer for Warwickshire Police and then the Senior Medical Officer City Hospital University of Birmingham. Living at 77 Lichfield Road at outbreak of war, he signed up to be the battalion medical officer. Each company had their own medical officer (Captain) and William, as the Senior Medical Officer (Major), coordinated the efforts of these officers in the battalion.

The Battalion Staff

Some officers have little historical records, such as the Adjutant of the Battalion, Captain Freeley, who we know only was commissioned from the ranks and was a quartermaster prior to his appointment. However, we know that Captain Harvey Freeman, who lived at number 12 Anchorage Road, served in the 5th South Staffordshire Regiment in the First World War and after being the intelligence officer for the first two years of the war, was made the civilian liaison officer and later liaison officer to the local heavy artillery anti-aircraft battery. Captain Frederick Sampson from Four Oaks was another liaison officer and had served in the Royal Warwickshire Regiment from 1916 to 1919, he would later become a staff Officer in the Warwickshire Sub-District. Captain Charles Harvey Sharpe from Eastern Road, Wylde Green, was the regimental signals officer. He had been in 33rd Siege Battery Royal Artillery as a signals instructor in the First World War. These officers had considerable experience and knew how to administrate and organise, these were key characteristics needed to ensure the battalion ran well. Key to all of these staff roles was the ability to talk to people and liaise with the other organisations, particularly in civil defence. This team, operating from the Royal Hotel in the centre of Sutton Coldfield were the nervous system of the battalion.

Supporting these headquarters staff were three key platoons, the Signals Platoon, the Regimental Police Section and the Battalion Headquarters Guard Platoon. These three platoons provided the day-to-day manpower to ensure staff jobs were completed. In Signals Platoon were phone operators, but also runners, often boy scouts or school boys from Bishop Vesey School over the road. The Guard Platoon had the thankless task of guarding the headquarters day and night for the duration of the war, constantly under the eyes of both the civilians in the town hall, but also the officers, many who were critical of appearance, going in to the headquarters.

Providing welfare support was the battalion chaplain, George Harvey, who lived at the Rectory in Coleshill Street. Reverend Harvey would spend many late hours visiting the soldiers on guard and on exercise, and would help those who were having a difficult time. A slightly different chaplain was Lieutenant (the Revenant) Leslie James Garrett, who commandeered No. 2 Platoon, E Company. From the Parsonage in Dosthill, which he turned into the platoon headquarters, he took a direct involvement in protecting his flock, taking a combat role in defending his village and congregation. Such a role was very unusual and spoke to the character of the man. He remained in the role until 1943, when he moved to 5th Battalion to provide a more pastoral service.

In the quartermasters' department, often behind the scenes, Quartermaster John Howard from Four Oaks had a team of veterans to support him. Arthur Rymond, also from Four Oaks, had served in the First World War in the Royal Navy Air Service. He was the battalion transport officer and worked in civilian life in a local haulage firm, so understood the role well. George Patterson, the battalion catering officer, also served in the First World War, but as a restaurant manager, understood the requirements of feeding large numbers of men. Working behind the scenes, this team of experienced men made sure that the battalion ran efficiently and was organised and equipped for any need. It would soon be tested as summer ended and the threat came from the air.

[i] For those who are unsure of the military terminology, a Brigade is a group of battalions, usually three or four, so around four to five thousand men. A Battalion is the building block of an army is around 600 to 1000 men. A Regiment in the British Army can be used synonymously with Battalion, but can also be an administrative unit which has a large number of independent battalions.
[ii] Details can be found in the War Diary of Auckland Infantry Regiment.
[iii] MV – a Merchant Vessel.
[iv] Details can be found in the War Diary of the 4th Battalion the Warwickshire Regiment.
[v] As quoted in the London Gazette.

Chapter 5

The Company Officers

The rifle company is the fighting building block of any infantry formation. It is the lowest level which a unit can operate in an independent context and is able to be grouped with other assets and administrate itself. The rifle company is commanded by the company commander and controlled by the company sergeant major and to many, this was a mother and father relationship in the traditional sense. In a very 1940s fashion, mother did the day-to-day routine, made sure you were fed and on time and told you off when you were naughty. The father was the master of the house, making major decisions and only disciplining or rewarding for exceptional reason. These company locations were initially designed to be the platoons of the battalion, however with the rapid growth of the Local Defence Volunteers, Sutton Company became a battalion, and Wilnecote Company became a detachment of two companies within the wider battalion.

A Company

A Company was formed to the north of Sutton Park in the area of Little Aston and Streetly. Moorland cottage was to be the headquarters, with platoon locations distributed across the area. Public houses, such as the Crown Pub, were popular locations, both from a military view, as they were often at key road junctions, and had feeding facilities, but they were often popular with the men also, with the ability to have a pint after duty.

The commander of A Company was Herbert William Hollands, who was born in Effingshall in Wolverhampton on the 21st of November 1896. The son of an accountant, at the age of 17 he spent two years at a technical college in London from 1913 to 1915. At the end of his course, he joined the 2nd Battalion Kings Shropshire light Infantry as a 2nd Lieutenant on the outbreak of the First World War. After receiving his initial training, Herbert was transferred to the 6th (Service) Battalion of the King's Shropshire Light Infantry based in Shrewsbury who had little equipment and were a second line unit training replacements at that time.

Herbert entered France on 21st February 1916 where the battalion had been moved in July of 1915 to begin training behind the lines. In 1916, the battalion became part of 60th Brigade, 20th (Light) Division and began a long year of campaigning, during which it lost 602 men. Each battle was taking a terrible toll on the soldiers. Herbert's battle did not last long as on the 24th February he was evacuated back to England after being wounded at Pilkem Ridge. He would remain in England for the rest of 1917.

Frustrated by his injuries, Herbert volunteered to join the new Royal Flying Corps where he was transferred to on the 25th November 1917. His technical education allowed him to start pilot training with No.1 Training Squadron, and he started learning to fly at the RAF training school in Hilborne in May of 1918. Herbert continued his training after the armistice was signed and became qualified to fly independently on the 4th March 1919. On the 5th March, Herbert was transferred to the reserve list, effectively demobilised, but retained in case of mobilisation. Herbert returned home to train as an accountant, but never lost his interest in engineering.

In April 1921 to maintain Herbert as a pilot, the RAF mobilised him for two months of active duty with No.3 Group, 39 Squadron in Shrewsbury. He trained to fly the Airco DH.9A Bomber over this period and was given the rank of acting Captain. Herbert returned home and married his wife Lilian, moving to Sutton Coldfield where he lived at 9 Bishop Road and became the Managing Director of Combustion Engineering Company.

Herbert signed up for the Local Defence Volunteer immediately once the call went out for volunteers. Both as an experienced officer from the war, but also as a senior manager in a local firm, he was determined to take on a leading role in the battalion. He was appointed as Officer Commanding A Company, despite 16 of the officers in the company having war experience in First World War, and of these nine of them being infantry. His experience and senior leadership, and also influence in civil society was seen as critical to command the men's respect. He would remain as the Company Commander for the duration of the war.

Backing up Herbert was his company second-in-command Albert Trechman. Albert was born in 1893 in Harlepool with his family and was training as a draughtsman for an electrical engineering company by the age of 17. He joined the Durham Light Infantry as a 2nd Lieutenant in May 1915 and served on the Western Front briefly before requesting a transfer to the Indian Army. He was posted to the 2nd Battalion of the 67th Punjabis, which had been formed only in 1915 for service in India. He arrived on the 17th of February 1916 and joined just as the battalion were signed off as being ready for active service by Brigadier Hardy, the Commander of 2nd Quetta Infantry Brigade. The battalion was posted to the Northwest Frontier and was based at Khajuri Kach, where in May 1917 they fought a bitter counterinsurgency fight with the local Pashtun tribes, with the battalion having 20 killed and 27 wounded. After this fighting, the battalion formed part of the Waziristan Field Force and were based in Tank, with constant patrols and operations over the harsh mountains.

In January 1918 Albert was made acting Captain and Adjutant of the battalion, responsible for discipline and administration. As Adjutant, Albert also wrote the war diary and was responsible for the battalion inspection regime. In 1919, an inspection report described the battalion as "smart and well up; they handle their arms well and move smartly."[i] Albert sailed back to England for a period of long leave in 1920 and returned in June on the SS Moria with his new wife Laura. On returning to India, he had to wait on the battalion returning from a short period of six months in

Iraq. The battalion became a training battalion in 1922 and was re-designated the 10th Battalion, 2nd Punjab Regiment.

Albert left the Indian Army and returned home to England, where he became a transport manager. He lived in Greenhill Road in Sutton Coldfield and was a special constable for a time. As the war started in 1939, Albert signed up as an Air Raid Precaution warden, but once the announcement was made in 1940 for the Local Defence Volunteers, he immediately resigned from the Air Raid Precaution Service and became a member of A Company. His experiences as both Adjutant, but also in logistics, meant that he was an excellent fit for company second-in-command. He commanded a mobile company in 1943 and was promoted to Major. Sadly, not long after standdown in January 1945, Albert died.

B Company
B Company was based to the east of Sutton Coldfield, largely around the White House, and Moor Hall. Again, public houses, hotels and golf clubs were used as key defensive locations, but also for administration. B Company had many experienced officers, including George Hackney and James Iveson, who had both been infantry company sergeant majors in the First World War and also Rupert Llewelyn Thomas who had been a Captain in the 5th Royal Welsh. George Hackney was made Company Training Officer, James Iveson was given a Platoon and Rupert Thomas was given an independent platoon at Wishaw, which was to the east of the main town. The presence of a platoon in Wishaw was critical to maintain communications between the main body of the battalion, and the three companies running north to south on the river tame.

The company commander in May 1940 was Levi John Albert Gay, known as John. John was an officer of the Territorial Army, who had joined in 1908, at the age of 26, on the founding of the territorial force. Born in Pembroke, Wales, John was very much middle class, and in time would become a senior insurance broker, who enjoyed his other 'career' as a TA officer, which gave him much stature in his professional and public life. By the outbreak of war in 1914, he was a subaltern in the Territorial Army battalion of the Royal Regiment of Wales. On the outbreak of war, the terms of service for the Territorial Army were that they were home duties only, meaning they were not expected to serve overseas. To that end, although many did volunteer to go straight to France, many did not, and felt their role should be as they signed up for, home defence.

Lieutenant Gay decided to remain in the Home Army and became a Platoon Commander in the 1/7th (Cyclist) Battalion. For the next few years, the battalion moved around the United Kingdom, tasked with defending the coast from German attack, first at Berwick-on-Tweed, then Ayton and Eyemouth in Scotland. In March 1915, the battalion moved to the east coast borders at Saltburn, where in 1916 John Gay was promoted to Captain. In early 1917, he moved to Seaton, finally settling for the remainder of the war to be part of Tees Garrison at Middlesbrough.

The rules changed for mobilisation in 1917 as the war dragged on, and many Territorial Army soldiers were moved to more active units and forced to go overseas. On 28th December 1917, John deployed to France as part of the 2nd Battalion The Royal Welch Regiment, likely as a Captain on the staff. The battalion fought at Lys, Arras and then the Hindenburg line that year, and although not a front-line commander, John would have seen first-hand the hard fighting on the Western Front. He returned later that year and as the war ended, decided to continue his territorial role as he returned to his civilian employment.

John and his wife Isobel Maud moved to Sutton Coldfield, living at 19 Cremorne Road, Four Oaks, for his work as a local manager the Scottish Metropolitan Assurance Company. He was promoted to command of the 5th (Territorial Army) Battalion of the Royal Warwickshire Regiment. His command lasted from 1929 until 1932 and after his command he was awarded an honouree rank of Brevet Colonel. When war broke out, John was 50 and was still on the books for the Territorial Army. He made the decision to sign up for the Home Guard and the Territorial Army to try and get involved in the war effort. He ended up as a Captain in both and was given command of B Company 6th Warwickshire (Sutton) Home Guard: an obvious choice for Wilfred Bigwood, who must have also seen John Gay as a potential competitor to command the battalion. It is likely that Wilfred's combat experience and gallantry award gave him the edge over this infantry Colonel.

Tragedy struck in 1942, when John's son, who was the chief stoker of HMS Ghurkha, died when the ship was sunk by German U-boat U133 off the Libyan coast. It was a terrible loss for John, and he never recovered from the sadness which came upon him. On the 24th February 1943, John Gay died and was buried at St James' Church in Sutton Coldfield.

B Company was handed over to a new commander on the 26th February 1943. Percy Cozens was promoted to Major and appointed company commander; he had been the company second-in-command since 1941 and was an experienced infantry officer from the First World War. Born in 1889, Percy had served in the 18th Fusiliers as a lance corporal in France from November 1915 until March 1916. He then commissioned into the 5th South Staffordshire Regiment and returned to France again in August 1916. An accountant by trade, Percy came from the Walsall (Streetly) side of Sutton Coldfield and therefore having joined a Birmingham Battalion as a soldier, was fortunate to commission into the territorial battalion of Walsall, which at this time was in South Staffordshire.

Percy's experience as a platoon commander was typical of many an infantry officer who has served. He joined the battalion, had been serving on the Western Front since February, in August of that year. He served with the battalion with distinction, being awarded the Military Cross for bravery in August 1917. His citation read:

> *His Majesty the King has been graciously pleased to confer the Military Cross in recognition of conspicuous gallantry and devotion to duty in the field. During a raid upon an enemy trench his platoon was held up by wire before reaching the trench. With complete disregard of personal safety, although already wounded, he crawled to the trench, and conducted a bombing attack upon the enemy, thereby preventing them from bombing that portion of the raiding party that had succeeded in doing this.*[ii]

Percy was a member of the battalion when they launched the final battle of the war, the assault by the 46th North Midland Division. The assault on the most heavily defended part of the Hindenburg line led to victory in the war and was the final mass offensive of that long terrible war. After the war,

Percy became an accountant, and knew John Gay through this work, so he was therefore an obvious choice for company second-in-command. These personal relationships were key to the selection of officer in the battalion.

C Company

The most controversial appointment made by Wilfred Bigwood was the appointment of Major Edward Christian Witt as Officer Commanding C Company. Edward had no experience in the military and his appointment was likely made as he was a member of the chamber of commerce and would have known Wilfred as part of the local community. This close relationship is reinforced when Edward later becomes the battalion second-in-command in 1944. C Company itself had an area of operations which overlapped with much of D (Headquarters) Company and also Battalion HQ. The Company Headquarters was at the Priory on Birmingham Road, opposite the Odean Cinema, with a platoon at Colbourne Antiques over the road. A platoon was based at the Rifle and Pistol Club on Coles Lane and the final platoon at Lind Vista Garage in Wishaw.

Edward Witt was born in 1901 in Balsall Heath to his father Christian who was a master tailor. By 1939 he was the managing director of three clothing companies and lived in Hill Village Road, Sutton Coldfield. He lived there with his wife Annie whom he married in June 1929. After the war Edward travelled a lot, including to Brazil on the SS Andes in 1945, and later he would settle overseas in Portugal.

This nonprofessional command of C Company was not the case in the other companies. But despite the risk of having such commanders, C Company also had a second-in-command who had never been in the military. Born 2nd May 1904 in Southampton, Gordon Stewart McDonald was the son of a soldier, Robert. As a young man, he travelled around the country with his father's postings including to Shrewsbury and Hertfordshire. Missing out of the First World War due to his age, by 1939 Gordon was a Chartered Civil Engineer and lived at 359 Birmingham Road, Wylde Green, with his wife Marjorie. As a professional, Gordon was given a commission in the Home Guard and given initially command of 12 Platoon C Company. In 1943, he was made second-in-command and in 1944 promoted to Major and Company Commander. A considerable rise in only four year and certainly testimony to excellent leadership.

It is noticeable that C Company had a lot less officers over the course of the war than the other companies. Of those with prior experience, Major (Retired) Charles Douglas Wetton joined as a platoon commander, despite being a previous Company Commander in the 3rd Battalion Machine Gun Corps during the First World War, prior to this being a platoon commander in 5th Battalion the South Lancashire Regiment. After 18 months, he moved to a staff role as intelligence officer of E Sector. Charles was the sales director of a radio manufacturing company, a senior role, and with such an underpinning experience, would be the natural choice for company command. The only other experienced officer was Lieutenant Cecil Pugh who took up the role of Company Training Officer. He had served from 1908 to 1919 in the 6th Battalion of the Manchester Regiment as a soldier and later in the 9th County of London (Queen Victoria Rifles) Regiment, as a junior officer.

C Company would become the company which was not to be used as a company if battle came. The orders throughout the war showed the company being used ad hoc for separate operations, but also later completely disbanded and turned into mobile companies with the C Company name remaining only an administrative function. It is telling that C Company was treated in this way in comparison to other companies in the battalion considering its choice of commanders.

D Company

D Company was both the Headquarters Company of the 6th Battalion, but also contained a large number of independent and specialist Platoons which gave considerable capability to the organisation. The Company Headquarters was co-located with battalion headquarters at the old Police Station on Station Road. With this headquarters were a Regimental Police Section, Signal Platoon and numerous staff in the Battalion Headquarters. However, of note, D Company also had two infantry platoons, numbers 13 and 14 and six independent sections (Electricity Department, South Staffs Water, British Legion, Boldmere Garage, Southaltons and Railway). Finally, the company had 15 Platoon, also known as the Mounted Patrol, which was based at the riding school in Sutton Park. More will be written of these individual units later, but the variety and scale of D Company was in itself a challenge to command.

In command of this considerable force was, in 1940, Angus McGregor G McCrae. Angus was born in 1883 to a large family that lived on the Coventry Road in Aston. His father James was a commercial traveller who had moved to Birmingham as a young man for work from Scotland. Angus, his six siblings and his mother Elisa lived in a small terraced house and had a tough upbringing. In 1910 Angus married his wife Gurtrude and worked in the family business of the wool trade.

Angus joined the Gordon highlanders in March 1916, however, was discharged in August 1917 with the Silver Wounded Badge as he was no longer fit to serve. After the war, he continued to work in the wool industry and grew the business, moving to a house in Streetly Lane. By 1939, he was the Chairman and Managing Director of a Wholesale Wool Merchants and well known in the town. The towering 56 year old Scotsman, despite being only a private soldier in the First World War, was given command of D (Headquarters) Company. In itself this appointment showed the pragmatism of Wilfred Bigwood: despite many men being much more senior or having fighting service, he understood the role of Headquarters Company was to supply, feed, administer and support the battalion; and the best person to do this was a man who understood the logistics and industry of the local area, and was used to commanding men.

However, after just a year, the redoubtable Angus McCrae moved to E Sector as a staff officer, to organise logistics and administration for the higher formation. Taking over command of the Company was Captain (now Major) John Joseph Slater. John was born in January 1892, so was just turning 60 when he took over command of headquarters company. He had been second-in-command of D Company since 1940, and was an experienced officer from the First World War, serving in the 8th Battalion the Royal Warwickshire Regiment as a Captain. In his day job, John was an estate agent and lived in Potloe, Moor Hall Park with wife Gladys and three children, with a live-in servant.

John joined the 8th Warwickshire Regiment at the outbreak of war, which was based at Aston Barracks next door to the famous Villa Park. For the next two years, the battalion was based in England as a depot and home defence unit, and when they departed for the front in 1915, John was involved in much heavy fighting on the western front, and despite this, survived to be promoted to become a platoon commander and lieutenant in June 1916 and then a captain and company commander in May 1917.

In 1918 John was attached to the 2/7 Battalion Royal Warwickshire Regiment, where an offensive was to take place at the River *Écaillon* near *Sommaing* on the 24th October. At this time, John commanded Z Company and as part of a general offensive, was tasked to launch an assault across the river. His company successfully completed the assault despite continual resistance by enemy machine gun fire. It was a year later that John found out he was awarded a Military Cross. The citation read:

> *Lieutenant (Acting Captain) John J. Slater, 8th Bn., attached. 2/7th Bn., R. War. R. (T.F.). - For conspicuous gallantry and devotion to duty near Sommaing, on 24th October 1918. During an attack he led forward several parties of men under extremely heavy machine-gun and rifle fire. He set a fine example to his company throughout the operation, and it was chiefly through his efforts that a bridge was erected across the River Ecaillon.*[iii]

After this battle, John was attached to the 1st Battalion the Lincolnshire Regiment, who had taken very heavy casualties and were in need of replacement officers. He ended the war with this battalion and was demobilised soon after. To have such an experienced officer as his second-in-command assisted Angus McCrae in his appointment commanding D

Company, but John's experience in command in combat made him an excellent choice to replace him in 1941.

Wilnecote Detachment

With the complexities of the River Tame and the open rural area to the east of Sutton Coldfield, the decision was made to form a detachment of two companies at Wilnecote. These companies would be under the command of James Cecil Mitcheson, an artillery officer. James was born in 1899 to his father George, a Mining Engineer, and his mother Alice, a nurse in Trentam, Staffordshire. Because of his age, when he turned 18 he immediately volunteered to serve and was commissioned as a 2nd Lieutenant in the Royal Field Artillery and deployed to France in February 1918 with 271 (Warwickshire) Battery, part of 68th (South Midland) Field Regiment. The battery had four 18 pounder field guns and despite firing from long ranges, James was injured on the 30th September 1918 by counter battery fire and entitled to wear the wounded stripe from this.

After the war, James became a mining agent and respected member of the local community. He was in charge of the Birch Coppice Collieries under Morris and Shaw Limited in Polesworth and his role was the Group Production Director. By 1939 he lived with his widowed mother and his wife Jene in Freasley, near Tamworth. When appointed as commander of the detachment, he made an opening address to the troops. The inspiring words show the urgency of the time and the real threat which was felt. James was humble and in his words his leadership shines through.

> *"It is a great honour and privilege to command this company of men who are detailed to protect this Division. I feel an honour*

especially great after looking through the records; some of you I know personally, some of you not, but I see that you are a body of men whom any man would be proud to have with him in a tight place. Old soldiers never die, once a soldier always a soldier. From your records of performance, I can see how unworthy I am to hold this position, especially unfortunately as I was trained as a gunner. But I can only say I will try my best to make a good infantry man and not let you down. I know you will not let me down or your section leaders. This is yours and my way of life and we must defend it"[iv]

The detachment Headquarters was to be at the old quarry, Glascote lane in Wilnecote, the work place of James. The scale of the two companies would increase throughout the war, but in 1940, E Company had four platoon locations and F Company had three.

E Company HQ – Personnel Office, Doultons Works, Wilnecote
1 Platoon E Company – Congregational Chapel, Glascote Lane, Wilnecote
2 Platoon E Company – Old Sunday School, Church Lane, Dosthill
3 Platoon E Company – Kingsbury Hall, Near Tamworth
4 Platoon E Company – Police House, Wood End, Near Atherstone

F Company HQ – Police Station, Glascote
1 Platoon F Company – The Dolphin Pub, Glascote
2 Platoon F Company – Amington Working Men's Club
3 Platoon F Company – Queen's Head, Newton Regis

As his detachment second-in-command, James had Thomas Jackson, known as 'Ellis' to his friends. Ellis was born in 1898 to the Schoolmaster of the same name at Kingsbury School. He was the youngest of five siblings and lived in a busy household with two of his cousins in residence. The First World War started with Ellis too young to join the forces, but when he turned 18, he immediately volunteered for his local regiment, the Royal Warwickshire Regiment, as a soldier.

He started training on the 24th of May 1916, but on the 14th March 1917 he was transferred to the 2nd Battalion Somerset Light Infantry bound for India. Over the next three years, Ellis served in the sub-continent, but he was constantly racked with illness, suffering from frequent bouts of malaria. He spent over six months in the King George General Hospital in Puna and was posted to the Controller's Office in Poona in an administrative role to recover.

Ellis was discharged in 1920 and moved back to Kingsbury where he married his wife Mary and moved into a cottage in Glascote. He became a bread salesman and settled into a more sedate life in the beautiful countryside. By the outbreak of war, he was living in 9 Clifford Street and volunteered immediately for service in the Home Guard. Through friendship and local association, Ellis was commissioned and rapidly promoted. He was made the second-in-command of the Wilnecote Detachment and in November 1942 was appointed Officer Commanding of F Company and then E Company.

Initially E Company was given to the command of the only officer who had any prior military service. Lieutenant Reginald Reaton Cleaver had served in 1919 in the army of occupation in Germany. However, shortly after this appointment, Captain Dirom Gordon Young was given command and although he had no military experience, he was seen as the best commander for the role. Captain G Williams was given command of F Company up to 1942, again with no prior military experience and although F Company had a number of soldiers who had served, there was a deficit of officers with experience.

In 1942 James made the decision that Ellis would command E Company and remain as detachment second-in-command, and he would command F Company and remain in command of the detachment. This arrangement made up for the lack of senior officers as the detachment grew in size during this time. Over this period James also promoted a number of experienced senior non-commissioned officers as platoon commanders, including James Bassford (Machine Gun Corps), Herbert Plater (Northumberland Fusiliers), Alber Davies (6th Battalion The North Staffordshire Regiment); Huber Joseph William Fisher (Royal Navy); William Henry King (Royal Engineers); William Newbury (South Staffordshire Regiment); and James William Price (Queen's Own Cameron Highlanders). These platoon officers gave much needed experience to the isolated platoons in the detachment.

G Company

G (Colehill) Company was the most southern company in the battalion, and was very much isolated in terms of its location. Like E and F Companies, it was made up of a series of isolated platoons which would increase in size as the war progressed. The first company commander was Lieutenant Colonel Leonard Holte-Smith. Born Leonard Smith in

Birmingham in 1880, he moved with his family to South Africa as an expatriate in the colony as a young man. He joined the British Army in South Africa in 1898, being a soldier in the 2nd Battalion Queen's Regiment. He served in the Boer War, fighting in Transvalle as a lance corporal in 1901 and after this serving in various roles in the battalion until becoming a company sergeant major in 1911 in the new forces of the Union of South Africa, formed in 1910.

On the outbreak of War there was a short-lived rebellion in 1914 with many in the military not believing South Africa should join the war and it was instead an opportunity for independence. The rebellion was defeated, and although the Union's forces were by law not allowed to deploy outside of the new dominion, expeditionary forces were created to deploy outside of this. South African units captured German imperial possessions in German South Africa and German East Africa. The Cape Corps was key to these operations. The 1st South African Brigade deployed to the Western Front in 1916, but the majority of forces fought in other theatres. Of the 250,000 South Africans who served in the First World War, 19,000 were casualties including 12,000 deaths.

Leonard continued to serve throughout this period, and although there are no records of his service now, we know that by 1936 he was a Lieutenant Colonel at retirement, and he chose to take his family back to England and Birmingham. On the 10th August 1916, the TSS[v] Fort Auckland docked in Liverpool and down the gangway came Lieutenant Colonel (Retired) Holte-Smith, his wife Joanna and his 11 year old son Ray. The family moved to Water Orton, just to the east of Birmingham and settled for a quiet retirement after an exciting life overseas.

On the outbreak of war, Leonard stepped up and with his vast experience he was appointed as Officer Commanding of G Company. However, on the 16th December 1941 Leonard died at the age of 60. The company was briefly commander by Major Gerald Walter Henry Walker, who was born in 1892 in Harborne Birmingham, to Henry, a Chartered Accountant and Blanch. The family moved to Castle Bromwich by 1911 and were well off, having both a live in servant and a cook. Blanch was the Company Secretary for Henry's company, and Gerald went into his father's business at a young age. At the outbreak of the First World War, Gerald joined the Royal Garrison Artillery as a Second Lieutenant and he became a Captain in the Royal Artillery during the war, deploying to France from March 1915. In 1919 he deployed to India and fought on the North West Frontier. By 1939 the family had moved to Chester Road, and Gerald, never being married, moved with them and had a varied career behind him. He was a Police Officer in Warwickshire Constabulary, and also and engineer (metal founder).

However, a few months later the company second-in-command the newly promoted Major Donald Samuel Griffiths, took command of G Company. Unlike his successor, Donald was a Navy man, having served from 1917 in the Royal Navy Volunteer Reserve. Donald was only born in August 1900 and therefore was only able to volunteer for service at the tail end of the war. He trained as a Midshipman and gained his commission on the 27th July 1918. His first ship was Motor Launch 239 which operated in Jersey, where he was posted from the 7th October. He served after the armistice on Motor Launch 145 and Motor Launch 169, before being demobilised on the 20th April 1919.

After the war, Donald worked hard and became the managing director of four companies by 1939 and lived in Knighton Drive. He joined the Home Guard as the company training officer, and then the company second-in-command . His business leadership qualities meant he had a lot of respect from his soldiers. It is telling that Donald took command, despite there being 16 officers in the company who had wartime experience. He clearly commanded the respect of both his superiors and of his men.

[i] Details can be found in various Regimental Diaries, such as that of the Waziristan Field Force.
[ii] London Gazette Issue 30234.
[iii] London Gazette Issue 31219 and 31583
[iv] Transcript in the notebook of James Cecil Mitcheson, found in the Warwickshire Archive.
[v] Turbine Steam Ship.

Chapter 6

The Enlisted Men

From the establishment of the Local Defence Volunteers until its stand down, at least 6541 men and women served in the 6th Warwickshire (Sutton) Home Guard Battalion. The vast majority of these were enlisted soldiers known as Volunteers. Until November 1940, they had their own rank system, at this point made to align to the regular army, in terms of traditional ranks. It is these soldiers that day in and day out attended training, went on patrol and stood guard. Most worked a wartime six day week, and therefore spent their seventh day on duty. It was a thankless task, but one which made a huge difference to the defence of Great Britain in its time of need.

On average the battalion had around 2500 soldiers active at any one time and by 1941, 2651 soldiers were serving, each company having well over the standard establishment of 140 men. A Company had 320 serving, B Company 252, D Company 364, Wilnecote Detachment (E and F) 812 and G Company 589. The considerable size of E, F and G Company were due to their establishment not being aligned as they were based in rural villages to the east of Sutton Coldfield. In 1942 the establishment was revised to 1781 soldiers, making the equipment scale of each company increase in line with this, however still at this point there were 2345 men in the battalion, well above this establishment. The numbers increased with the onset of conscription to 2590 in 1943, but then stabilised to 2521 in 1944. By standdown, 2234 men and women were still serving in the battalion. The turnover was considerable, most of the companies had a 200 percent turnover throughout the duration of the war. However, C Company was an outlier, with only 369 men serving, of the 320 men peak. This was particularly good retention for the men under Major Witt.

The platoons themselves varied in structure, even amongst those which were termed rifle platoons. Traditional rifle platoons were structured much like No.1 Platoon A Company. This platoon had four sections, A to D, each of ten men, but in reality, more than this at any one time. The platoon was commanded by a 2nd Lieutenant or Lieutenant, which in the case of No. 1 Platoon was Lieutenant William Haywood Matthews who lived on Heathlands Road. There would often be a 2nd Lieutenant as their second-in-command in the case of No. 1 Platoon this was Lieutenant Stanley Philips from Corbridge Road, and later 2nd Lieutenant Arthur Simmons from St Bernarde Road. The platoon sergeant, who ran the administration of the platoon, was in the case of No. 1 Platoon Sergeant Thomas Siger who lived on the Chester Road. The platoon headquarters that supported them consisted of an orderly, Private Matthews (son of the platoon commander in this case) and specialist weapons or signallers, who were Privates Paul Ellis, Eric Shanock and Eric Winspean. Private Paul Ellis lived two doors down from the platoon commander on Heathlands Road.

The Platoons' four sections were each commanded by a corporal and had a lance corporal as the second-in-command. 'A Section' had Corporal Victor Woolley from Jockey Road and Lance Corporal Ralph Walcot from Antrobus Road, 'B Section' Corporal Samuel Webb from Springfield Road and Lance Corporal Joseph Kitz from Redachre Road, 'C Section' Corporal Kenneth Scott from Melrose Avenue and Lance Corporal Bernard Baker from Jockey Road, and 'D Section' Corporal Stanley Wright from Jockey Road and Lance Corporal Murray from Buxton Road. The names and locations to any local of Boldmere will know how closely they all lived to one another in this platoon. The 50 private soldiers (volunteers) who were in these sections, also lived in a very small area were able to mobilise very quickly, and often knew each other from school, the Sutton Park Hotel (which was a pub!) and work.

In comparison to this simple structure, other platoons were much more complex. E Company, No.1 Platoon was large enough to be a regular company[i], split across three fighting patrols and one headquarters patrol. The three fighting patrols each had three squads. The platoon had headquarters at the Congregational Chapel in Glascote Lane, Wilnecote, but also had a battle headquarters at Wilnecote Police Station. Lieutenant King, the Platoon Commander also had an Ambulance Section of six men, a Specialist Weapon Section (eventually armed with light machine guns) of six men, an intelligence section, a bombing team and a signals section. This mini company was designed to defend Wilnecote itself and contained, at its peak over, 100 men. The introduction of a Platoon Sergeant Major, Warrant Officer Second Class Smith, shows the scale of the challenge with this size of platoon.

The Warrant Officers

The backbone of any fighting unit is its warrant officers' mess, in the Home Guard this was no different, but the selection of the warrant officers was by no means based on experience for seniority. Those who achieved the status of company or regimental sergeant major were likely to be in those roles due to their occupations in the civilian world, or their personal connections, rather than any military connection. But in many respects, this was a sensible decision, as anyone who was a warrant officer in the last war was likely to be in his 60s by 1940, and therefore a man who was used to a foreman's authority in the civilian world, but was also of middle age, was more likely to stand the rigors of such a key appointment. The records of warrant officers in the battalion are limited compared to those of officers, however 11 have been identified through research, of these only two of them are listed as company sergeant major, therefore there are at least five other company sergeant majors who have not been identified. Of the remainder, there are a number of platoon sergeant majors, but also the regimental quartermaster sergeant.

The regimental sergeant major is the most senior soldier of any battalion, the role is critical as the right hand man of the commanding officer, and the officer responsible for maintaining the organisation culture an discipline of the battalion. The role is very important to a battalion and therefore the selection of this role was of the utmost importance for any commanding officer, especially in such a new organisation.

The first Regimental Sergeant Major of the 6th Battalion was a man who had served just in the First World War and had achieved the rank of Lance Corporal in this time. However, as a middle manager in the commercial sector he was used to expressing his authority and was chosen due to his stature in the modern society of Sutton Coldfield in 1940. Joseph Clarence Burkin was born in 1897 in Rotherhithe, London. He was the fourth child, but oldest son of Joseph and Emily Burkin and Joseph was a dock porter. Joseph's father died by 1911, and the family of six daughters and two sons had a difficult life trying to make ends meet. At 16 his sister was already in the leather trade and Joseph was soon to follow. This hard upbringing steeled him for what was to follow.

On the outbreak of war, Joseph signed on as a Private in the 11th Service Battalion the Middlesex Regiment. He served in A Company and was promoted to the rank of Lance Corporal in September 1917. After just over two years of fighting, he was heavy wounded by a gunshot to his right shoulder. This wound caused a compound fracture which sent him back to England to recover. On recovering from his wounds, he volunteered for a more static role, but still fighting in the front line in the Machine Gun Corps. Joseph continued to serve for the remainder of the war until he was discharged in May 1919.

After the war, Joseph married his childhood sweetheart Gladys in 1922 at St Barnabas Church in South Kensington. He got a job as a sales manager and started to travel the world. In 1924 he sailed on SS Andania to the USA (where he was promoted to district manager) and in 1925 again to USA on SS Collaner (where he volunteered as a fireman as part of the crew). In 1926 he again travelled to New York on the SS Carmania, part of the Cunard line. He was only a 29 year old man but had travelled more than many in this period.

By 1939 Joseph lived at 321 Chester Road with Gladys and two children; he was the branch manager at an electrical cleaners and had many years of travel and life experience behind him. He joined D Company, and was appointed by the Commanding Officer to be his senior solder and once rank was established the Regimental Sergeant Major. After two years in post, Joseph was commissioned and became the training officer for D Company.

As the second regimental sergeant major, Colonel Bigwood chose a man who only had a small amount of experience in the military, but as a warehouse foreman commanded respect from the soldiers. Royston Abbot was born in 1898 to Victor, a draughts salesman, and Girtrude, who was from London. The family lived in Aston on Bowyers Road in a small, terraced house, and Royston was the oldest child. At the outbreak of the war, he joined the 9th (Queen Victoria Rifles) Battalion London Regiment and served in France from 12th April 1918 until 26th May when he was wounded. By the time he returned to France on the 28th August, the 9th Battalion had transferred to 175th Brigade in 58th (2/1st London) Division, the battalion was absorbed into the disbanded 2/9th Battalion and renamed 9th Battalion. Royston remained in France after hard fighting at *Villers Bretonneux*, *Tailles Wood* and *Bray sur Somme* until the end of the war, and was demobilised on the 24th February 1919.

In 1924 he married Annie and in 1926 they had a daughter June. The family initially lived with Annie's mother, Annie Moore who was a wages clerk, but by 1939, Royston and his family lived at 11 Clifton Road, Boldmere. Royston volunteered for the Air Raid Precaution Service in 1939 and quickly signed up to the local defence volunteers when they were established in May 1940. He was a foreman at the wholesale warehouse, for Jeghts Men's Clothing and commanded huge respect amongst the workers at this location. He initially was given the role of company quartermaster for A Company, which fitted well with his logistical skills, but in 1942 he was appointed as the second regimental sergeant major of the 6th (Sutton) Battalion.

The regimental quartermaster sergeant is the senior soldier in charge of logistics, and with the scale of the logistical challenge over the considerable area of the 6th battalion, it required a man who could delve into the detail. George Hinchley was born in 1875 and started his career as a young teacher in Aston, then moved to 88 Carol Lane in Erdington. He became a student at University of London in 1898, and with this qualification became a head teacher in schools across Sutton. He married his wife Anne Maria and lived with his sister Annabella and a servant in their small house at 17 Sutton Oak Road.

During the First World War he signed up to fight for the 1/12th London Regiment and then transferred to the Labour Corps. He served in France from the 24th December 1914 and would survive the war as a private soldier. Returning from war, he took up his role as a headteacher and got back into the routine of teaching, but never lost his experience of that terrible war. On the outbreak of the Second World War, he volunteered for the Home Guard, and with his organisational and administrative skills was appointed as the regimental quartermaster sergeant, a role he would continue throughout the war, in addition to his role as headteacher.

The company sergeant major is the senior soldier of the company, and a key man who gets things done. They run the subunit day to day and must command respect. In the Home Guard, the company commanders appointed their company sergeant majors, often because they knew them, or saw the command and authority they showed in the early days. Oliver James Smith was not a man to be trifled with. Born on the 29th January 1881 in Bidford, Warwickshire, he joined the police in 1909 as 7462 Police Constable Oliver James Smith. He served in the city police in Birmingham and lived with his friend another police officer, John Salisbury. In 1912 he was awarded a gallantry citation and given a guinea as a reward for his efforts in stopping a robbery. He did not serve in the war, as he was in a reserved occupation as a police officer. He married and had three children and retired in 1939 after 30 years of service. At the outbreak of war, he signed up to the Home Guard. He was not military, but as an experienced police officer, he commanded respect, and the company commander recognised these qualities immediately. In 1942 Francis Owen Smith took over the role of Company Sergeant Major of A Company.

The other company sergeant major known to have been appointed was Warrant Officer Class II J Esworth of G Company. The other warrant officers were largely at platoon level, with Platoon Sergeant Major WO2 C B Smith of No. 1 Platoon E Company. B Company had three platoon sergeant majors, Sergeant Major Louis Carl Spencer, of No. 5 Platoon who lived on Britwell Road, Sergeant Major Thomas Sydney luck of No. 7 Platoon who lived at Stonehouse Farm in Little Sutton and Francis Edgar Bates of No. 8 Platoon who lived on Whitehouse Common Road. These three were given senior appointments in support of the officers in those platoons, an unusual approach by the company commander.

In the companies were a large number of senior non-commissioned officer who performed many roles. Each company had a company quartermaster sergeant who was a colour sergeant, and responsible for the company stores and supplies. These senior soldiers, such as Colour Sergeant Harold Tomey of A Company, had considerable responsibility and although they were part of the company, worked for the regimental quartermaster sergeant on a day to day basis.

At sergeant level, the platoon sergeant conducted a similar role to the company sergeant major but at platoon level. These senior non-commissioned officers ran the platoons on a day-to-day basis and were critical to its success. However, in addition to this core role, many sergeants also took specialist roles, such as Sergeant Richard Bullock of A Company who was the Company Medical Sergeant, or Sergeant Henry Lister who was the Tank Hunting Section Commander in D Company. Signals sections in each company were generally commanded by a sergeant also, such as Sergeant Jack Ealing of F Company.

Through research of the battalion, 195 junior non-commissioned officers, at lance corporal or corporal level have been identified. These junior leaders commanded sections, and squads (half sections) as well as covering a multitude of other roles in specialist sections. In A Company alone, whose records are the most complete, there are listed 101 soldiers who made junior non-commissioned officer during the war period. Each one of these had a story, and many served in the First World War, such as Lance Corporal Ralph Hillard Walcot who lived at 62 Antrobus Road and was deputy section commander (1st Squad) of 1 Section, No. 1 Platoon, A Company. He served as a private in the Royal Warwickshire Regiment in 1918, and understood how to be a soldier.

D Company was the Headquarters Company of the battalion, it had a number of specialist platoons and sections which supported the administration and successful running of the battalion. Its structure meant that not only did it administer the key enabler platoons for battalion headquarters such as signals platoon, but it also contained a number of specialist elements. These included platoons at certain businesses which sponsored these units, allowed then to be on duty as part of their employment rota. Southaltons Factory, as well as five other factories in Sutton Coldfield sponsored sections, as well as the Electricity Department on the corner of Riland Road, and Colehill Road. Also, South Staffs Water had a section, another public service body who wanted to play their part.

The effect of guarding the railways was of particular significance, providing a very useful service to both the police and military. On the 21st June 1940, the Central Midland Area ordered the establishment of Railway

Platoons,[ii] in Sutton Coldfield this was to be based at the main train station, with patrols at each of the stations on the line between Birmingham and Lichfield, and also on the lines to Walsall and Tamworth. What was to become No.16 (Railway) Platoon was 82 men strong at its height, and was an independent platoon, commanded from Battalion Headquarters, and specific to tasks on the railway only. The Platoon was commanded by Lieutenant Walter Wheale Hall, who lived at 15 Maney Hill Road, Sutton Coldfield and his two section commanders, Corporals Dowdeswell and Rogerson. Most of the members of the platoon were railway workers, and they took their static guard duties on top of their normal shifts at work. Orders were clear that special companies and platoons of Local Defence Volunteers raised for the protection of building and vulnerable points, should remain earmarked for the protection of those places and should not in any circumstances be removed to other duties.

In addition to these department-based platoons were the musketry school, which led battalion marksmanship training, under the Chief Instructor Sergeant Perkins, and his three First World War marksmen, Privates Harols Pearce, George Puddey and J Bowskill. The battalion Guides Section also took on the reconnaissance task, under the Chief Guide Lieutenant John Ollis, of Walmley Road. The British Legion also managed to field its own platoon, made up of 43 veterans of the First World War, so it is no wonder that this was commanded by a senior non-commissioned officer, Sergeant Arthur Horton, who must have had a fun challenge rotating the men between duties and the legion bar.

Due to the pressures of mobilising forces quickly as possible for the defence of England, many informal structures took place and some novel formations were organised, especially in the early days of the Local Defence Volunteers and Home Guard. The presence of a mounted unit was not alone in the 6th Battalion, but particularly of note was the presence of the women's section of this patrol. By 1942 there were 24 county horse patrols across the United Kingdom which had a 15 shilling allowance per horse (ten when saddled by war office. There were 286 horses in western command.

In October 1940 Miss Mary Brancker a well known veterinary surgeon in Sutton Coldfield became a founding member of the mounted patrol. Mary came from a high society family and was the youngest of 3 children of Henry Brancker and his wife Winifred Caroline Eaton. Mary's brother Henry served in the Royal Airforce and would be awarded a Distinguished Flying Cross and Bar before being killed in action in 1942,[iii] her cousin was Air Vice Marshal Sir Sefton Brancker. Mary was one of the first women to attend the Royal Veterinary College in 1932 and was a force in the profession.[iv] Mary worked from 1938 in the practice of Harry Steel Bodger, who was the chairman of the British Veterinary Association, and due to the war, the Association moved also to Sutton Coldfield, she would 1943 become a partner at the practice.

Mary had joined the Air Raid Precautions team in Sutton Coldfield which were formed in 1938 to support military roles. In this dual role and her role as a vet, she campaigned to be able to treat wounded animals in Sutton Park caused by the bombing. She considered this role essential and was appointed to the National Air Raid Precautions for Animals Committee in July 1940. Ernest Fisher was the chief instructor at Sutton Riding School and knew Mary well. Together they persuaded Captain Bigwood to allow them to set up a mounted patrol for use in the park. The mounted patrol was responsible for routine patrolling of Sutton Park, the largest urban park in Europe, and day and night had a pair of riders on patrol. With Mary's influence, further ladies who were Auxiliary Territorial Service soldiers joined the patrol, and an arrangement was made that the ladies would patrol by day, and the men by night. "The presence of unexploded bombs added to our sense of ' being in it'."[v] The patrol consisted of 30 male soldiers and around ten Auxiliary Territorial Service ladies. They trained in first aid (human and veterinary), cooking and signalling and the riding skills needed for reconisance. A very considerable amount of clerical work was undertaken in support of the battalion and the battalion staff officers who rode also joined the patrol to be able to look smart when on parade.

The scope of activities increased, and then plans for using the patrol were included in routine orders. The role of Mary Brancker continued with animals reunited with owners after the air raids, and the killing of animals found injured or distressed. This agreement was formalised by an instruction written by the chief constable of Warwickshire Police who wrote to Mary and informed her that "during, or within 12 hours of hostile attack in the vicinity, to slaughter any animal which appears to you seriously injured."[vi]

The soldiers became efficient producing meals under almost any conditions and were often seen after air raids in the park looking for wounded animals. In July 1941, the Auxiliary Territorial Service was given full military status and Mary was promoted to 2nd Lieutenant, her roles were both with local military sector for veternary services, but also with the mounted section. In December 1941, all unmarried women were called up to serve in either the Auxiliary Territorial Service, Women's Royal Naval Service, Women's Transport Service or Women's Auxiliary Air Force. Some of the more informal members of the mounted troop became formal members of this Auxiliary Territorial Service unit at this point, as well as joining local anti-aircraft units. One Auxiliary Territorial Service member from Sutton Coldfield was Private W/14376 Clarice May Thorne, who was 39 years old, was killed on the 16th January 1942 during the Blitz. Clarice was married to George Hughes, a collier, and had two teenage children, they lived in Church Lane, Bidworth. Clarice did not have to join the Auxiliary Territorial Service, but volunteered her time in support of the war effort.

Elements of the routine of the mounted patrol were passed down by a hand annotated map of Corporal Albert Thomas Rudge of Baker's Lane. Close examination of this map reveals a large number of annotations, presumably made by its owner in connection with his Home Guard activities. It was obviously not an officially issued document but was more likely Corporal Rudge's private aide-memoire as he undertook various operational activities throughout the park. The annotations give some vague hints as to what was happening but represent no overall view of activity. The map would no doubt reinforce any official orders to which Corporal Rudge was under.[vii]

It is well worth noting Norman Wilkinson, of Crayford Road, Kingstanding, who joined for more than just patriotic reasons:

> *"I had my duties in the Home Guard to perform. However, I transferred to the mounted division (horseback) and on duty nights we patrolled Sutton Park. We were the only mounted division in the Midlands (possibly the country) though for me it wasn't all patriotism, it was a cheap way for horse riding experience. At that time, it was 8/- (40p) per half-hour to hire a horse at Sutton Riding School (just 50 yards from Sutton Town Gate) and this is where our HQ was. We were getting top class lessons from the Major (ex-cavalry Sergeant Major) for nothing"*[viii]

Another role which the Local Defence Volunteers adopted in their early days was the role of air defence. Although there were static defences around the Midlands based upon the 4th Anti-Aircraft Division, and No.5 Group of Royal Observer Corps, the Home Guard manned additional positions across the county, initially on an informal basis. Such positions were designed for multiple purposes, including to prevent the dropping of enemy agents. Guidance was given by the Warwickshire Subarea on the use of cars to guide enemy aircraft in, and that suspicious persons should be arrested.

Such was the zealous nature of engaging possible enemy aircraft, that General Headquarters had to issue direction on the 19th June when a large number of French Aircraft flew to the United Kingdom to escape the surrender of France. These preventative measures were in place to stop friendly fire incidents occurring.[ix] Direction on the markings of aircraft grew in detail with direction given on the details of under markings of Italian Aircraft under German Command on the 21st June. This was followed on the same day by detailed direction to identify the markings of

Royal Air Force aircraft, to explain the difference between them and the enemy.

Aircraft	Marking
Fighters and short nose Blenhams	Light sky blue under surfaces. Red, white and blue roundels on both sides of the fuselage. No roundels on undersides of wings
Night Bombers	Undersides black. Red, white and blue roundels on both sides of the fuselage. Red and black roundels on undersides of wings.
Day Bombers	Greyish blue in colouring. Red, white and blue roundels on both sides of the fuselage and also on undersides of wings.
Lysanders	Slate or sea grey in colouring. Red, white and blue roundels on both sides of the fuselage and also on undersides of wings.
Flying BoAuxiliary Territorial Service	Slate or sea grey in colouring. Red, white and blue roundels on both sides of the fuselage and also on undersides of wings.
Fleet Air Arm	Sky grey in colouring. Slate or sea grey in colouring. Red, white and blue roundels on both sides of the fuselage and also on undersides of wings.
RAF Training Craft	Yellow in colouring. Slate or sea grey in colouring. Red, white and blue

	roundels on both sides of the fuselage and also on undersides of wings.
Civilian Aircraft	All silver in colouring
Irish Aircraft	Orange in colouring

Table 8: Aircraft Markings for Home Guard 1940

Instructions were given to prevent the landing of enemy glider troops and also of agents by blocking landing zones. On the 25th June, instructions were given on how to put obstacles on lakes bigger than 300 yards to prevent flying boats, particularly important for the water courses around Kingsbury. Direction was given to ask farmers to block any fields longer than 300 yards with farm equipment. Many of the pools in Sutton Park, such as Longmore Pool, were drained, to reduce the chances of them being used by enemy seaplanes.

A further immediate response by the new Local Defence Volunteer units was to place observation posts out, often twenty four hours a day. These observation posts were designed largely to act as additional early warning for German parachute operations. The utility of such posts in the Midlands could be questioned, as in addition to these 'sky watchers' were the observers of the Royal Observer Corps, and the various units of Anti-Aircraft Command. However, they increased observation in the more isolated areas, and enabled a local response to the perceived threat of low numbers of agents being dropped into the country. Orders were given initially that parachutists of more than six will be seen as hostile, as they are more than a bomber crew. Therefore, these parachutists should be shot before landing. Such zealous orders were quickly calmed when it was realised that the majority of small scale landings were that of shot down aircraft crews.

Colonel Cash gave out further specific direction with regards to the manning of observation posts on the 5th June, ordering all church towers to be manned by observation posts.[x]

1. *All church towers to me manned as observation posts*
2. *Church bells to be rung as a warning when parachute troops etc. are seen*
3. *As churches would inevitably suffer in an invasion, we need to scruple to use them on the grounds that our scruples would protect them, they will not*

This use of churches as a military defensive location was against the rules of the Geneva Convention, but showed how the defence of the realm quickly became more important than the rules of war. There is clear evidence that the British Army on a larger scale was prepared to use poison gas to repel the invaders. General Alan Brooke noted in his diary against the entry for 22 July 1940 (as he was succeeding Ironside as Commander in Chief Home Forces): "I was relying on heavy air attacks on the [German] points of landing, and had every intention of using sprayed mustard gas on the beaches."[xi] Brooke's willingness to make pre-emptive use of chemical weapons therefore marks a deliberate decision by the British high command to disregard international law in the interests of national survival.

The enlisted soldiers of the 6th Warwickshire (Sutton) Home Guard represented a considerable number of the population across Sutton Coldfield. On top of the around 2000 members of the Civil Defence

Forces, the mobilisation of the population was an incredible achievement. It was the individual soldiers which enabled these units to exist at scale, and the call to arms was far beyond what was initially expected, which in itself caused many logistical challenges. Part II of this book lists the names of those who served, it is my hope that the stories of many of these will come to light through their families being able to research their involvement.

[i] For those unsure of the standard British Army terminology, a company is a subdivision of a battalion, and contained, depending on type between 80 and 160 men. A platoon is a subdivision of a company and contained from 20 to 40 men. There were generally four platoons in a second world war company, but this could vary.

[ii] Details on the establishment of specialist platoons and their command arrangements can be found in Warwickshire archive under S.C No.Z.5796/G.

[iii] The full citation found in the London Gazette is: *Bar to the Distinguished Flying Cross. Flying Officer Henry Paul BRANCKER, D.F.C. (84026), Royal Air Force Volunteer Reserve, No. 114 Squadron. In December, 1941, a low level attack was made on the enemy aerodrome at Herdla. Despite the difficult contour of the Norwegian coastline, the exact target was skilfully located and, according to plan, was heavily and accurately bombed. Hits were scored on both runways, the wireless station and on several aircraft on the ground. The skilful and courageous leadership of Wing Commander Jenkins, so ably assisted by his observer, Flying Officer Brancker, both of whom devoted much forethought to the planning of the flight, was largely responsible for the complete success achieved.*

[iv] Of note Mary became the Chair of the British Veterinary Association and also the author of the book Brancker, M. (1972) *All Creatures Great and Small: Veterinary Surgery as a Career (My Life & My Work)*. Education Explorers.

[v] Interestingly these arrangements and the presence of the women's platoon were lauded later in the war and are mentioned in full in the Birmingham Mail on 9th Oct 1944.

[vi] The letter from Chief Constable to Mary Brancker can be found in he autobiography: Brancker, M. (1972) *All Creatures Great and Small: Veterinary Surgery as a Career (My Life & My Work)*. Education Explorers.

[vii] The map can be found on the South Staffs Home Guard website - http://www.staffshomeguard.co.uk

[viii] This quote was found online in local memories within the Birmingham History Forum. The details within were accurate and therefore I have assumed it is genuine.

[ix] This document is amongst the correspondence of the Central Midland Area, send to Warwickshire Subarea held in the Warwickshire Archive, it was sent on the 19th June 1940.

[x] *Ibid.*

[xi] The original quote can be found in: Danchev A. and Todman, D (eds.) (2001). *Field Marshall Lord Alan Brooke. War Diaries 1939- 1945*. Weidenfeld & Nicholson, London. Although it has been extensively used in other books and articles.

Chapter 7

The First Three Months

The first three months of what was to become the 'Home Guard' were the period of the 'Local Defence Volunteers'. The summer of 1940 was a period of real threat from invasion, but also a time of mass mobilisation of the economy, of civil defence from sporadic German air raids, and of conflicting priorities. It was also a period before the more formal records began, and a period where legend and rumour collide. In Sutton Coldfield, the men of the Local Defence Volunteers came forward to do their bit, and quickly made their impact on life in wartime Britain known.

The first active operations of the Local Defence Volunteers were road blocks. Simple to set up, not requiring a weapon, and able to operate with the police in a joint way, they were seen as a quick win. Some dangerous incidents occurred in Sutton Coldfield, such as with the Wilnecote Platoon setting up a road block on the A5 during the evening of the 9th June. A large dark car travelled at speed up the road and refused to stop. The patrol open fired with a warning shot and the car screeched to a halt. The Company Commander, Major Mitcheson was quite worried by the incident; "We nearly shot up the Japanese ambassador in his large car (going to Liverpool along Watling Street). It only just stopped in time!" Such incidents were quite common, with overzealous protection of the streets around Sutton Coldfield, and many being worried about the armed men on the roads. That said, real concern by the population did not occur until later in the war as in June 1940, people were worried about invasion, and were expecting some disruption to their lives with defences being put in place.

Direction from Warwickshire Subarea to the various embryonic units, in the form of notes, built up throughout the first two weeks of June; on the 6th June Colonel Cash reminded Local Defence Volunteers personnel to work closely with the search light units which had been set up in Sutton Park and in Erdington. On the 10th June, a further memo followed, warning that the weather on the 14th June would be excellent for parachute drops, quite a bold statement at this point, as France had not surrendered. [i]

The direction of Warwickshire Subarea was calmed down almost immediately by more measured direction from the Central Midland Area under Brigadier Blackiston-Houston. On the 11th June, General Headquarters stated that sentries in church towers should not be armed. A further order from Warwickshire Subarea removed mission command from road block commanders and ordered Local Defence Volunteers to only stop cars at authorised road block points, effectively reducing the number of blocks. It made clear that platoon and company commanders should routinely visit these points. In addition, it was made clear that at road blocks Radio Security Service vehicles must be passed through without hinderance, as well as reminders that Morris commercial vans painted green were used by the General Post Office and needed to be unhindered. On the 15th June, the Chief Constable stated that only red lights are to be used to stop cars, due to the glaring of drivers. The Chief Constable at this point was still giving some direction to the Local Defence Volunteers units in Warwickshire, in addition to the Home Guard Zone under Colonel Cash.

The commander of Wilnecote Local Defence Volunteers, Major Mitcheson spoke to his men as he gathered then together for this first time. He was clear in his appraisal of what needed to be done, "Know your weapons, know your ground, this is local defence with parish mobility"[ii]. This sentiment was repeated across all of the disparate elements of the Local Defence Volunteers across Warwickshire, giving priorities for defence as firstly against airborne troops, then fifth columnists and then enemy mechanised units. There was a real expectation of invasion and firstly that any invasion would be from the air.

Orders came through on the 18th June regarding the use of road blocks. At this point instructions were getting quite specific, reducing the amount of variation and giving clarity on what was and what wasn't needed. Such standardisation, only a month after the formation was quite impressive. They key issue was around the delay of reinforcements, and preventing this, whilst still serving a defensive purpose. In many cases, a mobile type of road block was the requirement and instructions down to the measurements and type of materials were issued. The defensive nature was to stop a tank, therefore it was a difficult balance to strike. There was a division made between the various types needed including Defensive Permanent, Portable, Police Examination, which in turn gave the provision of resources in which to build them.

Such communication showed the conflicting view of the Local Defence Volunteers between the Subareas, such as Warwickshire which was concentrating on local defence and utilising the Home Guard in an effective way, and their formation commander at area level (Central Midlands Area) which concentrated on wider civil military partnership and saw the bigger picture. There were many factors. Brigadier Blackiston-Houston did his best to explain these in a measured way to the eager local commanders. On the 13th June he described the competing priority between factory owners and local zones. Many Local Defence Volunteer units had been formed on factories for their local defence, but such static positions did not allow mobility across the local area. The Brigadier asked zone commanders to work with factories to understand that 'keeping as many men as fluid as possible' would allow a better defence, and less chance that the factory will be defeated in detail by the enemy.[iii] The fact this was to be a discussion and not an order was significant showing the conflicting priorities which would play out during the war.

Other conflicting priorities were appearing, such as the methods of communication, which were limited at this point in the war. On the 7th June Colonel Cash gave guidance that wireless was not to be used as a communication method. There was in general a lack of available frequencies across the United Kingdom at this point, and the Local Defence Volunteers were not seen as a priority for its use. Of note, communications at this point were still the platoons at Sutton Coldfield, Coleshill and Wilnecote, from the Sutton Company Commander, showing that at this point, the Battalion had not formally formed. A further memo allowed the railway telephone system to be used by Local Defence Volunteers from any station or signal box.[iv] Such railway telephone systems had been found very effective in Europe, with communication being able to be made with people behind German lines using this system early in the war, due to the enemy not understanding its availability and extent.

The reticence for the use for the Local Defence Volunteers came from the very top of the military. General Ironside, who the Commander of General Headquarters Home Command, saw the Local Defence Volunteers as a side show against regular forces. His view of the Local Defence Volunteers was in direct conflict to that of the Prime Minster, Winston Churchill and would lead to his tenure in command, which only started on the 26th May, to end on the 20th July. Ironside wrote a memorandum on the 8th June which was to put the armed forces in the United Kingdom in a 'state of defence'.[v] This was in the context of the British Expeditionary Force being evacuated from France, but the French Army continuing to fight. He made it clear that the focus at this point was to re-equip the British Expeditionary Force to allow them to fight alongside the French forces on the continent. He asked the 'Local Defence Volunteers Corps' to take second priority over this re-arming of the British Expeditionary Force. This focus on the defence of France was followed by almost condescending advice to the Local Defence Volunteers, including that "shotguns are good for defence of towns and factories," whilst making it clear that it was important that "citizens were not obstructed by defence." Ironside did not believe that the war in Europe was over, and that the regular army was the most important weapon in defeating the Germans. His view was very much in contrast to the work of the wider defence structures in the Ministry of War, and also at political level. This was also come into stark contrast when Paris fell on the 14th June and France surrendered on the 17th June, when Britain stood alone.

Local Defence Volunteer units, including those in Sutton Coldfield, were immediately on patrol once formed. For many of those who had formally served, this was a natural action to be made in defence of their local area. It also came naturally to the police who were at this point responsible for this new force. In Huntley, the Beat Commander, Constable Green was issuing orders to the 'Local Defence Volunteers Platoon' in the style of a police beat patrol and static locations.[vi] Many of these patrols were along railway lines, to the extent that on the 14th June, formal direction was given for safe working on the lines to prevent accidents.

The growth of the local platoons was huge in terms of scale at this time. In the area around Amington, Alvecote and Glascote there was meant to be a section at each location, forming a platoon location. By the 14th June, the 'platoon' which was to be come F Company had 107 volunteers fully enrolled and a further 61 on the waiting list. Six police constables were attached as 'beat leaders' and had organised a series of patrols around the local area. The platoon headquarters was formed at the police station at Glascote, with the local sergeant working with Mr Williams to command the detachment. The first 'sections' were formed at The Dolphin Pub in Glascote, the police station itself and the Glascote and Amington Colliery. Further sections were formed at the Amington Working Men's Club, Alvecote Post Office and the Air Raid Precautions Post at Manor Farm in Shuttington. Other groups were forming in outlying villages, which were loosely affiliated at this time, such as at the Queen's Head Pub in Newton Regis. The locals in these units were appraised of international affairs but took a stoic approach to the issues of the day. On the 14th June 1940, Paris fell. "The news came through this morning whilst I was on guard duty. It was received by our section, some half dozen of us in the guard room without comment. Then someone proposed a game of darts."[vii]

From these local sections, a rota of patrols were formed. On the first night of patrolling two men patrolled Glascote Reservoir from 21:00 to 05:00 and three men patrolled Tamworth Colliery from 22:00 until 05:00. In addition, three men guarded the railway bridge at Alveson and moved between there and the bridge at Armington; six men were held in reserve in case of air raids. On each of the patrols, the lead man had a rifle with 20 rounds of ammunition, and the guard at Alveson was unarmed. This lack of arms did not make the operations ineffective. The patrols were able to dominate terrain and to provide an early warning of enemy approaches or landings. The key terrain of the railways and the bridges over the River Tame were now effectively guarded allowing regular and reserve forces to operate in other areas.

Threat from the air continued to be a theme of Local Defence Volunteer operations, to the extent that many sightings which were not the enemy were reported, and lots of wasted effort reacting.

> *"It appears that reports of parachutists having been seen dropping from aircraft have been due to individuals mistaking the white puffs of the bursts of AA Shells for parachutists, which they may resemble at times. It is essential that all ranks should be capable of recognising these AA shell burst puffs, and be on their guard so false reports are not circulated"*[viii]

On the 17th June, the first major alert came into A Company, stating that parachutists had landed at Elmdon Airport at Coleshill. The response was rapid, but also would have been an interesting and chaotic response to any German assault. "We got outside [of Battalion HQ] and saw police with rifles in their hands tumbling into a police car and we got into two following cars and were off."[ix] The soldier had ten rounds at this point and travelled at speed (80mph) towards the airport picking up armed police on route. The police officer commented "I was just having my bloody dinner and thinking of having three hours of sleep and this bloody call came in: but better bloody death than to live under Hitler." By the time they came to the airport it was seen as a false alarm on this occasion, but what would have been termed a quick reaction force from the battalion headquarters (which was collocated with the police station), would have delivered a small platoon of men to oppose an immediate landing and disrupt its effects.

Among the plethora of correspondence from Central Midland Area, Warwickshire Subarea and Chief Constable's Office were directions on administration, including that no summary punishment would be allowed within Local Defence Volunteers units and those who were falling below standard should be discharged instead. This was prompted by the increase in negligent discharges during rifle training, where a note of the 13th June reminded about supervision of soldiers. On the 14th June, a Central Midland Area telegram stated that woman could not enrol in the Local Defence Volunteers but "they may drive at their own risk."[x] Direction was given on powers of arrest, with the Chief Constable stating that Local Defence Volunteer personnel could make arrests on duty, but could not search premises and road vehicles and only search personnel if arrested. As time went on, the paperwork increased, with some direction seeming quite unnecessary or reactionary, such as the direction on the 25th June that "where possible bell ringers should be recruited, so bells are not rung by inexperienced persons."[xi] At local level, at the same time details were now listed down to the individual church and those qualified to ring the bells. A specific bell ringer form was provided for this purpose with considerable detail.

June was a complex time for defence and in the archives, notes show the early formation of many different units within the area. A battalion memo of the 27th June 1940 from General Headquarters Home Forces, talks about the presence of a General Headquarters Reconnaissance Unit, commanded by Lieutenant Colonel G F Hopkinson, (North Staffs), consisting of 29 officers and 250 men selected from different units of the army. The unit was equipped with armoured scout cars, motorcycle combinations, motor cycles, wireless vans and transport vehicles moving from the area. The role of this unit was to obtain information for General Headquarters Home Forces and for the Royal Airforce. It was ordered to obtain this through liaison and reconnaissance and would operate by units or detachments across the British Isles. The code name of the unit was Phantom.[xii] Such various units moving across the area of operations, added to the complexity and feeling of excitement at the time.

The complexities of arming such a vast number of men in a small period of time led to lots of changes in policy and much frustration for the police who were not keen to see a wider proliferation of fire arms. On the 22nd June there were requests from Warwickshire Police for the loan of all shotguns owned by the general population, for use by the Local Defence Volunteers.[xiii] At this point, the police were operating under the civilian rules for weapon ownership including licencing. Only on the 22nd June did a memorandum get released stating that fire arms certificate were not needed for persons in His Majesty's service and it would only be needed to acquire fire arms for personal use. It also clarified that Local Defence Volunteers were in his Majesty's service.[xiv] On the 24th June, the first major instructions on the use of Molotov Cocktails were issued:[xv] This included using a pint bear bottle made up of 25 percent petrol, and 75 percent Gas Tar and Water. Such instructions were on the back of numerous improvisations and were needed for the development of best practise.

There were night air raids over the Midlands on June 26th and on 30th June but these were small in scale and did not impact upon Sutton Coldfield. The Ministry of Information announced that the invasion was expected within days, perhaps hours and many members of the Local Defence

Volunteers, including Private Griffith, bemoaned the lack of preparedness and training so far, commenting "I am no more a "parashootist" today than before I joined."[xvi] There were some shortages in manpower in some rural Local Defence Force units, this led to a change of policy occurring on the 28th June, with Air Raid Precaution staff able to enrol in the Home Guard, particularly in these rural areas where there was a manpower shortage. There were general comments made that the close collaboration between the two organisations was very important to allow these to work in complimentary manor.[xvii] Another driver for the increase in recruitment was that financial grants to units were to be based on establishment on 30th June 1940, therefore there was a hurry to finish recruiting before this date.[xviii]

As June came to an end, there were a series of changes in the organisation of the Local Defence Volunteers. Army Command Instruction No.653 of 24th June 1940 made all existing companies into battalions, and all platoons into companies.[xix] In addition, to remove the alignment to police structures, orders on the 28th June denoted that Local Defence Volunteer divisions would now be battalions.[xx]

July started with dire warnings from the ministry of information stating that the invasion was imminent. The war was only getting worse for Britain with the setting up of the Vichy Regime in France and the first daylight bombing of England by the Lufwaffe. Italian Forces in Eritrea crossed into Sudan to attack British interests in Africa, and the Royal Navy attack on Mers-el-Kebir meant that what remained of France could join the Germans in conflict against Britain. The seriousness of the war situation had led Winston Churchill to order the biggest movement of wealth in history, the reserve gold of the United Kingdom to Canada, under

Operation Fish. The threat to the United Kingdom was real and invasion was certainly felt to be imminent.

July, for the Warwickshire Local Defence Volunteers, had been a chaotic journey of formalising structures, but now the battalion under Captain Bigwood had more of a semblance of order. More formal structures also followed, with ranks up to sergeant being now authorised, allowing sections and platoons to have more organisation and commanders to have recognised authority. The link with the police, although still co-located, was now no longer one of a command relationship.

With this change of organisational structure came a focus on defence from more static locations and a cessation of many of the mobile road blocks which had been used over the previous month. Orders were given that many of the current road block location would be turned into permanent observation posts or defensive locations.[xxi] Colonel Cash wrote to the units in Warwickshire that road blocks were to be built upon to form permanent defensive positions. This change in approach to defensive locations was very much driven by the sense that an invasion was imminent. There were reports on the 3rd July by intelligence that attacks were expected.[xxii]

The defensive positions were starting to be formalised, with a series of major company level road blocks, which were stretched from the north of the battalion area of operations to the south. In the north at Watford Gap, A Company built positions for 120 men to stand too. This key road junction crossed the A5 Watling Street and the Lichfield Road and was dominating terrain for any movement to the north of Birmingham. The position was initially a road block, but now was built up with considerable defense to dominate the terrain. Further south, the second main defensive location was formed at Ashfurung Hall on the Tamworth Road. This position dominated any movement into Sutton Coldfield from the east and would be a block to any forces which crossed the River Tame. B Company built up positions around the hall for a further 120 men, and had a permanent vehicle check point on the Tamworth Road.

The third rifle company defensive position was at Minworth, again designed to stop movement from the east, and crossing the River Tame. Minworth itself was just to the northeast of the major industrial area of Castle Bromwich, and therefore was a likely infiltration route for any enemy wishing to move to attack the key Spitfire factory. This was a 120 man position, again defended with new fixed positions. To the east of these positions on the River Tame, a new stop line was being built by regular forces, part of the new General Headquarters Line network. As this put Local Defence Volunteers forces in close proximity of the regular army, a memo was issued to remind that "all Local Defence Volunteers officers are subordinate to all regular officers and are in no circumstances to give orders to them."[xxiii] In Sutton Coldfield itself, the town centre was to become a strong point defended by 400 men of battalion headquarters and D Company.

The River Trent between Tamworth and Coleshill was the key defensive feature for any expected German assault from the east. It was a natural feature and the last significant obstacle for any force moving into Birmingham from the north or east. The General Headquarters Line was being built around the country to defend the south east and London, but to the North of London each of the Regional Commands were providing there own defensive lines, in Western Command, Command Line No.5 (Tamworth to Ashbourne) and Command Line No.6 (Tamworth to Stockport) were formed to the north of Tamworth, and at the start of the war the river line east of Tamworth was in Southern Command, and therefore priority was on the stop lines closer to the beaches in the south.

To mitigate against this lack of fortification, the Warwickshire Local Defence Volunteers ordered the formation of four strong points to the east of the River Tame, to delay any German advance from the east. These stretched from E Company and Wilnecote Strong Point, 300 men strong in the north of the area of operations, through Kingsbury (F Company also 300 men), then to G Company, which had a strong point for 135 men at Whitachre and 75 men at Follongley. This defence line, again first formed of road blocks, got considerable stores over time and became key defensive features for the Local Defence Volunteers.

The complexity of the defensive positions to the east of the Tame was not lost on the Sutton Home Guard, with all the logistical arrangements based in Sutton Coldfield itself. To mitigate against this issue, catering was requested for isolated battalions to cook at the local police stations. On the 11th July, orders came from Western Command, to the Central Midland Area then to zone and then to battalion. These orders stated that the Major General Director of Supplies and Transport had allocated the following for cooking at the local police stations near these detachments.[xxiv] It's worth noting these orders took two weeks to reach battalion level.

- One case of preserved meat (48 Ibs)
- Two cases of biscuits (100 Ibs)

- Two tins of tea (4 lbs)
- Two tins of Sugar (14 lbs)
- Three tins of Cheese (6 lbs)
- Seven tins of jam (14 lbs)
- Seven tins of condensed milk

These long-term stores were designed to sustain the force in these isolated locations when the invasion came, and allow them to operate independently. At this point on the 12th July, correspondence refers to Coleshill and Wilnecote as companies for the first time and part of the Sutton Coldfield Battalion, further clarifying the chain of command.

Concern continued over the amount of supplies for these defence locations, and on the 16th July, there was a conference with the now Major Bigwood, his company commanders as well as Colonel Cash. A number of key issues were discussed which highlight the issues of the day. This positive engagement is a huge change from only a few weeks before, when there was a lack of any kind of support in terms of equipment.[xxv] The end of the meeting came to the following conclusions:

- Lamps to support roadblocks (now being purchased by Territorial Army Association)
- Grenades (Territorial Army Association has in hand and sourcing)
- Cleaning Material (Territorial Army Association)
- Hotchkiss Guns (four now gone to Sutton Coldfield)
- Admin Officer (authorised)
- Small arms ammo (five rounds per man authorised for training)
- Petrol (some push back to ensure what is needed)

- Road Blocks (Commander Royal Engineers to visit to assist)

This conference made a real difference to the support given to the Sutton Coldfield Battalion, and at a time when invasion still looked very likely, it was a much needed confidence boost for the battalion and its men.

On the 18th July, the Central Midland Area noted that the forces in its area now had 49,000 rifles and 10,000 additional being issued in the area. However, as stocks arrived from the USA the .303 rifle would be replaced with the .300[xxvi]. This arrival of American weapons at this time shows that the impact actually was to the forces above establishment in the Local Defence Volunteers. General Alan Brook was becoming popular with the troops also, on the 19th July, 10 percent authorised expenditure of Molotov Cocktails was ordered to allow all ranks to train.[xxvii] This was followed up by further notes, which specifically stated that this has come from the Commander in Chief who had not seen them used at road blocks and thought they could be effective. The complexity of the defences continued to grow, with the Sutton Coldfield Battalion starting to liaise with the Birmingham Garrison in the defence of the city. There was a plan of road blocks on 'Line Red' as an outer cordon and 'Line Yellow' beyond this, to provide fire points into the city. The liaison with the Sutton Coldfield Battalion on these positions allowed a better integrated defence of the city, from the strong points east of the Tame, through the strong points outside Sutton and then into Birmingham proper.[xxviii] Even with the limited weapons available, this would be a considerable obstruction to any attack.

Towards the end of July 1940, the situation across the Local Defence Volunteers was becoming more stable, with a considerable influx of personnel, volunteers, equipment and weapons. General Alan Brook replaced General Ironside on 20th July. This led to a renewed focus on the additional forces gained by the Local Defence Volunteers, particularly as it was realised that London and the River Thames were a block for reserves moving to the south east or to the east.[xxix] Across the Central Midland Area, over 100,000 volunteers had joined up, all recruitment was now stopped by those with specialist qualifications.[xxx] Those in training and going through recruitment continued[xxxi] and to support the additional training of personnel, three staff officers were recruited at zone level from local regular units.[xxxii] On July 24th the name Local Defence Volunteers changed to Home Guard[xxxiii] and this change started the growth of the largest semi-professional military organisation in the history of these islands. The force would grow to 1,793,000 at its peak, in comparison to a regular British army of 2,920,000.

On the 26th July, in true military style, the now Lieutenant Colonel Bigwood wrote to the unit about dress, telling his unit to keep Local Defence Volunteer arm bands until new ones were issued.[xxxiv] On the 27th July 1940, the Earl of Dudley (Regional Commissioner) inspected the Home Guard in Sutton Park. He noted that the civil defence units were recruited above establishment. They were on parade with the Air Raid Precaution Service also present.[xxxv] Around 400 soldiers were on parade, as they marched through Sutton Park through thunder and lightning and torrents of rain. The small raids by the *Luftwaffe* over June and July actually allowed the Air Raid Precaution Service and other units to do rehearsals and get ready for the real strike to come.

On the 3rd August, in another sign of turning the force into a more professional organisation, the county cap badge was adopted by units. The badge of the Royal Warwickshire Regiment was taken on by those battalions in the Warwickshire historic county, and the Sutton Battalion became the 6th Warwickshire (Sutton) Battalion Home Guard. Following on from this formation, on the 4th August, Colonel Cash activated a practise of a 'stand too'[xxxvi] of all units across Warwickshire. It was a Sunday, and pre-planned, but this was certainly a step forward for an organisation which had only gone on its first tentative patrols eight weeks before.

[i] The correspondence of Central Midland Area and the Warwickshire Subarea (this example from the 10th June 1940, can be found in the Warwickshire Archive. CR 4367/2/1.
[ii] From the unpublished diary of Maj Mitcheson. CR 301/32.
[iii] Warwickshire Archive - Central Midland Area 13th June 1940. CR 4367/2/1.
[iv] Warwickshire Archive - Central Midland Area 7th June 1940. CR 4367/2/1.
[v] Secret Memmo from Ironside to all Local Defence Volunteers Corps, a copy of which can be found in the Warwickshire Archive CR 4367/2/1.
[vi] Notes on Huntley Local Defence Volunteers Meeting found in the Warwickshire Archive. CR 301/32..
[vii] War Time Sutton: Extracts from the diaries of Gwilym O Griffith 1940-40. Sutton Historical Society.
[viii] Warwickshire Archive - Warwickshire Subarea 25th June 1940. CR 4367/2/1.
[ix] War Time Sutton: Extracts from the diaries of Gwilym O Griffith 1940-40. Sutton Historical Society.
[x] Warwickshire Archive - Central Midland Area 14th June 1940. CR 4367/2/1.
[xi] Warwickshire Archive - Central Midland Area 25th June 1940. CR 4367/2/1.
[xii] Warwickshire Archive - SECRET CR HFI/3026(G).
[xiii] Warwickshire Archive - Chief Constable Warwickshire 15th June 1940. CR 4367/2/1.
[xiv] Warwickshire Archive - Warwickshire Subarea 22nd June 1940. CR 4367/2/1.
[xv] Warwickshire Archive - Southern Command Letter Dated 24th June 1940. CR 4367/2/1.
[xvi] As quoted in Flemming, P. (1958). *Invasion 1940*. Hamish Hamilton
[xvii] Warwickshire Archive - Central Midland Area 28th June 1940. CR 4367/2/1.
[xviii] Warwickshire Archive - Warwickshire Subarea 25 Jun 1940. CR 4367/2/1.
[xix] Army Command Instruction No.653 24th June 1940. A copy of which can be found in the National Archives under TNA WO 199/665.
[xx] Warwickshire Archive - Warwickshire Subarea 28th June 1940. CR 4367/2/1.
[xxi] Warwickshire Archive - Central Midland Area 2nd July 1940. CR 4367/2/1.
[xxii] Warwickshire Archive - Warwickshire Local Defence Volunteers 3rd July 1940. CR 4367/2/1.
[xxiii] Warwickshire Archive - Warwickshire Local Defence Volunteers 2nd July 1940. CR 4367/2/1.
[xxiv] Major General Director of Supplies and Transport Ref 53/General/5758 Dated 29th June 1940, a copy of which can be found at the National Archives under TNA WO 199/3457.
[xxv] Warwickshire Archive - Warwickshire Zone minutes of conference 16th July 1940. CR 4367/2/1.
[xxvi] Warwickshire Archive - Central Midland Area 18th July 1940. CRWC No.5 5/6899.
[xxvii] Warwickshire Archive - Warwickshire Subarea 22nd June 1940. CR 4367/2/1.
[xxviii] Warwickshire Archive - Birmingham Garrison 19th July 1940. CR 4367/2/1.
[xxix] Flemming, P. (1958). *Invasion 1940*. Hamish Hamilton
[xxx] Warwickshire Archive - Warwickshire Local Defence Volunteers 24th July

1940. CR 4367/2/1.
[xxxi] From Director General Welfare and Territorial Army 24th July 1940. A copy of which can be found in the Warwickshire Archive under 20/Misc/1763 (TA1).
[xxxii] Warwickshire Archive - Warwickshire Local Defence Volunteers 24th July 1940. CR 4367/2/1.
[xxxiii] War Time Sutton: Extracts from the diaries of Gwilym O Griffith 1940-40. Sutton Historical Society.
[xxxiv] From Director General Welfare and Territorial Army 26th July 1940. Warwickshire Archive -20/Misc/1763 (TA1).
[xxxv] Birmingham Mail 29th July 1940.
[xxxvi] 'Stand Too' is a military term in which all soldiers are ready for action. This usually takes place in the morning and evening, ready for an enemy dawn or dusk attack. It can be used in the more general sense to bring a unit to an alert status.

Chapter 8

The Home Guard

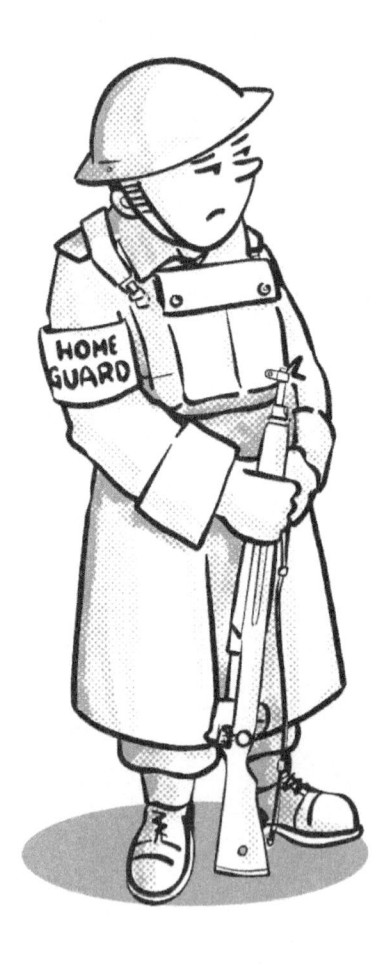

The Home Guard became the new name for the largest mass volunteer organisation in the history of Britain. From the 3rd August 1940, this organisation was now named and structured along the lines of a regular force, and started rapidly to look like them, with increased equipment and weapons. They started to gain a local identity with a wider regimental ethos, gaining the county badges of the other fighting soldiers from their homes. Over time the differences visually would be greatly reduced. The

Home Guard were now also providing operational utility, in terms of guard duties, patrols of vulnerable points and vehicle check points. These roles would have been conducted by other regular forces, and therefore allowed these forces to form a more comprehensive defence for the expected invasion.

The wider issue at this time for the entire British armed forces was the availability of rifles. This was not a shortage against the normal strength, but a shortage due to the huge demand for rifles and the huge increase in the size of the military in 1940. 'By the end of 1940, all the 1.5 million rifles in Britain were in use and 190,000 reservists were without arms at all.'[i] The scale of military recruitment was firstly felt in the regular army, which across all the campaigns up to June 1940 had lost over 300,000 rifles, much more than stated by Churchill.[ii] This was further exacerbated because the army's planned increase of 60,000 men per month, which it had based its equipment scales upon, had gone out of the window. Between June and August 1940, 324,000 men were enlisted. 'They were organised into 122 new infantry battalions,[iii] not because the army needed such a large increase in its infantry, but because the only weapons it had in stock were 300,000 First World War pattern rifles.'[iv] The re-equipping of the regular forces to both give an army to defend the United Kingdom, but also later to move to fight in North Africa, was critical to the war effort.

The supply of rifles was very limited due to production being almost entirely based at one privately owned factory, the British Small Arms Factory in Birmingham, and this was only supported by the cannibalization of old weapons by the Royal Small Arms Factory and the gun trade. In August 1940, an air raid destroyed the barrel mill and associated workshops at Small Heath, halting production, and further raids in November caused the machinery to be dispersed; the factory finally ceased production in late 1943. To supplement the limited reserves Churchill persuaded the Americans to provide half a million 'Springfield 1917' rifles of First World War vintage. These arrived in June and July and allowed much of the Local Defence Volunteers to be rapidly armed. The arrival of these rifles was signalled in true military fashion by formal correspondence from General Headquarters Home Forces to all the United Kingdom Commands on the 8th July 1940:

> *To H.Q. Eastern Command – Northern Command – Western Command – Southern Command – Scottish Command – London Area. From HOFOR 8-9 July 1940 Approx. _____ rifles will arrive at your command depots during next few days (.) Imperative to have distribution ready and that no delays are caused (.) Personal message on subject has been sent to your MGA but rifles will have to be degreased LDVs themselves (.) WO is issuing instructions how to do it. Eastern 24,000 – Northern 59,000 – Western 49,000 – Southern 49,000 – Scottish 29,000 – London Area 6,000*

One of the most critical factors in the shortage of weapons in the Home Guard was that it had recruited to three times the established size. By August 1940, Eden's broadcast of 14th May had generated over 1.6 million Local Defence Volunteers, rather than the 500,000 anticipated, and all of these men expected to be armed, disappointing two-thirds of the volunteers, who found themselves without rifles. There are many stories of pikes and truncheons being used in the early days, but mainly these were used for drill, and although the force was huge in scale, it was not envisaged that all soldiers would be on duty which would require large numbers of weapons at the same time. That said, Home Guard returns list an item 'bayonet, standard', from March 1942, which is the infamous 'pike'. 36,884 were already held at that date, along with 105,972 examples of the 'truncheon, various'. The numbers would eventually climb to over 45,000 pikes and 155,000 truncheons, in September 1942, before beginning a rapid decline.[v] Even with a good quantity of rifles across the whole of the Home Guard, at the end of July they did not have get Bren guns, armoured cars, mortars or any signal equipment:[vi] all key requirements in modern warfare.

The impact of the lack of equipment can be seen in the stores returns for E Company based largely around Kingsbury and Wilnecote at this time. The Company was scaled to be initially 120 men, but rapidly grew to be, at its peak, 544 men in strength. On formation the company was armed with only 12 rifles and 58 overalls, with 16 armlets. However, by the time of the first patrols at the end of the first week of June there were across the company 26 Rifles (with 83 rounds), 68 uniforms and 36 armlets. In reality most had sewn their own armlets, so they had the Local Defence Volunteers 'LDV' on their arm. The first patrols were either road blocks or observation posts, so not all men needed to be armed. Others on static guard could have a rifle for the man on guard and one man on rest without. The reality was that even with only one in five men having rifles (compared to establishment) at this time, the impact of the company in terms of defence was still significant, especially in terms of releasing other forces.

The situation by the end of June had not hugely improved, but there had been a considerable amount of self help. The armoury of the company at this point was 33 rifles, but also six private rifles and 37 shotguns, meaning 50 percent of the operational force was armed. It is noticeable that the first 19 tin hats were delivered on the 10th June, allowing sentries more protection in their roles. The rotation of troops, on a shift basis, and even within shifts, meant that most of the visible forces were armed now, even though in a defensive role they would be very limited. Improvisation was the order of the day, with vast amounts of Molotov Cocktails produced as well as other flammable defence systems. On the 12th July the company was fully armed at establishment with 125 rifles, and five rounds per weapons. The wider equipment was also on the increase, with 65 uniforms, 40 armlets, 15 tin hats, 800 sandbags, 240 field dressings, and 15 coils of barbed wire. However, the company had four times as many soldiers as established for at this point, so there were still many frustrated men and a real concern about equipment to train and having enough bullets to defend a position.

To help with these frustrations, communications were improved. From July Western Command issued a 'Round Robin' to inform people of mainly the supply updates, so they could see what was being done. It gave an honest appraisal of the difficulties of the times but was clear that efforts were being made to improve the situation. The tone is a lot more understanding and consolatory that the previous communication under General Ironside, especially as the situation was now one of expectant invasion, and the former arrogant statements of regular troops holding the line seem to have calmed down. At this point, General Alan Brook had taken over Home Command and a renewed emphasis on mass defence was given.

As the Home Guard started to build their capability for static defence and be prepared for invasion, the real threat came from a different direction. The threat of aerial bombing was always expected to occur, but the civil defence in the form of the Air Raid Precaution Service were envisioned to be the lead in this area. However, over the next few months the role of the Home Guard in this action would grow into supporting the civil powers, to taking an active part in the anti-aircraft defences. Direction came for the Home Guard for the actions on an air raid on the 29th June 1940,[vii] with a draft Command Order being issued.[viii] The key reasons for this were preventing an early reaction and stopping of vital war industry too early, both through factories unnecessarily pausing production and Home Guard personnel moving to their posts and leaving their regular work too quickly. Also, it noted that on Air Raid Red, troops should not take cover until "Hearing anti-aircraft fire or falling of bombs". This also was due to examples on the continent of parachutists landing immediately after bombing raids. At this point the sporadic attacks by air were causing disruption through alerts, but also allowing both the Home Guard and the Air Raid Precaution Service to learn their roles and understand how to respond to an incident.

The scale of the armaments industry in Birmingham and the West Midlands made it a prime target for the *Luftwaffe*. Key to this was the spitfire factory at Castle Bromwich, which produced large numbers of badly needed aircraft for the Royal Airforce. The factory had been developed under the Shadow Scheme, creating 15,000 jobs for the city. Other key production sites included the critical Birmingham Small Arms

Factory, which produced the majority of rifles at the start of the war, and all Sten Guns produced during it.

Name	Location	Production
Aerodrome Factory	Castle Bromwich	1,200+ Spitfires & Lancaster's
Austin "Shadow Factory"	Longbridge	2,866 Fairey Battles, Hurricanes, Stirlings & Lancasters
Austin Works	Longbridge	500 Military Vehicles/week
Rover	Solihull	Bristol Hercules Engines
Fisher and Ludlow	Birmingham	Lancaster Wings, Shell Casings, Bombs
Reynold	Birmingham	Spitfire Wing Spars, Light Alloy Tubing
GEC	Birmingham	Plastic Components
SU Carburettors	Birmingham	Aero-carburettors
Birmingham Small Arms Factory	Birmingham	Rifles, Sten Guns (100% of all made)

Table 9: Birmingham Factories of note

Sutton Coldfield was just north of the Spitfire Factory, and northeast of the industrial city proper, meaning that on bombing runs it was often a victim to overshot bombs on these factories. In addition, its location of high ground on Sutton Park meant that it was key for anti-aircraft defence and search lights, making it an obvious target for bombers beyond the black out of the city.

The first enemy action took place on the 9th August 1940, a day which the *Luftwaffe* was planning to be 'Alder Tag' or Eagle Day, the mission to destroy the Royal Airforce. However, the weather was dominated by heavy cloud and some rain at times, leading to a delay in the offensive. Some *Luftwaffe* operations took place, mainly mining operations on the east coast and a bombing raid on Sunderland, but mainly there were a number of reconnaissance flights. In it likely one of these lone reconnaissance flights which dropped a bomb over Erdington landing on numbers 16 and 18 Enstone Road.[ix] An 18 year-old cinema-projectionist called Jimmy Fry in Montague Road (off Tyburn Road) was killed in that first raid and was the first recorded casualty in Birmingham, six others were wounded.

> *"The second bomb fell in the back garden of a detached villa-type residence in Gravelly Lane, opposite the end of Goosemoor Lane. It created a small crater in the soft earth and shattered the glass of a greenhouse on the allotments that existed between the house and Oliver Road .... I believe the third and fourth bombs fell in the Church Road - Western Road area of Erdington. I saw fireman draping tarpaulin over the roof of a house in Erdington Hall Road between Alleyne Road and Croydon Road. I was told another bomb had landed in Montague Road but as it was downhill I didn't go to see it. It was the unheralded arrival of the aircraft that awoke me at about half past one in the morning."*[x]

The remainder of the stick of bombs landed north of the first impact, with one high explosive landing 80 yards along Blackberry Lane from Four Oaks Common Road at 01:10. There was slight damage to a house with windows broken but no casualties. At this point the 'Air Raid Purple' alert was sounded, when clearly the raid had started and it should have been 'Red'. Air Raid Red was not sounded until 02:02. Another high explosive landed in the gardens at rear of 47-49 Walsall Road giving a surprise to the family sheltering in the Anderson shelter, but thankfully they were not injured. However, shrapnel damage was reported to windows and doors and the telephone line at the front of the house was brought down. A further two high explosives landed in Sutton Park and were inspected by the park rangers early in the morning. On this night, the Home Guard were 'stood too' and told to parade at Town Gate of Sutton Park and await orders. This reaction was designed to allow the battalion to be able to support the civil powers in case of an incident, but the small scale of the attack meant that they were not used. The impact of this parade was also that the volunteers did not get much rest and were tired for the war work the next day. In addition, there was no shift system in place, so many men paraded in far greater numbers than could be needed. A further report were made by the Town Clerk and County Sub- Controller who wrote a report on the response, which showed the confusion which followed the first raid. The alerts (white and purple) were not received until after the first blasts, and red until later. At 1.30 am when the first blasts occurred most people were in bed, but few made it to shelters before the raid started.

These raids were sadly a sign of things to come, with the first major raid taking place on the night of the 13th – 14th of August. This was Eagle Day, and the largest raid yet hit airfields across the south coast. However, the raid on Birmingham was prioritized to cause maximum damage to Britain's war industry. Early evening, three waves of HE111 *Heinkel* aircraft left their bases at the French airfields at Vannes. These bombers of *Kamfgeschwader* 100 used radio navigation to travel at three-minute intervals at 19,500 feet in height. The fine weather allowed good navigation to assist the pathfinder aircraft leading the strike and at 21:00

they saw Birmingham in their right windows. It is likely that the Spitfire Factory at Castle Bromwich was the target, as well as the Dunlop factory down the road.

Two ambulances were reported at 21:00 available at the fire station. At Hill First Aid Post (Four Oaks), two ambulances and one first aid party were available. At Boldmere Depot, one First Aid Post and two Ambulances. At St Nicholas School, 2 Rescue Parties, one decontamination party and one road repair unit were available. The Home Guard has been posted to the gates of Sutton Park to prevent entry.

On the eastern side of Sutton Park, 378 Battery of the 45th (Royal Warwickshire Regiment) Searchlight Regiment (Territorial Army) had activated their large halogen lamps and were searching for the aircraft which they could now hear. Their lamps were in a defensive island next to the Crystal Palace in Sutton Park, near to Town Gate. Their lights shone into the clear night sky, providing a huge spectacle for those who had not taken cover, as at this point no sirens had sounded. The Observer Corps at Erdington had come under a lot of pressure for false alarms and did not wish to unnecessarily disrupt war production, so as they were unsure if the aircraft noises were friendly or enemy, they did not sound the alarm.

At 11:07 the first bomb fell, landing on Q and F Blocks of the Spitfire Factory. The first explosions killed five workers and injured 40 seriously, as well as over 100 with minor wounds.[xi] The *Luftwaffe* pilots did not report explosions or big fires, as many of the bombs landed inside of the huge warehouse facility, causing damage, but not igniting any equipment, due to the excellent air raid procedures inside. The bombs of this first wing of *Kamfgeschwader* 100 were accurate but did not yet alert the observer corps post in Erdington less than two miles away, or cause any anti-aircraft fire from 378 battery with their heavy guns.

As the *5th Staffel* (flight) moved towards their target of the Dunlop Factory slightly to the west of Castle Bromwich at 12:20, the lights of 45th Regiment caught them in their sights, causing simultaneously the heavy anti-aircraft guns to open fire and the Observer Corps in Erdington to sound the air-raid siren.[xii] Due to the many false alarms of the previous weeks, many residents chose to ignore the alarm and go back to sleep, but the more cautious went to their shelter or the public facilities. The Warwickshire Territorial Army Gunners were well averse with their 90 cm 'Projector Anti-Aircraft searchlights' and managed to catch some of the *Heinkels* in their gaze. This led to a high rate of anti-aircraft fire from the Heavy Anti-Aircraft sites at H5 (Sutton Park), H37 (Wylde Green), H34 (Walmley) and H35 and H11 at Castle Bromwich itself. These sites were formed of the units from 204th Battery, 95th Heavy Anti-Aircraft Regiment based at Saltley and 293rd Battery 95th Heavy Anti-Aircraft Regiment based at Washwood Heath. Across the city, there were sixteen, 4.5ich guns, fifty five, 3.7inch guns, about a third of these were part of 95th Regiment and engaged the *5th Staffel*. Although the weight of fire did not manage bring down any of the Heinkels, it caused the pilots to panic and disperse. Bombs were released in the action that followed as far afield as Hereford as the pilots dived to the west to escape.

The Crystal Palace was built in 1868 as a zoological garden for tourists. It was originally built with a hotel and stable for 50 horses. Prior to the war, it offered special attractions such as lions, bears, wolves, leopards and other novelties. The palace could cater for 1,500 people under cover for dinner. It was one of the main tourist attractions of Sutton Coldfield at the time. Gunner Edward Ruston was a 32 year old territorial soldier of the Warwickshire Regiment. He was married to Lydia Rose and lived in Aston. He was part of the team manning one of these huge search lights, allowing the anti-aircraft units to engage the enemy. At 38 minutes past midnight, three high explosive bombs landed on the search light position, destroying the light and smashing much of the glass on the Crystal Palace. Edward was badly wounded, along with two of his team. The position was connected by telephone cable to the local Police Station in Sutton which was coordinating the Air-Raid Precautions Response. A civilian Ambulance was despatched to the scene and quickly got the three men in the vehicle to take to the Cottage Hospital. Lydia Rose managed to get the hospital to see her husband and sung to him for a few hours and while he was in the hospital. Despite best efforts, Edward later died of his wounds.

The bombs continued to land across Sutton Coldfield and minutes after this first series of blasts in the park, the Boot Inn on Rectory Road had four high explosive bombs land to the side of it, with one wall demolished. Fortunately, the landlord was in the shelter and was unhurt. Bombs were landing across the area with bombs hitting Middleton Woods, Slade Road, Roughley Road and Lichfield Road. All in all, 26 high explosive bombs landed in Sutton Coldfield, with two people injured and one killed. It was the largest air raid so far of the war.

Members of the Home Guard conveyed one casualty to the hospital and a doctor dispatched a mobile unit to recover the other who was in grave condition. Both were military and connected to the search light in the park.

Road repair gang were despatched to deal with a crater in the road. This team were part of the Public Utilities Services. The Town clerk sent a reprimand to the Home Guard suggesting that they should have gone to the Air Raid Precautions post, as this broke down the recognised communication and coordination method. Referencing 'Local Defence Volunteers Instruction 6-1940' which explained this procedure. He also wrote to Dr J H Wright the Medical Officer of Health at the cottage hospital and told him to not deploy the mobile unit without authority.

The Home Guard response was still not as effective as it could have been, especially due to the scale of the raid and the number of incidents across the town. The volunteers had been ordered to muster at their posts on the sounding of an air raid, but as the alarm did not go until after the first hour, they found themselves reporting under the threat of bombardment from the air. What is more, as many of the Home Guard had not yet been issued steel helmets or respirators,[xiii] there was concern for injuries by such a response. Many of these items were held at the stand too positions rather than at home with the volunteer.

There were further complaints because the Air Raid Precaution Staff and fire officers worked on a rota so that different staff rotated and had some time off. However, the Home Guard stood too if there was an air raid and in the case of A, B, C and D company, they were still mustered in Sutton Park to allow them to respond to any needs. At first, with no equipment, this felt like a superfluous task. To concentrate such a large body of men in one place was also dangerous in itself. Many of those who would have responded had to work in the morning, in the new six day wartime week, and felt the task was very hard and not impactful at all. The reflections of this night were discussed by Captain Bigwood and his battalion staff and they then started the process of introducing a shift system and duty staff. It also encouraged better liaison between the battalion and the civilian powers in Sutton Coldfield Police Station, this would become the battalion tactical headquarters in case of an incident.

In terms of the wider response of the civil authorities, the raid on the 13th August was particularly bad and would come into much criticism for the poor response by the authorities. One Air Raid Precautions Warden S C Snape, was alerted to the bombing of Castle Bromwich airdrome, got changed and moved to the airdrome. He had to take cover en-route as bombs were still falling. It was very dark, and the danger was from machinery as well as craters. He joined the search for both the injured, the dead but also unexploded bombs. From 11:30 until 03:00, bombs fell every half an hour. Inspector Sutton told Snape to close the Kingsbury Road on the junction of Tyburn road and he took up duty there until 08:30. His feedback formed part of a formal report which would have considerable impact for the response to air raids in the future.

Castle Bromwich Air Raid Report – 13th August 1940[xiv]

1. **Conclusion 1**. Difficulties in securing admission to the factory, and, when admitted, in making contact with the appropriate officials to ensure rapid utilisation of services sent is indicated in following extracts from reports submitted by officers in charge of the rescue and casualty services which were sent to the factory.

2. **Conclusion 2.** The ambulances were admitted to the factory, but in the first instance sitting casualties by cars accompanying them were not permitted to enter. Apart from the difficulty of effective utilisation of the services sent, it would appear that a much larger number of rescue parties could have been used to complete a thorough search much more quickly had the request for help from the works given fuller particulars of the damage. Immediate and full co-operation between the factory Air Raid Precautions officer or another responsible official, and the incident officer, appears essential.

3. **Leader of the Rescue Party.** Contact with responsible officials was difficult to make, the layout of the works was unknown to the parties, and their equipment was not such as would be chosen for the particular job. It should be emphasised that the members of the rescue squads, the slightest conception of the general layout of the works or what they were likely to encounter and consequently their usefulness was extremely limited. In the case in point, there was no rendezvous point fixed, there was no one to meet the men, they were taken in amongst hundreds of machines in semi darkness by a person who they, themselves, had to persuade to guide them and by the light of the only effective electric lamp which their equipment is authorised to contain. Fortunately, the works organisation appears to have operated efficiently but had this not been so, the city's reinforcements would have had the greatest difficulty in coping with the task.

4. **Casualty Services** After great difficulty Air Raid Precautions Warden Snape managed to gain admittance to this factory and was

immediately struck with what the complete lack of co-ordination between their Air Raid Precautions services control, and the city Air Raid Precautions services. The response party was conducted to the factory Air Raid Precautions control centre, and there met technical adviser to Spring Lane rescue parties, and he informed the rescue party that it appeared practically hopeless to obtain either information or instructions as to where they had to go, or what had to be done. The Incident officer was a sergeant of the city of Birmingham Police who in turn knew nothing about the geography of this vast factory and was thus unable to direct our services to the ultimate destination in the factory-consequently he ceased to function as an incident officer. This appalling state of affairs was in no way the fault of this officer, but due to complete lack of co-ordination.

5. After being directed to various parts of these works, Air Raid Precautions Warden Snape ultimately gained contact with Captain Rivers who was the Air Raid Precautions officer. He gave the party certain information but could not decide without the authority of the works manager as to where casualties and clearance services should be utilised. The rescue party commander ascertained the rescue parties sent from Spring Lane had been instructed by the factory control to return to depot, and immediately after they had left, the Technical Advisor requested to recall one party for further service, and when Air Raid Precautions Warden Snape arrived at the depot, they had been standing by for nearly an hour waiting for instructions. Air Raid Precautions Warden Snape asked Captain Rivers if he still wanted the aid of

these men, and here again was met with the answer that he could not decide until he had seen the works manager. Having in mind the fact that the works rescue party had been considerably augmented during the period which had elapsed since the bombs had fallen on these premises Air Raid Precautions Warden Snape agreed with the technical advisor that these men should return to their depot.

6. It was thought possible that there were still workpeople buried underneath debris but owing to the dangerous condition of the building struck by bombs, no one in authority would give consent for rescue personnel to enter these ruins. Air Raid Precautions Warden Snape understood from the technical advisor that our men were quite willing to go in and see what they could do, but the necessary permission could not be obtained for me to do so."

The lessons of these early raids were critical for the development of the civil defence services and of the Home Guard who would support them. Although this first major raid caused limited impact on Sutton Coldfield, the lessons from Birmingham allowed those in the wider area to learn how to respond effectively. The lessons of Air Raid Precautions Warden Snape read like a training document today in how not to respond to an incident, (in peace time there would have been a public enquiry about such a disaster). But with a war going on, lessons were learned and new procedures implemented quickly to ensure the mistakes were not made again.

In preparation for the next attack, the Air Raid Precautions teams increased construction of air raid shelters, and rehearsed firefighting with locals. On Goldeslie Road, ladies who did not work were being trained in firefighting by the fire service ready to help out. The Home Guard arrangements were also improved, with companies being given more autonomy in their muster locations, and the start of a shift system being introduced to prevent the constant call out every night. Colonel Bigwood was conscious of the impact on morale but also of physical exhaustion of the constant alerts.

The training and establishment of the Home Guard continued, with another Round Robin (No.7) being issued by the Central Midland Area on the 16th August. There were both positive stories but also brutal truth in the document and it helped these men who were training against invasion and were stood too most nights due to the threat of air raids, despite wartime sensitivities to telling the truth. The difficult news was around the lack of equipment, even to the extent that there was a shortage of paper to print manuals. However, the scale of recruitment, with 517,000 Home Guard volunteers in Western Command alone, was simply incredible.

There were now over 1,500,000 Home Guard in service. To support this force over 75,000 uniforms were being made a week and over 2,000,000 arm bands had now been issued. In addition, each rifle now had 50 rounds and many automatic weapons had been issued, with a scale of 750 rounds per gun. Defensive stores were the new shortage as the strong points in the battalion area of operations were being built up. Advice was given that sandbags should be painted with a weak mixture of cement which made them stronger. Also, the lack of barbed wire was named as the top priority for General Officer Commanding, Western Command. This was a substantial improvement to the units, and now even machine gun and mortar training were included as standard, showing the extent of the improvement. 36 new instructors had joined battalions in Western Command, giving regular army guidance to the new formations.

The first night of heavy bombing gave clear focus to the Home Guard that there services would not just be against invasion, and that they must prepare to defend the wider community from the threat from the air. Training programmes were amended to include more on gas, and various bombs and air recognition, to assist in case of emergency. In addition, the links to the local police stations, which were starting to reduce with the new independence of command of the Home Guard, were reinvigorated, in preparation for further bombing raids. Sadly, this major raid was only the beginning.

[i] For those who wish to look into extreme detail on the weapons within the Home Guard, I can recommend the series of books by Ian Skennerton which provides all the technical and numerical data to support this. For this data, I used Skennerton, I.D. (1988). *British Small Arms of World War 2*. SAIS.
[ii] Churchill, W. (1955) *Finest Hour*. Houghton Mifflin Harcourt, gives a figure of 90,000 rifles 'left behind at Dunkirk', but Skennerton, I. D. (1993) The Lee-Enfield Story: The Lee-Metford, Lee-Enfield S.M.L.E. and No. 4 Series Rifles and Carbines, 1880 to the Present. Greenhill Books, London.
looking at all the campaigns up to the end of 1940, puts the loss at over 300,000
[iii] As David French explains in his book French, D (2008) *Military Identities: The Regimental System, the British Army and the British People 1870 – 2000*. Oxford.
[iv] Again from Skennerton, I. D. (1993) The Lee-Enfield Story: The Lee-Metford, Lee-Enfield S.M.L.E. and No. 4 Series Rifles and Carbines, 1880 to the Present. Greenhill Books, London.
[v] An analysis of this can be found in MacKenzie, S. P. (1996) *The Home Guard A Military and Political History*. Oxford Uni Press.
[vi] A low level view from, War Time Sutton: Extracts from the diaries of Gwilym O Griffith 1940-40. Sutton Historical Society.
[vii] Southern Command order 5/2147. A copy can be found in Warwickshire Archives.
[viii] S.C. No. 5/2147 Draft Command Order. Action to be taken on Air Raid Warning Yellow, Red or sounding of Public Warning. A copy can be found in Warwickshire Archives.
[ix] Huge amounts of detail of the wider raids in Birmingham can be found in Richards, S (2019) *The Luftwaffe over Brum*. I highly recommend this book for a full understanding of the Blitz in Birmingham.
[x] This quote is from an E. Wilkes in Brummagem magazine. The archive of these magazines can be found in Birmingham Central Library.
[xi] Again I have taken this detail from Richards, S (2019) *The Luftwaffe over Brum*.
[xii] *Ibid*
[xiii] From War Time Sutton: Extracts from the diaries of Gwilym O Griffith 1940-40. Sutton Historical Society

Image 1: B Company.
Photo: Sutton News 1942

Image 2: Colonel Wilfred Bigwood, Commanding Officer.
Photo: Sutton News 1943

Image 3: Gunner Edward Ruston killed in action on the night of the 13th/14th August 1940.
Photo: Eddie Knight, grandson of Edward Ruston

Image 4: No.14 Platoon, D Company. The Platoon was stationed at the old Police Station (9 Station Road) and was tasked to provide a guard force to Battalion Headquarters at The Royal Hotel.
Photo: Phil Doulgas

Image 5: Sergeant Edward James Douglas and Lance Corporal Peter James Douglas both served in No.14 Platoon, D Company.
Photo: Phil Doulgas

Image 6: The visit to Royal Sutton Coldfield during 1942 of King George VI. The visit took place on 26th February 1942. The King and Queen visited the town hall and inspected Home Guard units at Sutton Park.
Photo: Philip Butler

Image 7: Member of the mounted patrol, based at the Riding School in Sutton Park.
Photo: Sutton News 1943

Image 8: The female section of the Mounted Patrol.
Photo: Sutton News 1943

Image 9: The Mounted Patrol on exercise, Sutton Park.
Photo: Sutton News 1942

Image 10: Howard Butler joined 11 Platoon C Company. The Platoon was based at the antiques shop on the Driffold.
Photo: Philip Butler

Image 11: Lieutenant John Alfred Ollis, known as the officer that kept on going, when others have stopped.
Image: Steve Woodward

Image 12: Arthur Crutchley was one soldier who served in the 6th Warwickshire (Sutton) Battalion Home Guard. I have not yet found his records, but his family have provided me a photo of him in his uniform.
Photo: Leigh Crutchley

Chapter 9
The Blitz

The Blitz and the associated history has become almost legendary in the minds of the people of England. The Home Guard had a key part to play in this story; 1206 Home Guard soldiers were killed in action, mainly during air raids during the conflict. In addition, by the middle of the war the Home Guard and associated units such as the Auxiliary Territorial Service were to man many of the anti-aircraft units across the country. 43,500 people were killed in blitz with 71,000 seriously injured and 88,136 slightly. Many didn't report their injuries.

Across Birmingham there were 365 air raid alerts, and 77 actual air raids, eight of which were classified as major (in which at least 100 tons of bombs were dropped). Official figures state that 5,129 high explosive bombs and 48 parachute mines landed on the city. Along with many thousands of incendiary bombs, this equated to around 1,852 tons of bombs, making it the third most heavily bombed city in the United Kingdom. Of the high explosive bombs, around one fifth failed to detonate and one third of the parachute mines were left suspended after the parachute cords became caught in various obstacles such as trees. In total, 2,241 people were killed and 3,010 seriously injured. A further 3,682 sustained lesser injuries. The attacks destroyed 12,391 houses, 302 factories, 34 churches, halls and cinemas and 205 other buildings. Thousands of other properties were damaged.[i] During the Second World War Sutton Coldfield was bombed during 40 separate nights, of which 31 were recorded as major raids by the Air Raid Precautions Services. During these 4358 bombs landed on the town, of which at least 330 were High Explosive. Ten people were killed (of which three were service personnel) and 28 injured.

As summer turned into autumn 1940, the scale of the German bombing raids on the United Kingdom started to increase substantially. Birmingham was a key target and even at this point in the war where German bombers targeted military factories, the large concentration of war industry in the city meant it was key in their sights. That said, there was considerable push back from the government to explain that fear was the aim of the bombing, and therefore the population should not overreact. In the pamphlet 'Nerves Versus Nazis'[ii] the message was clear, "Don't exaggerate the danger of air raids." It stated that "The bomber is booming about all over the place, covering a hundred miles of the country, but he has only a dozen or so bombs. The chances of my house being hit is no bigger than if he dropped them in thirty seconds and went away." It explained further about the messages sent through newspapers, stating that "You see a photo of two or three houses smashed to pieces. What you do not see, what you do not think about, if the hundreds of houses in the same street which were not touched." It made clear that the evacuation was needed by that "Children should be protected to ensure the morale of adults, not for safety." Despite this messaging, as the first signs of damage from this raid were seen in the light of the morning, people did begin to fear, but for the next few nights, the skies above Sutton Coldfield were quiet as the *Luftwaffe* concentrated further south.

The next attack came on the night of the 24th August 1940 and the attacks would continue none-stop for the next two weeks. At 21:50 the alert was sounded and the German waves came in again led by the *Kamfgeshwader 100* pathfinders using their radio beam to hone in on the target. Volunteer Griffith was out on that night on sentry duty at Wylde Green station "to watch the sky. It was a great spectacle for the searchlights and anti-aircraft guns were in full play. The interlacing beams of the searchlights, sweeping up to a tremendous height, were really beautiful, and the sparkle of the bursting shells, twinkling like sudden stars, was fascinating to watch."[iii] The Air Raid Precautions staff had a considerable number of resources available this night, including three ambulances at the Fire Station; two ambulances and two first aid parties at 'Hill' in Four Oaks; two rescue parties at St Nocholas School; one rescue party on Riland Road; and two first aid parties at Boldmere Garage.

As the first waves of bombers came under fire from the anti-aircraft guns and were lit up by the huge search lamps, the low cloud also made an impact on the accuracy of the bombing. Volunteer Private Sydney Barley was at work at the Reynolds Tube Works in Small Heath when it was hit by the bombers who had flew off course. Sidney was married to Lilly Clara Oldham and was only 37 years old. As a serving member of the 6th Battalion, he was the first to be killed in action and was given a military funeral. An unexploded bomb which fell on Orphanage Road, exploded causing a number of deaths in Erdington. As the bomb had not exploded, residents, soldiers and Air Raid Precautions Wardens had gathered around and were unaware of the serious danger of delayed action fuses. The reaction team were digging down to find survivors when it exploded.

With the bombers going off course and being confused many more bombs landed on Sutton Coldfield. 324 were recorded landing on the town this night, but the vast majority, including 300 incendiary bombs, landed on Walmley Golf Course. Fortunately, despite a noisy night and broken sleep, no casualties were recorded in the town. However, across the Birmingham and wider Midlands the raid was particularly bad, and many of the fires could be seen from the town. Of note was the news that a raid had occurred on London (later to be found to be an accident) which was to have huge impact on the targeting going forward, as the Royal Airforce reacted by bombing Berlin.

The next night, a larger raid was planned, with 50 bombers leading a raid aimed at the metal works in Witton and Aston areas. The bombing on Birmingham was intense, causing over 60 fires and destroying the market hall in the town. The impact on Sutton Coldfield was considerable with 22 large bombs landing on the town including a number of unexploded, which the Royal Engineers had to deal with. The Royal Engineers, tasked through the Subarea destroyed their first bomb at 02:25 at the side of Rectory Road.

A whistling bomb fell on Goldeslie road, with shrapnel landing in the neighbour's garden.[iv] Another high explosive bomb landed on a house at Coppice Farm at the back of Four Oaks station at 23:15 demolishing the whole house. The rescue party was deployed from the town hall, including with some Home Guard volunteers and attended the scene at 23:33. Sadly amongst the wreckage was found 35 year old William Ralph Philip Haywood who had been killed in the blast. The rescue party checked on neighbours and the gas company arrived to ensure there were no leaks and the pipe works were safe. These bomb parties were becoming more efficient at their trade, and even started to have a Women's Voluntary Service tea van to provide much needed hot tea for those who had to work as well as those who had to leave their properties whilst they were made safe.

Whilst Volunteer Leonard Perkins of C Section, 4 Platoon, A Company was on duty supporting the recovery parties in response to the raids, a call came out that a high explosive bomb had hit a house on Lichfield Road, Four Oaks. As the vehicle arrived it was found to be number 400, Leonard's house. Fortunately, his family was in the shelter and the damage was only superficial with shrapnel on the walls. In the air above, the tracer rounds, from the heavy and light batteries, continued to fire causing a great spectacle interspersed with the bright beams of search lights. Although no enemy were shot down, the impact of knocking them off course certainly prevented serious damage to the factories providing for the war effort.

For the next few days, night raid continued daily from around 22:00 every night. Anderson shelters were rapidly being constructed, with a six-person shelter made for the Griffith family, with a reserve of coal to keep them warm on the damp ground. The main impact of the raids was on the inner city areas of Birmingham, but the attraction of the lights of Sutton Park, and the overshoots from the targeting of the Castle Bromwich Spitfire Factory and the surrounding factories, were leading to many hits on Sutton, and considerable risk. Even those who were sceptical at first, decided to take shelter over the next few nights.

The night of the 26th was another raid on the Spitfire Factory at Castle Bromwich, another group of 50 Bombers led by *KampfGeschwader 100* aiming for the factories around northeast Birmingham. They dropped incendiaries on the large ammunition factory ICI Ltd in Witton and the Erdington Birmingham Electric Furnaces Ltd was set alight.[v] Again large amounts of anti-aircraft fire disrupted the German formation and many of the bombs overshot to the north into the vicinity of Sutton Coldfield. The first stick of incendiary devices hit Sutton Oak Road at 00:50, including one which hit the garage attached to number 72, setting it on fire. The Air Raid Precautions Service and Fire Brigade scrambled to the road, with troops moving from A Company Headquarters to support, however en-route a further string of incendiary devices landed on Bakers Lane parallel to Sutton Oak Road, hitting the road and gardens at 01:00. The Home Guard and Fire Brigade used sand to extinguish the phosphorus charges and inspected the gardens to ensure that no more fires broke out, the Fire Brigade concentrated their pumps on the garage of number 72. Volunteers Harold Howard Atkins, who lived at Number 77 and Volunteer L Wedgebury who lived at number 67, were quick to check their own homes to make sure their families were okay. 11 volunteers from A Company lived on Bakers lane and were quick to respond to the action, particularly Colour Sergeant Harold Tomey, A Company Quartermaster Sergeant and his son Volunteer Harold Tomey who lived at number 41, were first on scene.

At 02:00 it was D Company who responded to the next incident as a high explosives bomb landed on the island in the centre of Wyndley Pool, much to the anger of the swans. The Park Wardens reported fires in the surrounding trees, but with higher priorities, they were left to burn. On the boundary with Birmingham, C Company responded to a delayed action bomb at Pype Hayes Park, on the Penns Lane side. A cordon was put in place after a quick search to ensure no one was in the area. C Section, 12 Platoon, C Company responded to the bomb under Corporal Edwin Power, with Volunteer William Harry Hands of 62B Penns Lane concerned for his home. At 04:45 the bomb exploded causing damage to the sewage system, but thankfully no casualties. It had been a busy night for all concerned, but thankfully in Sutton Coldfield there were no casualties.

The raids continued for the next two nights, with two more high explosive bombs landing on Pype Hayes Golf Course on the night of the 27th. One failed to explode and was later detonated by the Royal Engineers. Corporal Power's section made itself comfortable on the golf course and sent runners home to get hot tea. One bomb landed on Whitehouse Common Road, damaging a water main and causing much disruption.

On the 28th, New Hall bore the brunt in Sutton Coldfield with six high explosive bombs landing in the area just after midnight, but no casualties were caused. Even the most stoic of Home Guard soldiers were now taking shelter, Volunteer Griffith commented that on the "31st August, sirens sounded at 9.30pm and the all clear was given at 4am. We went into the shelter for the first time. It was still damp and reeking and we crumbled the concrete steps as we descended. We had an oil stove and sat uncomfortably on deck chairs. The discomfort for the womenfolk was so great as the hours past that at about 2am I led them back to the house where we had tea and went to bed. The banging went on to 3am."[vi]

The night sky was alive with anti-aircraft fire, with the guns claiming 16 kills during August, not a considerable number considering the huge weight of fire which was used. However, both the disruption of German formations was important, but also morale impact on the population fighting back. The Royal Air Force night fighters, of which there were six Bristol Blenham Squadrons, also had limited impact at this point in the war and although they managed 828 night sorties, these resulted in only three confirmed kills.[vii]

The training within Home Guard units continued over the summer, as well as the preparations for defensive locations. In August there was still a very real threat of invasion, and the main effort of the Home Guard was to be prepared to repel this. This included the draining of some of the pools in Sutton Park and Kingsbury to prevent landings. The lack of ammunition for training was creating much concern amongst those who had not fired before. One volunteer commented that on a range "the rifleman shooting next to me failed to put any of his five shots onto target. At the rate of two practise nights per week we should reach some stage of proficiency by 1945."[viii] That said, the quality of the training was on the increase with children assisting the soldiers by acting as Germans in Sutton Park, [ix] and some units building up to offensive action in training. The equipment situation had also improved. By the 4th August scale of equipment for each soldier was considerably improved:[x]

- 1 suit of denim overalls
- 1 respirator
- 1 eye shield
- 1 helmet steel
- 1 field dressing
- 1 Field Service Cap
- 1 greatcoat
- 1 pair of boots
- 1 bayonet frog
- 1 pair of gaiters
- 1 belt
- 1 haversack
- 2 arm bands
- 2 blankets per 4 men
- 1 ground sheet per 4 men

Training for winter of 1940 was being planned for by the autumn, with the Territorial Army and Airborne Forces Association offering to foot the bill for any indoor facilities, even for socialising as needed. They also offered to reduce friction with the Ministry of Education if needed to use school halls.[xi] On the 23rd August 1940, County of Warwick Zone held a demonstration, with 30 vacancies allocated per battalion. The demonstration showed field signals, field formations and pinning hostile parachutists with offensive fire. Smoke screens were used and training was given on how to generate these effectively. This demonstration was a good method of showing large number of people the type of actions which the Home Guard were designed to perform.

Despite the danger of air raids, between the major raids there was an over zealousness to the enforcement of the air raid procedures by some Home Guard. This led to a memo being released stating: "During periods of Air Raid warning drivers of civilian vehicles who have good military reason for going on will be allowed to do so. Military or Home Guard Posts posts will not, repeat not, stop civilian vehicles except for specific purposes."[xii] In addition, a circular went out from Warwickshire Zone asking volunteers to be aware of parachutists being friendly also, and to make sure identity is checked before firing,[xiii] there was a reality now that it was realised that most sole parachutists were aircraft crews rather than enemy agents.

On the 3rd September 'Home Guard acting in aid of civil power was issued' under the authority of the Police and only in emergency, which specified three tasks for local units. These were to assist the Police and Civil Defence organisations in segregating areas rendered dangerous by unexploded bombs; to assist the police in traffic control and air raid warnings being sounded and to be prepared to assist the police, and specifically detailed regular army police, in dealing with panic evacuation, should it occur. These specific tasks gave more clarity to the role of the Home Guard during an air-raid, and although no major attacks had reached Sutton Coldfield since the attack on the 27th August, every night an alert was sounded and men were stood too. The rostering of troops to shifts, and clarity of roles was much needed. Road blocks were becoming obstructive, and orders were given that road blocks would only be put down if immediate action was needed and a direct order was given from the Subarea commander (noting not the zone).[xiv] The 9th September was the first night without raid or alert in many weeks.

As September continued, it became clear that the overwhelming victory by the *Luftwaffe* envisaged by the Germans was not occurring, and this was more evident as bombers started to move from bombing airfields in the south, to bombing the industrial cities. That said, the attitude of the Home Guard was becoming more relaxed towards the bombing. When at 21:59 on the 12th September a large incendiary landed on the Co-Op store on the corner of Holland Street and The Parade, it did not explode but shattered windows. D Company sent three men with brooms to clear up the mess. A much more muted reaction than only a few weeks before. Another high explosive bomb landed at the rear of St Peter's Church in Maney causing slight damage to the roof of number 10 and shattering the glass in the greenhouse. Lieutenant Walter Wheale Hall, who commanded No.16 (Railway) Platoon, lived at number 15 Maney Hill Road, opposite number 11, and came off duty happy to find his green house had not suffered the same fate. Maney Hill and the Co-Op did not have much luck during this week, with more high explosives landing on the 13th September, destroying the nets on the tennis court, and probably of more significance, destroying the Co-Op fully this time. However, despite this there was slightly less concern than if the bomb hit the pub over the road.

On the 15th October a *Staffel* of *Heinkels* bombed Sutton Coldfield, possibly targeting the railway line at Wylde Green. The first bombs fell at 21:00 and Volunteer Griffith from No.4 Platoon A Company was on guard at the station when the first blasts occurred. At the base of the station bridge "A shopkeeper [Vove's Shop] was in his wooden shop, which was slightly damaged, whereas I would have expected it to be blown clean away as it had no foundations. The explosion threw tons of earth from the road over the railway bridge onto the line, yet this wooden shack stood up to the blast." The bombing around the station was very heavy, "one bomb dropped so near that, as it was falling, we thought it must be upon us. It made a crater in the road by the railway bridge [Station Road Wylde green], put our gas fires out of commission and held up the train services next morning."[xv] The work of the railway platoon and the gas board were critical for such incidents coordinated through the Central Air Raid Precautions Command. Quickly the soldiers from the platoon set to work repairing the line and ensuring that the trains could travel as soon as possible.

No. 4 Platoon had a difficult night responding to blasts in the region of Wylde Green station, "our sub section leader told me that his father's house had been bombed twice and rendered untenable. His father is 77 and mother invalided. Neither had taken shelter. The old couple were packed off to their cottage in Aberdovey."[xvi] This bomb had landed at 184 Station Road at 22.05 whilst No.4 Platoon were dealing with the explosion at the railway bridge and securing the gas mains. Another high explosive had landed to the rear of the houses on Sunnybank Road causing shrapnel damage and smashed windows to many houses on the road.

This raid on the 15th was the start of a major effort by the *Luftwaffe* to destroy the industry of the Midlands and Birmingham itself was hit very hard at this time. A new variant of *Heinkel* allowed 500 kilogram bombs to be slung, which could cause immense damage to houses. [xvii] The raid on the 16th was considerable in scale and across Birmingham 59 people were killed and 43 seriously injured, with the raid lasting from 21:00 until 16:00.

The first alert of bombs landing came into the Police Station at 20.55. High explosive bombs had been reported as landing at along the Chester Road, including a direct hit on number 396. Private Jock Pardem of No.11 Platoon lived at number 400 and return home from his shift with C Company to see his neighbours house turned to rubble, fortunately with no loss of life. Princess Alice Orphanage on Chester Road had two high explosive bombs land in the grounds, destroying telephone wires, electrical cables and smashing glass. Fortunately, the children were in the large public shelter in the basement and were all safe and well.

Concurrently two large 500kg bombs landed on Kings Road, destroying the houses from number 20 to number 30 to such an extent that they had to be demolished. Volunteer George Bullock of No. 2 Platoon D Section lived at number 28, and was hugely impacted by these bombs, with all of his worldly possessions lost. Thankfully all the residents had been sheltering and no casualties were caused, but the local council had to provide them with temporary accommodation. Lieutenant Watson who Commanded No.2 Platoon and Corporal Robert Seaborn who Commanded D Section were quick to provide support to Volunteer Bullock and his family. Despite the terrible circumstances, clothing, food and toys were provided to help. On the scene immediately were the ladies of the Women's Royal Voluntary Service with hot tea and a bun, much needed on a night like this.

As the raids continued in Birmingham, and the anti-aircraft units worked hard, a second stick of bombs straddled the town at 00:50. George Frederick Road was hit by two high explosive bombs, landing in the gardens of number 60 and 65. Another landed at 25 Bakers Lane where Volunteer Harry Kemp lived, but failed to explode. The Air Raid Precautions service responded and set up a cordon around the area with the support of A Company, evacuating the nearby houses. A Royal Engineer explosive team was called in to make it safe, much to the relief of Volunteer Kemp who now had a large hole in his roof, which could have been worse. Another bomb had landed in some silver birch trees off Bakers Lane, causing shrapnel damage to a number of roofs. In addition three large high explosives landed to the rear of Westwood Road. One bomb landed near the Parson and Clerk Hotel hitting a gas main and causing a small explosion. The Air Raid Precautions Service organised the Volunteer Fire Brigade and Gas Works to move to the scene, screened off by Home Guard troops. . There was a lot of luck on this night considering the large volume of ordinance dropped. It could have been much worse.

The Birmingham Mail reported that "a town in the West Midlands had another experience of Nazi frightfulness on Saturday night .... On Friday night a cinema received a direct hit and a number of casualties, some of them fatal, were caused."[xviii] This was the Carlton Cinema[xix] (the movie Typhoon playing) on the 26th October.[xx]

> *"The two houses at an angle facing the old village centre at the end of Dudley Park Road were very badly damaged by a direct hit. Dorothy and I had often admired the charm of these two houses,*

with their carefully tended gardens and neatly cut dwarf hedges. Oxford Road had a bomb and quite thirty houses had windows broken. He [the Germans] came early tonight, 5 past 7, and big fires were started immediately. From 7 to 11 guns and bombs and noises of planes were about continuous. The glare from fires in town was terrific. We came into the house from the shelter at 1 a.m., but the all clear had not gone then."

On the 28th October 1940 there was another medium sized raid, with large scale incendiary bombing. Around 200 incendiary devises landed across Sutton Park, which set fires in the dry autumn undergrowth. A Company mobilised to move into the park and assist the rangers putting out the larger of the fires. In addition, the Mounted Section moved out to help and assist with any wounded animals. One of the wardens was injured putting out an incendiary and was helped to the cottage hospital where he received treatment.

In addition to the incident on Sutton Park, three of the incendiaries also landed at 21.50 on 146 and 148 Streetly Lane, home of Volunteer James Alan Donn and Volunteer Revill Edwards. The fire damage to these houses was considerable, with the Volunteer Fire Brigade deployed to bring the flames under control. Three high explosives landed on 54 and 62 Thornhill Road, causing considerable damage to the properties. Again, despite the high levels of physical damage, Sutton had been fortunate to not suffer casualties on a larger scale. The next night, the town was lucky again with over 100 incendiaries landing to the rear of Oakwood Road in the Spiny, missing the houses by a few metres.

The Birmingham Mail with wartime restrictions reported on the fire bombing incidents in its daily news;

> *In a West town hit by enemy raiders, incendiary bombs fell in able numbers, damage was caused to various kinds of property, business and domestic, and hotels and churches were among the buildings to suffer. Once again, valiant work was done by the fire-fighting services who upon there fell a heavy burden. Two soldiers staying in premises near where a shower of incendiaries fell, were personally responsible for extinguishing nearly 20 of these fireraisers. They also got 18 cars out of a garage which was ablaze, and not content with this they further salvaged hundredweights of sausages and scores of hams from a nearby shop. Numerous pork pies were among other things they saved, and some of these were distributed to the firemen while they were at work on the blaze. Close by four Home Guards another shower of incendiaries hit a building beneath which they knew was a public 'shelter. The building immediately went up in flames. The men dashed across the road, pulled away fallen debris from the mouth of the shelter, and then got out the people, 35 in all, without a scratch.*

Although there is some flourish in the statements made by the Birmingham Mail, and some of the incidents are likely within Birmingham itself, the description brings to life the actions of the raids which were ongoing.

As the late autumn weather set, in the scale of the bombing slowed as the *Luftwaffe* concentrated on the coastal cities, however there were incidents two or three times a week which had to be responded to. On the 1st of November, a bomb destroyed 25 Anchorage Road, and on the 9th November, Over Green Farm was hit by three high explosives and one incendiary. Wylde Green station was hit again on the 6th November with eleven high explosives damaging the line. Over 100 incendiaries hit Park Lane in Minworth early evening on the 20th November and high explosive bombs laned in the road on Coleshill Road, Marsh Lane and Park Lane throughout the month. That day the prime minister visited Birmingham, and recorded his observations.

> *"The next target was Birmingham, and three successive raids from the 19th to the 22nd November inflicted much destruction and loss of life. Nearly eight hundred people were killed and near to two thousand injured; but the life and spirit of Birmingham survived the ordeal. When I visited the city a day or two later to inspect the factories, and see for myself what had happened, an incident, to me charming, occurred, it was the dinner hour and a very pretty young girl ran up to the car and threw a box of cigars into it. I stopped at once and she said `I won the prize this week for the highest output, I only heard you were coming an hour ago'. The gift must have cost her two or three pounds. I was very glad (in my official capacity) to give her a kiss. I then went on to the long mass grave in which so many citizens and their children had been newly buried. The spirit of Birmingham shone brightly, and it's million inhabitants, highly organised, conscientious and comprehending, rode high above their physical suffering."*[xxi]

On the night of the 23rd November the danger was brought home again to the Home Guard while Volunteer Graham Brooks was on duty, his home at 9 Frederick Road was destroyed by a 500kg bomb. As always, the Home Guard rallied together to help one of their own, and support was given both by the chain of command, and the local authority to help him in this difficult time. One of the saddest events of the war was the death of a child. Ruby Maureen Bunford, aged only 7, died when a bomb landed on 33 Little Green Lane on the 26th November 1940. She was the daughter of Edith Buffery (formerly Bunford). Words cannot describe this tragedy.

The last raid of 1940 came on the 21st December, when 100 incendiaries landed at Water Orton near the bridge and 50 Incendiaries landed at Vicarage Lane in the village. Fortunately, there were no casualties and no significant damage. 1940 went out with a bang as a large 500kg bomb landed in Minworth by a Heinkel avoiding anti-aircraft fire, but no damage was caused. From November, there had been an increased night fighter provision by the Royal Airforce. The Hampden Patrol of No.5 Group consisted of five squadrons in Lincolnshire to do night fighting many were Hampden bombers acting as night fighters.

By the end of 1940, 41 percent of the German bomber force was available (551 machines)[xxii] mainly due to maintenance, accidence and repairs. At that same time, the weather was getting very hard for bombing, therefore the *Luftwaffe* reduced the campaign to allow a reset. By this point in the war, 70,000 Birmingham homes were damaged, however 50,000 of these were only minor damage and could be repaired. The bombing had caused considerable damage to the city, and the impact in Sutton Coldfield was such that it felt it was also part of the war. The front line was now at home, and people were motivated to help in every way. Although the individual stories are tragic and horrible, the overall impact on both the war industry and the population was minimal. There were terrible losses, but not overwhelming, and can be summed up the message that "The bark of the bomb is worse than its bite."[xxiii]

[i] This summary is quoted from Brazier, C. & Rice, S. (2018) *Condition Red.* (West Midlands Police).
[ii] The pamphlet is: Langdon-Davies, J. (1940) Nerves Versus Nazis. HMG.
[iii] Another quote from War Time Sutton: Extracts from the diaries of Gwilym O Griffith 1940-40. Sutton Historical Society.
[iv] *Ibid.*
[v] Richards, S (2019) *The Luftwaffe over Brum.*
[vi] War Time Sutton: Extracts from the diaries of Gwilym O Griffith 1940-40. Sutton Historical Society.
[vii] Richards, S (2019) *The Luftwaffe over Brum.*
[viii] War Time Sutton: Extracts from the diaries of Gwilym O Griffith 1940-40. Sutton Historical Society.
[ix] From Evening Despatch 29 July 1940.
[x] The information on this was written in Central Midland Area Round Robin No.5 Dated 4th August 1940 found in the Warwickshire Archive. But also importantly the headquarters were communicating the fact through this effective method and holding themselves to account.
[xi] Written by Colonel Erskine Murray from Warwickshire Territorial Army and Auxiliary Forces Association – Warwickshire Archive.
[xii] Central Midland Area Memo No. O 1605 – Warwickshire Archive.
[xiii] Headquarters Warwickshire Zone 6th September 1940 – Warwickshire Archive.
[xiv] Headquarters Warwickshire Zone 19th September 1940 – Warwickshire Archive.
[xv] War Time Sutton: Extracts from the diaries of Gwilym O Griffith 1940-40. Sutton Historical Society.
[xvi] *Ibid.*
[xvii] Richards, S (2019) *The Luftwaffe over Brum.*
[xviii] Birmingham Mail - 26th October 1940.
[xix] A memorial garden was opened on the old site in 2007.
[xx] From the Acocks Green History Society Website - a diary entry by a resident.
[xxi] Churchill, W. (1955) *Finest Hour.* Houghton Mifflin Harcourt.
[xxii] Richards, S (2019) *The Luftwaffe over Brum.*
[xxiii] From Langdon-Davies J. (1940) *Nerves Versus Nazis.* HMG.

Chapter 10
Training

After a hard-working autumn, it was clear that the invasion was unlikely to come over the winter, and as the Blitz calmed down with the poor weather, the Home Guard set in for a winter of training and preparation of defences. Many write of the actions of the Home Guard after 1940, however a cursory glance at world events show that Germany was still not even near the peak of its strength, and Japan had not even entered the war. It was still likely at this point that after the winter, Britain, who stood alone, could be invaded. In addition, the support given to the regular forces by the huge manpower available in the Home Guard to guard, patrol and maintain an effective deterrent, allowed the build up of additional forces to support the campaigns in North Africa, East Africa and later in the Far East.

In January 1941, authority was given to the Home Guard to appoint colonels in charge of sectors and zones and to conduct mobile offensive patrols. Lieutenant Colonel Bigwood was making an assessment of his forces and bringing his structure and training in line to efforts needed across the Central Midlands Area. There were always conflicting priorities of the immediate requirement of assisting the civil powers during air raids, the need to maintain troops in critical war industries, and to provide an effective force for anti-invasion actions, including now mobile offensive units to respond where needed. The priority was anti-invasion, but the threat of air raids was real and had been lived by all the men over the last few months. Leadership was needed to persuade men of the needs of training and maintaining a high standard of effectiveness.

The situation with equipment and weapons had improved substantially by winter 1940, but still in general there were only arms for two thirds of the men, with the third not on duty or standby being ineffective in combat. This, however, did not prevent them being in support of administrative and civil contingency tasks. By December 1940 the situation on clothing had improved with most soldiers having either battle dress or denim uniform, boots, a field cap, helmet, anklets and belt as a minimum issue. Each company was now issued equipment and administrated through the procedures listed in the Warwickshire Territorial Army and Airforce Association. In true military style, a large book was purpose made for the issue of each item and 'Form HG' was required by each company. Each individual Volunteer was issued a 'Form G.1054.A' to account for their personal items. However, with this bureaucracy did come substantially more equipment and stores, giving confidence to the troops in the 6th Battalion to defend their homeland.

The first formal defence order was written by the then Captain Bigwood on the 30th January 1941. In everyone's mind was an invasion in 1941, so this plan was written as if it was a very likely occurrence. The orders were written in a very clear and concise way following military procedure, being very explicit on boundaries and responsibilities. This was considerably important with the large number of troops on the group, both Home Guard and Regular, but also the plethora of irregular, auxiliary and civil defence units. It was important to have clear lines of responsibility and command. The orders outlined the reinforcement of defensive positions, particularly the strong points of each company, but also the section and platoon stand too positions in local areas. In addition, it outlined the priority of training for the battalion to follow over the relatively quiet winter months.

"The defence scheme was a series of defensive points with 'all posts capable of defence against attack from any direction and should be supported by covering fire from emplacements on flanks and trenches sited for grenade and cocktail throwing."[i] Runners were allocated between company and battalion locations. Many of these were boy scouts or schoolboys from Bishop Vesey Grammar School. The fact of these boys serving with the Home Guard provided a convenient excuse for a beleaguered Sutton headmaster, defending himself against his Governors. In 1941, "thirteen out of twenty-nine boys from form 5M1 failed their School Certificate but the Headmaster explained that they 'were giving a good deal of time to Home Guard duties."[ii] Arm bands were issued in red for runners, orderlies and cyclists to clearly identify them amongst the hustle and bustle of an incident or emergency.

As well as the company defensive position, a new independent defence area was allocated by the Warwickshire Sub Zone at Castle Bromwich aerodrome. The defence position was of critical importance as the airfield was used to fly completed Spitfires from the factory. The defensive position bordered C Company's southern boundary, but was under the independent command of Major Simpson MC MM. It included the 'Kingsbury Road Block' and 'Railway Point', and was a likely point for assault by German paratroopers, so was a likely task to be reinforced by the remainder of the battalion.

Further details were given on the action of the invasion including the destruction of petrol pumps, these were outlined in orders, showing a scorched earth policy against the enemy invader. Details were given for the smaller defence islands in the multiple villages to the east of the River Tame. The Coleshill and Wilnecote defence scheme would be in village circles. They would hold out as defensive islands to delay and disrupt the enemy. These positions would be isolated and not linked to the wider defence scheme. Details were given that all soldiers should carry 48 hours of rations which were not to be eaten unless orders were given to, and gas masks were to be carried. It must be noted that this was not just for defensive action, there was a real likelihood that poison gas would be used by the British Army in defence of the United Kingdom as a last resort. Adding further to the isolated nature of the defence, orders stated that in case of casualties A, B and D Coy would use the Battalion aid post, but C, E, F and G Coy were to make their own arrangements.

The purpose of these defensive positions[iii] were listed to have a main effort of firstly destroying the enemy by all means and forces at the point of landing before they could collect and organise and secondly, if available forces were weak, to pin the enemy until reinforcements can be sent. It was very clear that if regular forces arrived, the regulars would take command and the Home Guard would give every assistance. Orders stated that "Six men in 30 minutes do more than will 50, two hours later" so aggressive counter attacks against the enemy were particularly needed.

Lieutenant (Reverend) Garrett taught a lesson to E Company on 30th December 1940. This was about anti-tank warfare and the use of the Molotov cocktail. He talked about how to recognise the main German column ahead of its recce force, due to it having four tanks in its column. He described the vulnerable air intake vent and valves and how to use a Molotov to attack. This was a recent invention from the Finnish army in the winter war of 1918 (a present to Molotov from the Fins, not made by Molotov as some people presume). He described also how to make a 'plumb pudding' or sticky bomb using two cartons of High Explosive, and where to place this. What is striking is that there was an absolute expectation for these to be used in combat, and the bravery of being willing to approach an enemy tank in such a way is incredible.

No. 2 Platoon, F Company were responsible for the positions around Shuttington, and from the Platoon Command Post at Amington Working Men's Club, Lieutenant Arthur Derby would command the Platoon, not far from his house at Number 8 Main Road, Amington. Sergeant Banister would have his platoon ambulance post at the Alvecote Post Office. The coordination of the defensive arcs was supported by Sergeant Brown, who was the Company Intelligence Sergeant. Considerable detail of the stand too positions were listed in the orders, an example of this was the section defending Shutting Bridge at Amington, which had the three weapons slit trenches listed, two with rifles and one with a Browning machine gun. Each of these had a grid reference and details of the defence. Other defensive slit trenches were listed at Hangman Corner, Newton Regis, Nomans Heath and Austrey. These were all built up to defensive stand too positions dominating the ground. Although they were static in nature, they would have caused much disruption to any enemy movement.

Lieutenant Cyril Henry Ball was in Command of 3 Platoon F Company, and lived in the vicarage in Nomans Heath. He had allowed a stand too position in his home, as it had dominating arcs of fire over the surrounding area. He instigated a demanding series of training for his platoon over the winter, an example of this is one week's training from the week commencing the 16th December 1940:

- Monday 1900 – 2100 – Newton Reges Rifle Inspection and cleaning by section commanders
- Tuesday 1900 – 2100 – Normans Heath, Shuttington Austrey. Field Signals, semaphore with flags. Rifle inspection by section commanders at own HQ
- Wednesday – Duties. Newton regis. Bayonet fighting, talk on patrols, inspection of ID Cards
- Thursday – Duties. Oustrey / Nomans Health. Revision of musketry by own squad commanders
- Friday – Duties. Shuttington. Revision of Signalling and musketry. Instructor 2nd in command of Platoon
- Saturday 1430. Browning Rifle Firing

- Sunday 1030 – 1230. Austrey and Normans Health. Platoon Drill. Shuttington, Bayonet fighting and section drill.

The training focused on the basics of firing, signals and administration. This quickly brought the basic standard of the soldiers to a point in which they could handle their weapons effectively and man a defensive position, the core role of the Home Guard.

As the summer of 1941 passed, the threat of invasion again receded, but the situation was certainly not relaxed for Britain. Russia was under attack and the Panzer Divisions were well on their way towards Moscow. It did not look like the Russians could hold out, and the first Arctic convoys were being used to transfer led lease equipment to the Soviets. The whole of the Balkans were now under Axis control, with Greece and Yugoslavia conquered in the spring, and then Crete in May. In the desert the British Army was under siege in Tobruk and the Africa Corps had forced the 8th Army back to Egypt. The build-up of forces in the Far East continued with noises coming from Japan. This grew in September when French Indochina was annexed by Japan, moving Japanese forces closer to the sub-continent and Malaya. The battle of the Atlantic continued throughout 1941, and although the Royal Navy was holding out, huge losses were still occurring from the U-Boat threat.

On the home front as the Blitz reduced in scale, the focus of Home Guard units returned to training. The winter training plan had given the Home Guard a focus on recruiting, training and getting specialists. The focus of 1941 had been to produce training manuals to standardise procedures ad to introduce proficiency badges to bring them in line with the Territorial

Army's principles of training. Early 1942 was to be a more formal introduction of regulations for the Home Guard, bringing in a level of bureaucracy and standardisation to sustain the force into the future. This reorganisation was to leave behind much of the variation and improvisation of the early days, but still allow for what could be another potential invasion in 1942, however unlikely this now looked. In addition to this new focused training and administration came a renewed focus on anti-aircraft units, where the manpower was needed to release those soldiers fit for service overseas.

The urgency of all of these issues rapidly increased with the entry of Japan into the war in December 1941, and the immense losses across the Far East, including Singapore, Burma and the Dutch colonies. These defeats, although they were given hope by the entry of the USA into the war, saw an immense drain on the manpower of Britain, especially in fighting troops. Anything that could be done to move troops from the British Isles to the front line, needed to be actioned urgently.

On a national scale, Home Guard Instruction No.38 1941 outlined the training requirements for the winter of 1941. It gave commanding officers direction that although the threat of invasion must be in their mind, training was needed to ensure they were ready for any invasion in the clearer weather of 1942. The object of the training would be twofold: for trained men, training in the more mobile forms of defence as applied to their operational role; for untrained men, individual training. The instruction gave direction that collective training should focus on night operations, patrols, anti-tank actions and that the training of specialist would also be a priority.

Detail was broken down on each element of the training, including how to improve skills in both rifle and machine gun training, and the use of bombs and gas. It is noticeable that the order states that attendance on parades are usually a direct reflection of the standard of the training, much like that of the Territorial forces. It commented that across the various Regional Commands, 4000 instructors had been trained by the end of 1941[iv] allowing a high quality of training across the Home Guard.

The wider issues of mobilising a regular infantry force was shown by the fact that Infantry Training Centres were not able to give as much support to the Home Guard, due to focus on regular forces at this time. However, 'Travelling Wings' of War Office Schools are able to give assistance. War Office Lectures were touring the country talking about camouflage, small arms, and scouting. Orders explained that training must be of the next highest unit to which junior officers and non-commissioned officers currently command[v] and that Army Cadet forces and the Home Guard should work closer together for training and recruiting purposes. It was clear that only limited ceremonial duties should be conducted, but church parades were encouraged for reasons of morale.

These instructions on defence were supported by clear instructions on operational activity, including stating that a proportion of training time must be used to improve defence and replace camouflage on the defensive positions manned by the Home Guard. Although further clarified as the war continued, the principles of Home Guard defence were now being confirmed, including:

Principles of Home Guard Defence [vi]

- Defence is final. A defended locality must fight to the last man and last round.
- Defended localities must be sited in depth. The enemy may infiltrate between localities, he may overrun one, but the impetus will be slowed down as he advances and he can be dealt with by vigorous counter-attack.
- Aggressive defence. Defence must not be static. Every commander must have his mobile reserve to dominate his front by fighting patrols and snipers and to destroy the enemy by counter-attack.
- Defence must not be concentrated. Seeds, not soldiers, survive distribution in penny packets. It is fire power that stops an attack. Keep the size of a locality small enough to produce concentrated weapon fire. Defend essentials only.
- Mutual support. Enfilade fire by machine guns and anti-tank weapons is more effective than frontal fire. It often assists concealment. It allows one locality or strongpoint to support the neighbouring ones.
- Concealment is paramount. A post located can often be neutralized. A vital element in successful defence is surprise. Conceal yourself, your positions, your weapons.
- Don't let the enemy draw your fire. Hold it until he attacks in force.

In the 6th Battalion these regulations on training and operations were considered and applied by Colonel Bigwood and his battalion headquarters. An individual training record was issued to every soldier in the 6th Battalion to ensure they were qualified and proficient. The training had to be signed by both the instructor and also the company commander. The training was divided into the various weapon systems, and marksmanship at different position, target indication, duties of a sentry, anti-gas drills, map reading and fieldcraft. It is noticeable that this basic infantry training had not changed from the modern military view of basic soldiering. Judging distance and range cards are common pocket book lessons to be taken by a junior non-commissioned officer. This mandatory training list showed that a focus on the basics being done brilliantly by the 6th Battalion, which was an excellent method of conducting training.

On the 11th October 1941 a major exercise took place in Sutton Park with E Company acting as a sabotage force. No.1 Platoon acted as a penetration force with the aim of infiltrating the goods yard at Sutton Park Railway Station, which they succeeded to do. The soldiers enjoyed the exercise and there was an insatiable appetite for more of this type of training.

In addition to the exercises conducted by the companies and the battalion, troops also supported regular army training. A major exercise took place in February 1942 in Marston Green, utilising an urban training facility. The attackers, who were commanded by Major P. N. Dinglev MC, attacked and captured various objectives in the role of paratroopers. Regular troops and aircraft participated in the exercise defending from the Home Guard acting as Germans.[vii]

There were still many shortages at this time, and the availability of publications to train from was very limited. A number of unofficial books were recommended reading, in a time where limited focus could be given to Home Guard tactics. These were available to buy, but also were recommended by the war office, these included:

- Home Guard Training Manual. John Langdon Davis
- Home Guard For Victory. Hugh Slater
- New Ways of War. HE Graham
- Home Guard Pocket Book. Brig Gen AFU Green
- General Knowledge for Home Guards. GS Mackay

Also, simple games were produced to improve skills, such as when on guard. Such as 'War Planes' a card game for aircraft spotters, made by Temple Press Limited. A popular guide to the German Army No.5 was issued in November 1941, again showing an increase availability of producing pamphlets for use in training. The first official pamphlet widely available was the elementary map reading 1941 publication for Home Guard.

Soldiers were invited to attend a large amount of individual courses across both the Central Midlands Area, but also nationally. Courses varied in name, but can be themed into those which were for instructors to allow 'train the trainer' activity, but also those which gave specific lessons in technical trades such as signals or ammunition. There was a considerable focus on leadership, with various leadership schools across the country.

Category	Courses	Locations
Ceremonial	Drill Course	Burbrooke
	Funeral Course	
Instructor	BAR Course	
	Bombing Course	
	Browning Machine Gun Course	
	Gas Course	
	Grenade Course	Humberslade Command School
	Physical Training Course	Birdbrooke
	Short Mortar Course	
	Vickers and Lewis Course	Elmdon
	Weapon Course	Altcar Command Weapon Training School
Leadership	Command Course	Powells Pool / Sutton Command School
	Commanders Course	
	Commanding Officer's Course	Donnington
	Home Guard Commissioning Course	Malvern Officer Cadet Training Unit
	Junior Commanders Course	
	Junior Leaders Course	Denbies
	Leaders Course	Leaders School 1941
	Medical Officers Course	
	Platoon Commanders Course	Sutton Coldfield / Ludlow / Warwick / Knutsford
	Senior Officers Course	Donnington
	WO1 Instructors Course	

Logistics	Ammunition Course	Barthomley Rectory / 54 CAD Hewell Grange
	Travelling Wing	Nuneaton
Staff Training	Umpiring Course	
	Intelligence Officer Course	Hagley
	Liaison and Intelligence Course	Birmingham
Tactics	Anti Sabotage Course	Kjackbrook
	Anti Tank Tactics Course	Harborne
	Battlecraft Course	
	Camouflage Course	Devisis
	Field Tactics	Knutsford
	Patrolling Course	
	Street Fighting Course	Street Fighting Wing Birmingham
Technical	Intelligence and Security Course	Hasley
	Pioneer Course	Blacon
	Security Course	Birmingham university
	Signals Course	ITC Budbrooke Barracks
	WTS (Wireless Telephone and Signals) Course	Unberslade

Table 10: Home Guard Courses

Of particular note was the establishment of the Urban Training Facility in Birmingham, also known as the Home Guard Street Fighting School, run by the General Headquarters Town Fighting Wing. The wing utilised the areas in the triangle of Wrenthan, Gooch and Essex Street Birmingham which had been destroyed by the *Luftwaffe* bombing. The Chief instructor was Captain Abert Dick Edwards (Royal Leicestershire Regiment).[viii] The facility had an increasing number of aids, including a German headquarters, mock tank and German equipment. The course opened with a Home Guard film shown and details of equipment and structures. The course then had lessons on observation and cover, crossing obstacles, company defence. There was a 'Tactical Exercise Without Troops' or TEWT which allowed commanders to go through the theory of house clearance, and then defence, but this was followed by a practical assault on a house to test what they had learned on clearing houses. As equipment became more available later in 1941, such training facilities became more common, and much of the previous Territorial Army infrastructure was being utilised by the Home Guard.

A Tactical Exercise Without Troops (or TEWT) is a common method to train young commanders in how to conduct a plan (or estimate) in the military. It is used today, as it was used in the Second World War, often when resources are not available to train with troops, or to allow commanders to test their theory before trying it in practise. Many will remember their time as a junior officer on the side of a hill, planning an attack, in the rain under a poncho, watching their clock for the dreaded directing staff. TEWTs were used by the 6th Battalion to train their commanders. The sites in one exercise by E Company consisted of local areas such as Wilncote Hall and Watling Street, however, the twist is of course that when this TEWT was done in 1941 the threat of invasion was still very real, and the role of the Home Guard was to fight to the death, for their homes and their villages.

The Gort Scheme exercise took place on the night of 11th October 1941 in Sutton Park. The exercise was very secret in nature with soldiers not told of its nature prior to attendance. This was a night exercise in Sutton Park with Wilnecote and Coleshill Company acting as parachute troops. Headquarters were mentioned often in the instructions for the exercise, giving a hint at the type of attack. It was noted that ammunition was not to be used, nor bayonets fixed and that casualties would not be taken beyond company headquarters. An insight again into the rank heavy nature of training and large numbers in the units at this time, can be found in the handwritten orders for No.4 Platoon E Company. The platoon was divided into four sections, each commanded by an officer or senior non-commissioned officer. No.1 Section Commanded by Sergeant Smith and Corporal Beacon was given the crossroads of Monmouth drive, in the direction of Stonehouse Road to deny to the enemy. No.2 Section commanded by 2nd Lieutenant Allton and Sergeant Buckler with three squads were to be in an observation post at Wyndley Pool. No. 3 Section under Sergeant King and Sergeant Rettanly were to move on patrol from Holly Hurst to Stonehouse Gate. Then finally No.4 Section under Lieutenant Adams and Sergeant Phillips were to support the others in reserve. Lieutenant Allton commented in his report that he felt that "the men took their part a little seriously! Especially the mounted patrols. The Marines captured each of the mounted patrols by creeping up in cover and then dismounting them and enjoyed the rest of the exercise as troopers."

The strength of the battalion by the end of 1941 had stabilised, with some leaving to join anti-aircraft units, but others volunteers joining from leaving school. The total strength was 2651, hugely above their establishment of a thousand men. The six rifle companies were well manned, A Company (320), B Company (252), C Company (314), E and F Company (812) and G Company (589). The rural companies east of the River Tame being now even larger with smaller village sections now established as platoons. Wilnecote Detachment (E and F Company) now had 12 village platoons across the two companies. D Company (Headquarters) had reduced in size to 364 men and women, with a large number moving to anti-aircraft units in the park, and a reduction in the administrative staff who were above the recommended age.

Sport was an important part of unit life in the Home Guard. It was used for team building as well as fitness. Many of the sub-units had football teams, but also a battalion team was formed to play the local amateur teams. The first match between the Home Guard XI and Boldmere St Michaels took place, after the club paused playing due to the outbreak of war, in February 1941. Boldmere Swimming Club organised a swimming gala for the local members of the Royal Artillery (anti-aircraft units), Royal Airforce and members of the Home Guard in August 1941.[ix] In December 1941 a inter-company boxing match was organised at Boldmere School by the 6th Battalion, with Private F. Hales of Coleshill Coy winning the welterweight contest. Prizes were presented to the winners of the contests by the Mayor of Sutton Coldfield.[x] The scale of the tournaments gathered pace as more time was available. In 1943 a Mounted Gymkhana was conducted "Horse Leaping and Novelty Races, Open to Novice and Children. Musical Chairs, etc." Lieutenant Fisher organised the event at the Equitation School.[xi]

In addition to sport, the Home Guard was now more involved in the civilian community of Sutton Coldfield, especially in terms of music and charity events. Most of the Home Guard platoons had their own charitable funds to support both their welfare but also to support the members who now were in the regular forces overseas. Application was made for the registration of the 4 Platoon 6th Battalion Warwick (Sutton) Battalion Home Guard Comforts Fund with the objects of "which are shortly as follows: (a) To raise money for the benefit of ex members the Platoon serving in his Majesty's Regular Forces and their relatives or dependants. (b) The preliminary financing functions promoted to raise money for charitable purposes. And the Administrative Centre which situate at Lorn E. Hillwood Common Road, Four Oaks. Sutton Coldfield". Another welfare fund was created in 1941 "in connection with Sutton Coldfield Battalion of the Home Guard as a result of two concerts, which, with many generous donations, realised £213 15s."[xii]

Dances for the local population to join also were established, with Lieutenant Hickman, of 69 Antrobus Road, being tasked to organise a band for the dance on 6th February 1942.[xiii] Such dances and events were remembered fondly by the local population and were making the Home Guard a staple part of wartime life in Sutton Coldfield.

Relations with the United States of America had improved over the winter, with Churchill writing to Roosevelt to ask for help in December 1940, leading to the proclamation that the United States of America would become the 'Arsenal of Democracy'. Some prior agreements had taken place, such as the 'Destroyers for Bases' agreement in September 1940 which saw the transfer of 50 old US destroyers in return for leases to British Naval Bases across the Atlantic. On March 11th 1941 the Lend Lease Act was signed into law and started the movement of large scale weapon exports to the United Kingdom. However, despite these good intentions, the majority of arms would not arrive until later in 1941, with the first lend lease period occurring from October 1940 to June 1942. The intentions of Germany at this point in the war were to continue to isolate Britain and prepare for the invasion of Russia after securing the Balkans. Fighting in Africa was largely between the forces of Italy and of the Commonwealth, with Rommel's Africa Corps only arriving in March of 1941 to shore up the Italian forces.

The next changes in the regional command structure came in early 1941 with the creation of South East Command. This command was designed to concentrate the forces to the southeast of London, the closest area to the Channel and most under threat. In the Midlands, Buckinghamshire was moved into South East Command, and a new Welsh Boarder Subarea was created in Shropshire, allowing a simpler command structure in this relative backwater area. Within the West Midlands, Warwickshire Subarea gained Dudley from Worcestershire as part of Birmingham garrison, allowing a more consolidated urban defence of the Midlands itself.

In Sutton Coldfield, winter training of civil precautions had improved the responses of the local systems to the air raids, and the Home Guard units, as well as now being better equipped, were more integrated into these organisations in a shift system. The training of civilians also continued through the winter, with public training sessions on first aid, bomb disposal, rescue training held across Sutton Coldfield at many locations by the Air Raid Precaution services. This included the showing of films at the Odeon Cinema. 6,600 volunteer fire guards were trained in Sutton Coldfield, 3,500 individually enrolled and 3000 received a course or training. In December 1940 it had been made law that every man working less than 60 hours, and women working less than 45 must do a 48 hour shift every month of fire watching, which explained this huge increases in courses attended.

Training for the impeding invasion was still the priority, but in the back of the volunteers' mind was the very real threat of an air raid and the death and destruction from above to their homes. On the evening of the 11th March 1941, the sky above the Midlands was lit up in the dusk by the search lights and flashes of anti-aircraft fire as 135 bombers of *Luftflotte III* flew in from the west, using the Irish Sea and Welsh hills to avoid the main anti-aircraft fire of the south and east. Newly trained air raid precautions staff move quickly to the standby positions, and Home Guard soldiers on duty to their standby locations. Dull thuds could be heard to the west as the first bombs landed in the industrial areas of Birmingham. The winter training was over and the Blitz had started again.

[i] Orders by Captain Bigwood MC Dated 30 January 1941 – Warwickshire Archive.
[ii] This quote is taken from Osbourne, K. (2000) *A History of Bishop Vesey's Grammar School - The Twentieth Century*
[iii] Orders by Captain Bigwood MC dated 30 January 1941 – Warwickshire Archive.
[iv] Home Guard Instruction No.38 1941 a copy of which can be found in the Warwickshire Archive.
[v] *Ibid.*
[vi] Home Guard Instruction, No. 51, Battlecraft and Battle Drill for the Home Guard, Part III, Patrolling. GHQ Home Forces, January 1943. A copy 1941 a copy of which can be found in the Warwickshire Archive.
[vii] Evening Despatch 16th February 1942.
[viii] One of my favourite books I found in lockdown, McKay, S. (2021) *Secret Britain*. Headline, is highly recommended for a general history of locations around the United Kingdom during the war.
[ix] Evening Despatch 17th August 1942.
[x] Evening Dispatch 7th December 1942.
[xi] Birmingham Mail 16th July 1943.
[xii] Evening Dispatch 18th June 1941.
[xiii] Birmingham Mail 21st January 1943.

Chapter 11
The Second Blitz

After a winter of training and reorganisation, the *Luftwaffe* launched strikes again on a massive scale in March 1941. The war was still going well for Germany with the Axis was still growing to now include Bulgaria, Hungary and Romania, with new conquests in Yugoslavia about to start. Unknown to the Allies, preparations were also taking place for the invasion of Russia on a massive scale, and this was where the majority of resources were being built up. The fighting in North Africa continued, and

British troops were being diverted there via the Cape to build up the forces to defend the Suez and eventually to go onto the offensive.

The *Luftwaffe* campaign to destroy the industrial and naval output of the United Kingdom had continued throughout the winter of 1940 to 41, but had been scaled down due to poor weather. A large scale campaign however, restarted in March 1941 with over 4000 sorties being flown by the *Luftwaffe*, with the aim of destroying the British industrial might and crushing the will of the civilian population. That said, despite the huge increase in bombing in the spring, a large proportion of the *Luftwaffe*'s forces were diverted to the Balkans, and this would only increase as the time for the Russian invasion came closer.

There were some further technical improvements to the *Luftwaffe*'s equipment with X and Y Garet beams[i] used over false targets, and radio silence now utilised until bombs were dropped. That said, the reduction in the number of heavy bombers available for the raids with the move to the Balkans meant that many shorter range, lower altitude bombers were also used against Britain which were more susceptible to night fighters and to anti-aircraft fire.

Since the raids in autumn 1940, the Royal Airforce had increased the scale of its night fighter protection across England. There were by mid February 1941, 13 squadrons of night fighters operating across the country, and new techniques and procedures, as well as advances in technology were having some impact. At first the Defiant and Blenheim were used in the night fighter role, however over the winter only a few very primitive airborne interception radars were available and search lights were the main method to intercept bombers, to limited success. However, in early 1941, the twin engine Bristol Beaufighter was used for the first time, equipped with the Airborne Interception Mark IV Radar, which allowed pilots to be guided to their prey within two miles of target. The new system worked very effectively with 22 German bombers shot down in March 1941, 48 in April and almost 100 in May. The exploits of the night fighters and using the veterans of the battle of Britain was utilised as a morale boost for the population:

> *"At least two night raiders were destroyed, one of them before it could leave its base. Details of the latter were given in an Air Ministry News Service account. An R.A.F. pilot who has already won the D.F.C. for his night exploits against enemy raiders flew to an aerodrome in France, stayed there for 25 minutes, then dropped bombs. One of these was seen to hit an aircraft on the edge of the aerodrome, it burst into flames, and ammunition and verey lights flew out, and the petrol tanks exploded. The other raider, a Heinkel, was shot down off the East coast of Scotland during the night. The machine sank, and three members of the crew, including one wounded, were rescued from a rubber dinghy"*[ii]

Anti-aircraft fire was still the major killer of German aircraft, however their impact was still marginal representing only 1.5 percent of the enemy sorties which flew over the United Kingdom. Only around 600 bombers were shot down from June 1940 to March 1941 and many of these crashed due to operational incidents. There was an improvement of the accuracy of anti-aircraft fire, with 20,000 shells needed to shoot down an enemy bomber in 1940 reduced to 4087 in January 1941 then 2963 in February. There was still a shortage of anti-aircraft guns, particularly heavy guns, with some units being moved around the United Kingdom to support where the perceived German effort would be.

On the evening of the 11th March 1941 at 21:40, the Mounted Patrol of D Company were riding across Sutton Park when a whole Staffel of He111 aircraft released their payloads on the park. Over 500 incendiary bombs landed on Westwood Coppice, setting it alight, but thankfully hurting no one. The Mounted Patrol reported the bombs, but took no action, letting it burn itself out. At the same time, volunteers on the boundary of B and D Company saw a second Staffel dropped 300 incendiaries across Walmley Golf course, some landing on the Birmingham Road. Those bombs on the road were quickly smothered in sand by the Air Raid Precautions staff and Home Guard, but the devices on the golf course could wait until the morning to be checked.

After this initial impressive but largely ineffective bombing run, the cloud started to settle in further, but the anti-aircraft fire continued unabated, making many of the German aircraft take evasive action. Lieutenant Percy Llewelyn Adams was on duty with his No.4 Platoon F Company at Atherstone, based at the police house. The platoon had not been hugely impacted by German bombs previously, with few landing to the east of the River Tame. His focus was on defence and training, although in the back of his mind he was aware that there were few Air Raid Precaution Service facilities in the area, and only a village doctor for support. At 21:55 a German 250 kilogram *Flammenbombe* landed on a house in Boulters Lane in the village, the device partially ignited on impact, but the speed it hit the house smashed the roof and one wall. Lieutenant Adams heard the impact from the police station and immediately moved his men down the road to assist. The found two injured people in the house, an elderly couple. The platoon moved them to the village doctor, and put a cordon around the house, where there was still the majority of the bomb unexploded. The *Flammenbombe* were ineffective, and later withdrawn by the *Luftwaffe* due to not often exploding.

The air ministry reported that the raiders lost four of every five incendiary devises as they were extinguished by the voluntary fire fighters without any assistance from the fire brigade. "The service, which has quadrupled in the past three or four weeks, did valiant service during the raid." And this is not all, the work of the fire watchers in the West Midland district concerned (the Nazis claimed it was Birmingham) was specially praised in the official Air Ministry account of the night's activity."

Across the town, a further seven high explosive bombs landed, causing the Air Raid Precautions staff to scramble and deal with the damage and risk from gas mains and electric pylons. Bombs landed on Boulters Lane, Hill Hook and Wood End as well as hitting Shustoke Hill Farm and Pype Hayes Golf Course. Fortunately, there were no further injuries and by midnight the all clear was sounded by a confident observer corps, who understood how important an early stand down was for the emergency services. Volunteer O'Griffith of D Company commented that he "Joined the wardens standing on the railway bridge: some eight or nine middle aged men in civilian overcoats, mufflers and black tin hats, all silhouetted against the moon lit sky. Now and then a bomb swished and whistled uncomfortably near; not one of them ducked."[iii]

The Birmingham Post reported on the raids stating that:

> *"The official Air Ministry report states: Enemy aircraft crossed the South Coast last night and penetrated in fair numbers to the Midlands and as far as the North-western Counties- Bombs were dropped at a number of points in these areas, but damage was not heavy. In one North-western district some buildings were set on fire, and a certain amount of other damage done. All the fires were extinguished or under control before daybreak. A few isolated incidents were reported from other parts of England and Wales Starting soon after dark early raiders scattered incendiary bombs over a wide area. High explosive bombs fell in the West Midland town, damaging house property, and there were some casualties, a few fatal. A warden's post was hit. and five people were injured. Another bomb severely damaged some houses and six people were killed."* [iv]

After this large raid, only a few nuisance raids occurred for the next month, however two major raids occurred on consecutive nights of the 8th to the 9th April, then the 9th to the 10th April. On the night of the 8th, 237 *Luftwaffe* bombers headed for Birmingham in what would be the most damaging raid of the war for the Midlands. Many bombers aiming for the Spitfire factory at Castle Bromwich missed and their bombs hit Sutton Coldfield, but Birmingham bore the brunt with 1121 casualties occurring in the city. The casualties in Goosemore Lane Erdington were very bad with the bombing on this night. 13 people of all ages were killed; a terrible loss for one street.

Surname	First Name(s)	Age	Killed At	Air-Raid Job
Bradnock	Elsie Heath	18	Number 35	None
Evans	William Everett	58	Number 44	Fire-watcher
Fidoe	Norman Edward	36	Number 46	None
Foster	George	62	Number 69	Fire-watcher
Gilmor	John	61	Stones Laundry	None
Goodwin	Alfred John	34	Number 66	None
Green	George	46	Number 78	Fire-watcher
Harris	Bert	25	Number 85	None
Harris	George James	62	Number 52	None
Morgan	Elsie	26	Number 29	None
Morgan	David John Edwin	18	Number 29	None
Stanley	Albert Edward	56	Number 98	None

Table 11: Casualties Goosemore Lane 9th / 10th April 1941

Volunteer George Alfred Webster was aged fifty and had served in the 3rd East Surry Regiment in the First World War. He was a gardener by trade, was married to Mary and had two teenage children Audrey and Robert. They lived at 106 Tower Road, Mere Green. At 00:57, 250 incendiary bombs hit Hill Green Farm on Coton Road and about 100 incendiary bombs hit Worcester Lane. George was on duty that night helping with the wardens and fire services, living just two roads down on Tower Road. He was killed that night helping evacuate houses.

During the second night of the raid, the bombs continued to hit Sutton Coldfield, testing the responses of civilian organisations across the town. At 01:15 on the 10th April, 11 high explosive bombs hit Jockey Road and Redacre Road, causing significant damage to the infrastructure, including water systems and gas mains. Bombs also landed on Wylde Green Road, Marston Lane, Coton Road, Tamworth Road, Lindridge Road and Fox Hollies Road. 12 high explosive bombs landed in open fields near Curdworth also.

The pattern of heavy raids continued throughout the spring of 1941. The gaps in between raids allowed the local authorities to plan and improve their systems and approaches. A significant change came on the 18th August 1941 when the local fire brigades formed into a national structure to respond to raids across the country. This allowed the movement of fire units to those cities that needed the most support. The new No.24 Fire Force covered Birmingham and the Black Country, allowing a better coordinated response across the region.

Throughout this period, the training of units continued and preparations for a 1941 were considered a priority by Home Guard Units. The Commander of Wilnecote Detachment, Major Mitcheson descried the quality of his troops in an inspection conducted in May 1941.

- 1 Platoon. Wilnecote. Sentries conducted themselves very ably and showed excellent knowledge of their duties. No railway guard at station. Barracks room for guard needed a tidy and blankets to be changed.
- 2 Platoon, Dosthill. Inspected mounted of guard, six volunteers and Sergeant, conduct very good. Men gave good knowledge of duties but no password given. Bedding and equipment in good condition.

- Kingsbury Platoon. Four men and one corporal on duty. Sergeant Smith did guard mount. Soldiers had good knowledge of duties. Best headquarters in the company without doubt. Good visibility by leaders.
- Woodend Platoon. Three men and Sergeant Buklin on duty, slackness on post of one sentry, cigarette glow could be seen.
- 4 Platoon Piccadilly Section inspected. Bedding and equipment in excellent condition. Sentries alert and challenging excellent.

The quality of the Home Guard soldiers in their duties had not slackened and there was a perception of a real threat of invasion. The German army was still winning victories and were poised to invade Russia, there was no reason to see the chances of invasion being reduced from a British perspective. The scale of exercises and their reality was also improving. Volunteer Griffith was now working in D Company Headquarters and described the training taking place now on the 16th March 1941.[v]

> *"At 9am a Home Guard runner called with the order to report at once to company headquarters. I got into my uniform and down to headquarters in time to be detailed for office work for a large scale try out. The company commander and his staff were there, and runners came in with dispatches – casualties here, prisoners there and reinforcements urgently wanted yonder. It gave me a hint of what staff work was like, even though this was a minor and local affair. There were errors too. Battalion headquarters orders us to send up reinforcements that were far beyond the limit of our reserves"*

Routine patrols were continuing too with the sub-units increasing in scale as more volunteers were completing their training. No.5 (Hurley) Platoon F Company, was now 7 NCOs and 107 Volunteers strong, against an equipment establishment of 40 men. The platoon was under the command of Lieutenant Hubert Joseph William Fisher, and had a second-in-command Lieutenant Harry William Payne. These officers were supported at section level by three experienced veterans as sergeants, Sergeant Pridmore, Beacon and Rickard. The isolated platoon in the village of Hurley was now established with a signals section to allow efficient communications to both the civil authorities and also to company headquarters at Glascote Police Station. The platoon also had an ambulance section, reflecting the isolated nature of the village command to the east of the river Tame.

The patrol routine for Hurley Platoon was constant, but only utilised a small number of available troops, allowing attendance on patrol once per week, but also to training once per week. Each night, a seven men patrol would leave early evening and return at 04:30, this would be commanded by a section commander, and would be supported by either an officer or platoon sergeant in the headquarters. A second section would be on standby, sleeping after their evening training. The patrols would take place over Peacadhill twice per week, Woods End twice per week and Hurley itself twice per week, (these were the three section locations of the platoon). However already the number at training were not as full as during the winter, with attendance at Peacadhill Section being descried as poor, Wood End Section as moderate and Hurley itself as fairly good. This would be a pattern which would only get worse as the threat would diminish later in the war.

Across the Wilnecote Detachment, the activity continued at a high tempo. In a sense this was unsustainable for a volunteer force, who were, as time went by, encouraged to focus on war production over defence. These conflicting demands started to have some impact on attendance. However, the increase in equipment, facilities and opportunities, and the fact that companies were hugely over-manned, allowed the companies to continue to be effective both in the civil defence role, and for their core role of home defence. The diary of Major Mitcheson shows one week of training in May 1941 for this company, with a clear focus on leadership, marksmanship and core skills of the infantry soldier:

>Sunday 25 May 1941 - Wilnecote 1030 Parade
>Monday 26th May 1941 – JNCO Passing Out 1900
>Tuesday 27th May 1941 – Away Training NCOs
>Wednesday 28th May 1941 – 1830 AA Rifle Fire Training
>Thursday 29th May 1941 – Kingsbury NCO Training
>Friday 30th May 1941 – Shuttington 1900 Passing Out Parade
>Saturday 31st May 1941 – Wilnecote NCO Training

On the 17th May a major raid took place against the Wolseley Motor Factory, with bombs landing on Jockey Road and Lindridge Road. The bombs on Jockey Road caused considerable damage, smashing a 12 inch water main and blocking the road for a week whilst repairs were made. However, mainly the raiders were not hitting the north of Birmingham routinely at this time, with little activity reported.

On the 5th June a major raid took raid which led to the worst fears of the local civilian defences coming true. At 01:50am on the 6th June a high explosive bomb directly hit a house in the Tamworth Road in Kingsbury. Kingsbury had largely avoided the Blitz to this point, but the devastation of this bomb was immense, destroying the house and burying the occupants. With limited air raid precautions staff in the village, it was down to the men of 3 Platoon and Company Headquarters of E Company to react the incident. Lieutenant James Henry Fullord was the Company Intelligence Officer and lived on the Tamworth Road; he quickly ran to the incident and tried to help. Captain Alfred James Basford was the commander of 3 Platoon. He ran from his home on Whitehouse Farm and joined the platoon who had responded under Sergeant Frank Smith who commanded the E Company Ambulance Section. The soldiers tried their hardest to dig through the rubble, but the toll was high. Four members of the family had been killed and six injured. Children were amongst them. Such a terrible sight was etched on the memory of those who responded that night, and a deep hatred for the enemy that caused such evil to occur.

The bombs continued to fall across Sutton Coldfield and the surrounding area that night, with two houses on Redacre Road being shattered by bombs and another landing on Jockey Road damaging a gas main. A high explosive landed on Bodymoor Lane, Minworth at 02:15 and two incendiaries severely damaged a house on Chester Road. Fortunately, as people had gone to the shelters because of the scale of the raid, no further casualties were reported despite the huge devastation. On the morning of the 6th June, Volunteer Griffith from D Company noted that he "turned into Redacre Road today and was surprised to see two houses shattered by bombs. Then on to Jockey Road where [he] knew there had been devastation. The surrounding houses were almost unscathed and in one of them a very large and handsome doll had been put in the window with its head turned archly to look at the damage. And now the sirens once again."

After this raid there were some complaints that in public shelters many of the men inside could have been put to better use, and could have been "compelled to participate fire watching in danger areas." However, in Erdington a voluntary post has been established and manned by rota served by proprietors, managers, clerks and assistants, many of whom are already serving with the police, Home Guard, and Air Raid Precaution Services. The duties are being carried out from dusk until dawn, with men from Sutton Coldfield, Streetly, Castle Bromwich, Solihull, Hall Green, as well as Erdington.[vi] A resident in one of the badly bombed areas, wrote some words of praise for the Home Guard in the Birmingham Mail. She wrote that:

> *"We all know that the Home Guard are officially a body of men who are to guard our land against parachute troops, but would like to give few instances of their courage, resource fulness and spirit in other spheres. They go on patrols through the blitz, guard delayed action bombs put out incendiaries and fires, hell in rescue work, and if need be the do first-aid. Apart from these things there a case of two elderly ladies who were sitting in their front room, very frightened and shaking when there came a knock at the front door, and some members of the Home Guard entered. They knew these ladies were the only residents for a good distance around that they were still living in, and they had come to see that they all right before carrying on with their patrol. Then there was the time*

when a raid was on, bombs had been falling, and we were enjoying a brief respite, when through the suddenly still air rose half dozen voices sing Land of Hope and Glory. Hearing that I can assure you our spirits rose enormously. These men asking no reward, seeking no praise wanting only to do their duty, are to us in these times invaluable."[vii]

Clearly the Birmingham Mail did its best to praise soldiers and raise public moral, however the sentiment and love for these volunteers in 1941 was very much true.

After this last and most deadly raid on the 6th June, the majority of *Luftwaffe* forces started moving to the eastern front to fight the Russian Army. For the remainder of 1941 the town was spared, and as the year went by, the threat of invasion became less likely, with the Germans focused on their new enemy. As the threat from the *Luftwaffe* diminished, the need for soldiers for the fighting in Africa increased. In addition, there were stirrings in the Far East, and the Indian Army needed reinforcement too. This manpower crisis led to the formation of 'mixed batteries' in the summer of 1941 for anti-aircraft units. These batteries would be manned jointly between the Home Guard and the Royal Artillery, allowing the territorial forces to be posted overseas. A key staple of these defences would be the simple Z Battery concept, which used Unrotated Projectiles (Uncle Percy) Rockets which were a 3" simple and cheap missile. The batteries were constructed of 4 troops, each with 16 rockets and Home Guard volunteers, many who were present above establishment in their companies were moved across to these new units. One such battery was formed in Sutton Park this was 199 (M) Z anti-aircraft Battery under the

Command of Major R Cooper. The battery was headquartered at Greyfriars, Tudor Hill, Sutton Coldfield and formed part of 10th Warwickshire (Mixed) Anti-Aircraft Regiment, transferring to 18th Anti-Aircraft Regiment in 1942.

In addition to the Z Batteries, the Territorial units which manned air defences were reinforced by Home Guard on a voluntary basis. The 105 Warwickshire Home Guard Rocket AA Battery was based at the Walmley First School, on Walmley Ash Road. They never fired a shot in anger above Birmingham at this point in the war because of the reduced number of air raids, but did so when sent to Liverpool, London and Cardiff. This mobilisation of voluntary Home Guard units led to a more flexible organisation and produced Home Guard units who were effectively full time. However, in most anti-aircraft units, the soldiers worked seven days a week for the war effort and manned the guns once a week on rota. Anti-aircraft duty started at 19:45 and finished at 06:00, just before work the next day.[viii] The Commanding Officer of 105 Warwickshire Battery was Major AE Palfreman.

For the 6th battalion, training continued throughout the spring and summer of 1941. The threat had reduced, but Germany could change its focus, and the rapid success in Russia meant that quite quickly they could have changed focus and again threatened Britain, who was still fighting alone in the west. The first major battalion level training took place on the 7th July 1941[ix] in Sutton park, with well equipped Home Guard soldiers, including with Lewis Guns and mounted troops. This battalion training event was very public, with wide spread press coverage and utilised all the equipment in the battalion to give the impression of a fully fighting force. The addition of Lewis Guns to the battalion were likely the only ones present at this time in the Zone and utilised in this way to ensure that the wider impression of Home Guard strength was given to both the public and the enemy. That said, the companies at this point did have considerable equipment and were to scale of a normal infantry battalion, but the reality was that the 6th Battalion was six times the strength of a normal battalion, so many soldiers did not have their own issue of weapons and equipment. The report for No.1 Platoon, E Company stated that in their 70 man platoon of five sections, they had 58 American Rifles, one Lewis Anti-Aircraft Gun, one pistol, four Grenades and ten rounds per man. In addition, the entire platoon had uniform and they had some surplus.

The battalion defended the park from a simulated enemy parachute drop. Three hours of intensive training for the men from the 6th battalion included dive bombing, tanks and road blocks. "If all battalions are as keen and exercised as this one, few fears may be entertained to how the home defenders will react to any real test"[x] The zone commander Colonel Cash was present to see the troops train. Many spectators watched including the Mayor of Sutton Coldfield. Comments were made on the successful use of dummy positions and camouflage, as well as the use of anti-tank mines. B Company under Major Gay assaulted the two tanks during the exercise. C Company under Captain Witt then launched a counter attack using home made smoke grenades, finishing off with a bayonet charge.

The Birmingham Mail reported on the exercise:

> *" For three hours the local battalion of the Home Guard, the Sixth Warwick (Sutton Battn.), engaged in continuous full-scale*

exercises—a tribute to the fitness of the men. Most of them, like so many others in this spare-time army, are middle-aged men, many with greying hair. A year ago they were stiff of limb for want of exercise. War Pensions Some were developing a comfortable corpulence. Certainly they were as short in wind as in memory long. Among woodlands and open spaces of a Midland beauty spot, Sutton Park, there was some big game hunting yesterday. But the big game were mechanical monsters, marauding men, and that highly dangerous animal, the paratroop. Yesterday they seemed fit as fiddles, and certainly in tune when it came to concerted action. I saw one man, in an exercise in which they had to deal with enemy paratroops, run 50 yards at top speed with equipment, the sweat streaming down his face so that it blinded him. But he carried on towards his objective. He was 50 at least. On Saturday, for all I know, he was sitting in an office, or maybe, sleeves rolled up, in his garden tending the roses. Yesterday he was a soldier, putting ail the energy he had, and more perhaps than he thought he had, into the job of attacking the enemy that had dropped from the skies. That man, a home-loving, hard-working men in soldiers' clothes for the day, was the symbol of these and all the other exercises that' went on in the byways and highways of England yesterday. They showed cunning and skill that won the praise of those who know."

D Company under Major McCrae had a tank hunting section under Lieutenant Miesmann. They sneaked forward and took out the sentries "before the enemy had time to say Heil Hitler… Captain Holland with A

Company pinned the enemy to give the cu de grace." The Birmingham Mail continued that

> "*their own commander, Colonel Wilfrid Bigwood, a former Mayor of Sutton, praised their performance as excellent." Their Zone Commander, Colonel Cash, specially commended the way they dealt with two enemy tanks. That was in the first exercise of the day. A plane had come over from the direction of Derby before an attack on a munition factory. It dive-bombed the road block and went back for tanks. The first enemy tank came up, but the defenders had prepared a surprise for it. The second tank arrived and being alone was also quickly despatched cunningly camouflaged troops. Equally skilful was the following exercise, in which a tank which put into a copes as a refuge for the night was captured. The enemy scout, who had come on ahead to find a suitable hiding place, was spotted. Information was sent to headquarters in the park and the tank was captured by men who-creeping through the grass in the dusk, disposed of the sentries and took the sleeping crew by surprise. The way the sentries were tackled was a typical piece of Home Guard tactics. They pounced on each man and brought him to earth by dislocating his neck with the strap of his helmet and finishing him off with a bayonet.*"[xi]

The battalion then formed a hollow square and gave three cheers to Colonel Cash. A recent change was that zones and battalions were now allowed Colonels, so Major Bigwood was made Lieutenant Colonel. The event served as propaganda, but also morale boosting purposes for the wider Midlands. It really was the pinacol of training for the first stage of the Home Guard. In less than a year, a volunteer force, the greatest in size and scale in history, had built up and whilst helping the civilian population from a new type of warfare from the air, built a capability which could match, in terms of training and equipment, that of a regular fighting force. All whilst doing their critical day jobs to keep Britain going alone against a real threat of enemy invasion. The Home Guard has a chequered image in popular media, but this achievement simply cannot be understated.

This letter from Colonel Cash summed up his views of the 6th Battalion.

> *"To Editor of The Birmingham Post Sir. I want to thank the citizens of Birmingham, especially those in the Home Guard and Civil Defence Services who took part in the combined military and civil exercise this weekend, for their splendid co-operation. The Wardens Service and the Home Guard turned out in great strength, and although the inability of the enemy to penetrate deeply resulted in large number of volunteers remaining inactive, nevertheless the efficiency of the city's defence forces under special conditions was fully demonstrated. I have received from the military commander for the area most appreciative references to the work of the citizens generally and with particular reference to the Home Guard. He asks me to convey his grateful thanks to the thousands who participated. The exercise has provided most valuable material both to the Military and Civil Services."*[xii]

[i] The idea of "beam" based navigation was developed during the 1930s, initially as a blind landing. The basic concept is to produce two directional radio signals that are aimed slightly to the left and right of a runway's midline. Radio operators in the aircraft listen for these signals and determine which of the two beams they are flying in. This is normally accomplished by sending More Code into the two beams, to identify right and left. For bombing, the *Luftwaffe* built huge versions of the antennas to provide much greater accuracy at long range,
named *Knickebein* and *X-Gerät*. These were used during the early stages of the Blitz with great effect.
[ii] Birmingham Mail 23rd January 1941.
[iii] War Time Sutton: Extracts from the diaries of Gwilym O Griffith 1940-41. Sutton Historical Society
[iv] Birmingham Post 10th April 1941.
[v] War Time Sutton: Extracts from the diaries of Gwilym O Griffith 1940-40. Sutton Historical Society
[vi] Birmingham Mail 23rd January 1941.
[vii] Birmingham Mail 21st December 1940.
[viii] Sutton News 10th October 1986.
[ix] Birmingham Gazette 7th July 1940.
[x] Birmingham Post 7th July 1941.
[xi] Birmingham Post 15th July 1941.
[xii] *Ibid.*

Chapter 12

The Americans Arrive

On 21st December 1941 the Japanese attacked Pearl Harbour and the United States of Amercia entered the war on the side of the Allies. Britain was no longer alone, and the might of the largest economy in world meant that victory was now a real possibility. However, the change was not immediate and 1942 was a series of losses on an incredible scale. On the 9th January the Philippines were invaded and the islands were captured by the 9th April. Singapore, the impregnable fortress, fell on the 15th February, followed by the Dutch East Indies on the 8th March. Despite the failure of the Germany Army to take Moscow, a renewed offensive saw the German forces in Russia pushing into the Caucasus and approaching the gates of Stalingrad. In north Africa, Tobruk fell on the 21st June and the Germans again entered Egypt, at the gates of the Suez. By the summer of 1942 the Allies were in retreat on all fronts, and huge numbers of American ships were sunk in a second Happy Time for German U-Boats.

On the Home Front, the limited air raids over the winter of 1941 and the diminished threat of invasion had allowed the reallocation of resources to beef up the anti-aircraft units and civil defence. The chances of an invasion were now very low, but they remained a possibility if the Russians were defeated. More importantly, manpower for the fighting armies overseas was now critical, especially after the loss of 80,000 men at Singapore. All measures would now be taken to release fit young men for front line duty, and the Home Guard took on additional responsibilities to allow this to occur.

By 1942 the defensive locations of the Warwickshire Subarea were in a more formalised state. The Zones A to F had consolidated defence plans, both for invasion, but also for assaults by enemy paratroopers and such. It must be remembered that this was before Stalingrad and El Alamain, the Germans were still expanding, despite their difficult winter of 1941, and Japan had now entered the war and again was about to overrun the British Empire in Singapore and Burma. Despite the invasion likelihood being reduced, it was still very possible that Russia would be defeated, and that it could occur in 1942 or even 1943. These orders were first written in

January 1942, but were refined as the strength of the Home Guard grew in terms of manpower and equipment.

The orders for the defence scheme in 6th Battalion were updated again in 1942, giving a clear plan of operations. At this point command was very clear through the General Headquarters Home Forces, Western Command, Central Midlands District, Warwickshire Subarea, then E Sector to the 6th Battalion. A number of companies had changed hands with E Company under Captain Young, F Company under Captain Jackson and G Company under Captain Griffiths. The battalion staff had also stabilised at this point, with clear liaison roles for Lieutenant Freeman and Lieutenant Sampson, intelligence under Lieutenant Turner and signals under Lieutenant Sharpe. Logistics and transport were again distributed under a number of lieutenants, with Lieutenant Rymond in charge of catering, Lieutenant Collins ammunition and Second Lieutenant Thursfield motor transport. The battalion headquarters would be divided in two now with the now Lieutenant Colonel Bigwood commanding with his adjutant located in Sutton Coldfield, and an alternate command under Major Dingley, the second-in-command, with his own adjutant Captain Ross, located in Coleshill. This was also useful as this was the location of the sector battle headquarters and would give good coordination at what was expected to be the main defensive position along the River Tame.

Within Zone E, a boundary between the 6th (Sutton) Battalion and the 2nd (Nuneaton) Battalion was placed to the east of the River Tame. The defence of this river would prevent any flank attack into Birmingham from the northeast and considering intelligence reports suggested East Anglia as a likely invasion point, this was a sensible defence location. A formal military 'Stop Line', part of the General Headquarters Line was formed from Coventry and stretched the Peak District in Derbyshire, using the terrain to defend. This south edge of the stop line was defended by the strong points on the river manned by Home Guard units of the 6th Battalion. Stretching north to south, garrisons were placed at Wilnecote (300 men), Kingsbury (300 men), made of up of soldiers from Wilnecote Detachment as well as Whitacre (136 men) and Fillongley (75 men) made up of soldiers from Coleshill Company. In depth to these positions, strong points were formed to the north and east of Sutton Coldfield, at 'Whatford Gap' (110 men), Ashfurlong (110 men) and Minworth (110 men).

These company positions were supported by a battalion reserve held in Sutton Coldfield itself of 400 men. In addition, a detachment of 58 men was deployed to Elmdon (Birmingham Airport today) in case of parachute attack, and a further detachment of 86 men were allocated to Castle Bromwich to defend the spitfire factory. These two latter locations were in F Zone (Birmingham Garrison) but were seen as critical to the defence. In case of an assault from the northeast, 'H Zone' was formed in Aldridge, with elements of the South Staffs Home Guard coming under the command of Warwickshire Subarea for defence. Logistics were in a much better place but were still reliant on relinquished transport at this point. Eleven cars and six motorcycles had been allocated as relinquished vehicles for emergency use. These vehicles were allocated to the key battalion staff to enable movement across the area of operations.

Guidance was given on the strength of defensive position with Warwickshire Subarea issuing guidance around the suitability of pill boxes considering the advances in modern weapons. Earthworks are more successful in terms of defence. These would be improved within anti-tank island defensive through Home Guard pioneer platoons.[i] Company stores were quite comprehensive by 1942, with a considerable number of engineering tools, such as detonators, axes, crowbars, saws, sledge hammers, plier and wire cutters issued to companies for their defensive locations.

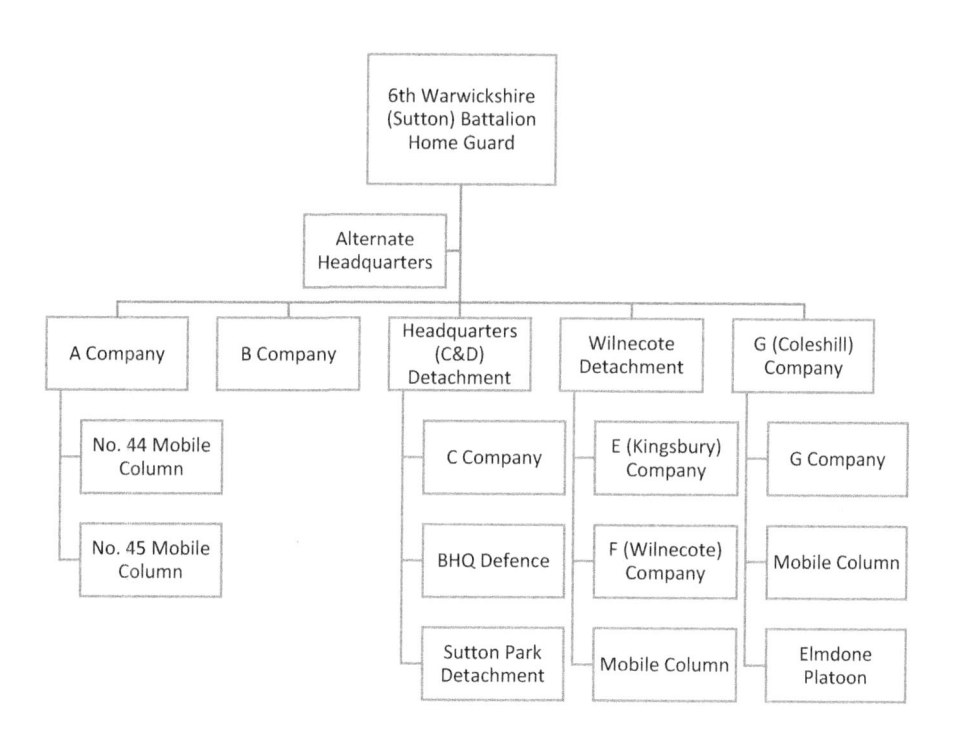

```
                    ┌─────────────────┐
                    │ 6th Warwickshire│
                    │ (Sutton) Battalion│
                    │   Home Guard    │
                    └────────┬────────┘
                             │
                    ┌────────┴────────┐
                    │    Alternate    │
                    │  Headquarters   │
                    └─────────────────┘
```

A Company	B Company	Headquarters (C&D) Detachment	Wilnecote Detachment	G (Coleshill) Company
No. 44 Mobile Column		C Company	E (Kingsbury) Company	G Company
No. 45 Mobile Column		BHQ Defence	F (Wilnecote) Company	Mobile Column
		Sutton Park Detachment	Mobile Column	Elmdone Platoon

Table 12: 6th Battalion Structure 1942

The breakdown of strong points and the mobile reserve was detailed outside of the normal administrative structure. A Company Group commanded by Major Hollands now consisted of three key elements. The company headquarters had its own logistical support and catering, with one officer and 24 other ranks. Then two mobile columns would provide a mobile reserve across the area of operations. No.44 Mobile Column under Lieutenant Dunnett would have a small mobile Headquarters and three platoons, then No.45 Mobile Column would have the same structure under Lieutenant Pulsford. These two columns were ordered to operate inside or outside of the battalion area of operations. As a force they were well supported logistically, with four medical non-commissioned officers and 12 stretcher bearers, as well as motorcycles for reconnaissance and their own signallers. However, the reality of the vehicles was slightly less impressive; A Company had allocated six Midland Red buses, four lorries, six cars and 12 motor bikes for its mobile force. Additional vehicles were requested through the civilian population also, with advertisements in the Birmingham Mail for a 12 to 24 horsepower car or chassis for converting into armoured car. "Many citizens in Birmingham appreciate the efforts of the Home Guard now is your chance to do your bit and help us".[ii] Of note, each man was to be issues with £1 for incidental expenses.

B Company was earmarked for a static defence task under Major Gay. The company would be split into two subunits of around 110 men, one at a strongpoint at 'Watford Gap' and the other at 'Ashfurlong'. These strong points would consist of static guards, reserves, forward reconnaissance and fighting patrols. These strong points were located to the north of Sutton Coldfield, in Four Oaks, and were based around Mayfield House on the Lichfield Road and company Headquarters at the Whitehouse, Whitehouse Common. The method of getting the company to these locations would be the same red buses as A Company would use as the reserve, which could have presented problems as the reserve would not be able to deploy until B Company was in place. The logistical support would be through the civil defence logistical system and Hardings Wearhouse in Mere Green would provide food for the company. Of note, the company had Spigot Mortars, flame throwers and anti-tank mines at this point to be used in defence, a considerable improvement on their arms from 1940. Again, they had a comprehensive medical detachment under Dr Tait, with its own allocated car, stretcher bearers and equipped first aid post. In addition, the company had signallers and despatch riders.

In defence of Sutton Coldfield itself was a composite detachment of 633 soldiers. This headquarters detachment would be under the command of Major Witt (normally Officer Commanding C Company) and would consist of the combined C and D Company manpower. The company headquarters would be at the Priory, and an under the administrative supervision of Major McCrae at 9 Station Street. This considerable force would provide firstly a sub detachment at Sutton Park under Captain Slater, which would consist of three fighting patrols, each 80 men strong, one at Powell's Pool, one at Blackroot Pool and the final at Rowton Cottage. Powell's Pool itself was being rapidly turned into a civil defence camp for the volunteer fire units, Air Raid Precaution Service and other units. This sub-detachment would be supported by a 25 man (and women) mounted patrol to provide reconnaissance support. A fighting reserve would remain in the town centre at Linda Vista of two platoons, in addition a guard force for the battalion headquarters would consist of two sections, as well as specialist personnel such as signallers, intelligence, guides and police for the battalion. Again, the detachment would be supported through requisitioned vehicles, including five cars, six motor bikes and a lorry. Civilian support was provided for feeding, with Wrights Stores, Hughes Jockey Stores and George Mason Limited all providing food for the troops.

Wilnecote Detachment would still consist of E and F Companies, and these would be across two centres of resistance. The first under Captain Gordon Young, would be made up of E Company, 270 men, and be based around Kingsbury Hill. The second, F Company, was under Major Mitcheson himself, and consisted of 420 men based around Doulton's works. In addition, a mobile column of 120 men, made up of a headquarters and three platoons would be under Lieutenant Newbury in reserve. This mobile column would be based at battalion headquarters when established, as part of the reserve and had allocated three Midland Red buses and three lorries. Unlike the other companies, Wilnecote Detachment was spread across 12 villages, with individual strong points. This task would be very difficult to command and control, therefore each strong point had an allocated civilian supplier for food and soldiers were issued £1 to pay for food if needed. The dispersed nature of this defence would always be difficult, but with preprepared positions, it would be a considerably difficult objective for any enemy to clear, and block all movement across the River Tame.

G Company at Colehill was again given a fixed point defence location at the Whitacre Works, but also at Fillongley to defend, each with 100 men. In addition, a mobile company of 120 men, with headquarters and three platoons was again allocated to the battalion reserve. Finally, a platoon of 50 soldiers was allocated to Elmdon Airport for its defence. Like other companies, G Company had three Midland Red buses in support, other vehicles, and local suppliers for food, as well as a comprehensive medical plan.

The logistical support of the plan was very comprehensive, with allocated petrol points for vehicles and a plan to destroy these under codework 'Bardia'. Such steps as a Chemical Warfare Officer (Lieutenant Fisher) were in place, but now seemed less likely as the war continued. Civilian liaison to the Air Raid Precaution Report Centre at the Council House in Sutton Coldfield was the responsibility of Lieutenant Freeman. Military Liaison was under Captain Sampson, his role as well as liaison with sector and other units, was to vouch for leaders of military reinforcing units: a considerable task if needed.

Direction on training now gave more of a focus upon time spent in civilian employment, to prevent disruption to the war industries. Home Guard Regulations 1942 made it clear that training and duty should not exceed 48 hours in a four week period.[iii] There were also changes to some of the duties which the Home Guard took on, such as some ceremonial duties and additional movement into anti-aircraft units. By the end of 1942, half of the anti-aircraft units in the United Kingdom were run by the Home Guard, with 150,000 men on these duties across 28 anti-aircraft regiments and 200 independent light anti-aircraft platoons. In addition, by 1944 there would be 90 'Z' rocket batteries manned by the Home Guard.

Battalion events continued, often with a local political angle, and especially within Sutton Coldfield itself. The Birmingham Mail reported in December 1942 that "The Sutton Coldfield Battalion of the Warwickshire Home Guard paraded for inspection yesterday. Captain Wilfrid Bigwood, the Commanding Officer, who raised the Battalion, inspected the men from the four companies of the borough. Captain P. N. Dingley, second-in-command, was in charge of the parade and led the Battalion in the march past."[iv]

It seems at this time a rationalisation took place with both inflow and outflow. Despite the manpower issues, the decision was made to discharge all those over the age of 65 at zone and battalion level, seeing therefore a reduction in numbers across the battalion. However, at the same time conscription was expanded to allow direct conscription into the Home Guard itself. This was not universally popular, as it was not considered to be aligned to the volunteer ethos of the organisation. However, with additional anti-aircraft duties and the requirement to maintain a credible defence, these measures were deemed appropriate.

After over a year with no considerable air-raids, a second Blitz occurred in July 1942 over the Midlands. The *Luftwaffe* was focused on the Soviet Union, but these raids were a reaction to Royal Airforce raids in Germany of increasing intensity. The first major raid took place on the 28th July; it was made by 40 bombers which approached from the east across the Welsh mountains.[v] 468 pumps from the National Fire Service were deployed across the city, dealing with over 1000 homes damaged across Birmingham. Seven factories destroyed and 65 damaged. Un-exploded bombs also caused disruption. Two German bombers were shot down by night fighters.

That night a strong Air Raid Precautions team were on duty once the Air Raid Red was abounded at 01:35. This included a total of three ambulances, five first aid posts, one rescue party and one mobile unit. The Home Guard on standby that night could hear the raiders over

Birmingham. The night passed without much incident, but Lieutenant Freeman based with the civil defence command in Sutton Police Station, awaited any incident. A report came in at 02:07 from D Company, numbers 24 and 28 Stonehouse Road had received direct hits from a stick of high explosive bombs. 13 Platoon D Company had responded under their Platoon Sergeant Charles Kibby. The devastation was vast, but the Home Guard supported the Air Raid Precaution staff and volunteer ambulance crews digging through the rubble. The volunteer fire fighters doused the rubble to ensure no fires started or gas explosions were caused. Five people were pulled from the rubble, three of which were driven to the Cottage hospital. Three other houses received damage, including number 34, home of Volunteer Percy George Middleton from No.13 Platoon, but thankfully those residents were safe.

One of those recovered was William Frederick Holcroft, aged 62 and living at number 24 Stonehouse Road. Although he survived that night, he died of his wounds on the 9th August. A local Annie Hooper remembered that night:

> "We lived nearly opposite the Park Hotel - I was told a bomb landed in Stonehouse Road - I was asleep in my carrycot in front of the windows of the flat and every window went up and crashed down without any injury to me. Mum was an ambulance driver and dad in an essential job, fire watcher (too old as was in WW1). Ma was watching a plane caught in the searchlights in Sutton Park - she was in the middle of Boldmere Road jumping up and down when a voice came from the shadows "get under cover you bloody

little fool"[vi] *- the air raid warden was on the pavement watching her!"*

A further German bombing raid took place on a large scale two nights later on the 30th July. This would be a huge test of the town as over the course of the night, the raid killed one resident and injured 11. The bombs started landing just after 02:00, with an incendiary bomb landing behind Boldmere shops at 02:15, injuring two residents who were taken by volunteer ambulance crews to the Cottage Hospital. The fire gutted one shop but was prevented spreading by the volunteer fire fighters. Further incendiaries landed at 35 Ivy Road 15 minutes later injuring one resident, John Cooper, who had not taken shelter, again they were evacuated to the Cottage Hospital. A nigh explosive hit 802 College Road, and John Pearson was rushed to hospital with minor wounds.

Boldmere would bear the brunt of the bombing that night, with high explosives landing on the high street, on the corner of Boldmere and Sheffield Road, on Oakwood Road, as well as direct hits on the houses of 29 Cofield Road, 2 Heathlands Road, 19 Ivy Road and 28 Antrobus Road. With the latter the house burst into flames, and the wardens broke in to extinguish it, as the gas pipes were damaged and threatening to cause an explosion. Chris Gracey remembered that "one of the incendiaries went through the roof of our former home, 189 Boldmere Road, leaving scorch marks and a breakage in the floorboards. We realised what had caused the damage a few years ago when I read articles of Boldmere in the Blitz. There was a fire warden's hut in the garden of 191 and think that Mr. Charles Stephens (of Stephens building firm) was one of the wardens." [vii] A string of high explosive bombs hit Boldmere Road, with number 6 and number 10 badly damaged, and their occupants Mr Charles Brown and Mr Ernest Moore being hospitalised. Another high explosive bomb hit number 24, and Mr Arthur Briant was killed in the blast.

Six incendiaries landed on the golf course in Boldmere near Darnick Road, causing a large fire to break out. One of the fire watchers was Charles Edmund Brown, age 41, who stood by the shops dousing the incendiaries as they landed. He was badly injured by the blast and evacuated to the Cottage Hospital, sadly he died later. He was married to Caroline Elizabeth Brown. Another two houses on Antrobus Road were hit and set on fire. These houses and many surrounded were evacuated and the residents sent to Britwell Hall at 02:25. Here the redoubtable head teacher of Boldmere School mobilised an effort, supported by the Women's Royal Voluntary Service in her Group I feeding facilities. Mrs Stansfield organised hot food for all, and even decided to break out the emergency tea and biscuits. The loss of a life in this local community had a huge impact, and with so many houses destroyed the community came together in a way which people hoped they had left in the dark days of 1941.

Wylde Green was heavily hit with a large number of incendiary bombs at 02:30, these caused fires and some minor injuries to emergency responders. Number 3 The Boulevard took a direct hit at 02:35 and 12 incendiaries landed on Green Lanes and Emmanual Road soon after, and a further landed on 317 Chester Road causing a large fire and damaging the stairs inside the house. The bombs continued to fall across the wider Sutton Coldfield area, most landing in a small window between 02:00 and 02:30 am, causing the civil defence to rapidly multitask. Fortunately, the remainder of these bombs, despite there wide distribution and damage, caused no loss of life, but they all required response from Fire, Ambulance, Air Raid Precautions and Home Guard units. These blasts include a bomb crashing through the ceiling of 1 Warden Road, 3 Barker Road and 6 Mulroy Road. Incendiaries also landed on Westwood Coppice in Sutton Park, but these were left to burn out, with the Mobile Patrol and Lieutenant Mary Brancker deploying to check for injured animals in the early hours. A total of 27 unexploded bombs were found across the town after the raid.

The Birmingham Mail reported on the raid the next morning:

> **ANOTHER ATTACK ON MIDLANDS - HOSPITAL HIT**. *Nine enemy planes were destroyed during last night's raids. Eight were brought down in this country and one near its base in France. Soon after midnight enemy aircraft crossed the East and South coasts of England. They flew inland across East Anglia and the West Country, and the main objective of the attack appeared to be a West Midlands area. The raids, however, were generally on a much lighter scale than those of the previous night, and were again widely scattered. Of the casualties caused a small number were fatal. One West Midlands town experienced one of its sharpest raids of the war. High-explosive and incendiary bombs were dropped and several fires started, some in business premises. A number of people were admitted to hospital. in their previous visits the raiders were greeted heavy gunfire, in which the new batteries were again prominent. The effect kept them to channels in which had few opportunities of attacking targets of consequence, for they rarely showed a disposition to attempt to penetrate a barrage. Announcing the target of last night's raids,*

the German News said to-day that strong bomber formations again raided Birmingham. It added: "In good visibility the bombers broke through the defence system and dropped heavy and very heavy bombs, as well as incendiaries, on numerous war objectives, which had been already heavily hit in the earlier big attacks." The agency also claimed that later reconnaissance to-day showed a score of fires. Some of them extended over an area of nearly one mile from to south-east, covering the entire target area." Of the fires which broke out in the West Midland town only two were of serious proportions, and these were quickly dealt with. Many of the incendiary bombs 'dropped were the explosive type. Delayed action bombs were also dropped at various points. A bunch of incendiaries fell on a hospital, and everybody who could tackled them. Nurses, porters, and engineers worked untiringly, and even two Boy Scouts, who were acting as messengers, gave a hand. As the bombs fell on to the roof, an official told a reporter, fire watchers kicked them off on to the ground, where other people put them out. A few bombs fell into the kitchen of the out-patients' department and the engineers' shop, but all were quickly extinguished. An outbuilding used as a store was, however, badly damaged. Walking and sitting patients were removed to shelters. Fortunately, no bombs fell into wards occupied by patients.

It will come as great encouragement to people in the Birmingham district to know that many local Home Guards are now engaged on these apparently successful defences and are, as it was put to Mail reporter, "now able to have a pot at Jerry." The raids seemed to be almost a repeat performance of the attack on Monday night (writes an air correspondent). On that occasion between and 70 enemy aircraft scattered themselves over Britain. Last night their raiding was very similar, but small groups managed to concentrate over the Midlands. Others operated singly over other areas.

The 23rd April 1943 was the last raid on Birmingham but the raid on the 30th July 1942 was the last on Sutton Coldfield. Birmingham suffered on a greater magnitude to Sutton during the Blitz, but the impact on the Royal Town was at least 28 wounded and 8 killed, a terrible loss of life. The records are incomplete, but we know the names of five of these killed to be Ruby Maureen Bunford, Charles Edmund Brown, William Ralph Philip Hayward, Arthur Briant and William Frederick Holcroft.

Despite the busy period of 1942 with the renewed bombing and intense training, the 6th Battalion still found time to have fun. In particular, Colonel Bigwood was always ready for a society occasion and to boost his profile in the civil community. Colonel Bigwood present at opening of Borough Restaurant on south parade in 1942, along side the Mayor and local society. He joined his companies for dinner nights, encouraging officers and all ranks to dine together and build bonds. Colonel Bigwood was a guest at a dinner at the Swan Hotel, Coleshill on the 7th February 1942, of Major G. Walker and the officers of Coleshill Company.[viii] Colonel Bigwood's instincts for politics supported the battalion in many ways, from equipment to uniforms and to opportunities at training. He was very politically astute.

To support the battalion, a charitable fund was set up under the above-mentioned Act on 27th February 1942, for The Sutton Coldfield Battalion Home Guard Welfare Fund "the objects of which are shortly as follows; to provide comforts, amenities, etc., for the members of the Sutton Coldfield Battalion Home Guard, and the administrative centre of which is situated at 25, Highstreet, Sutton Coldfield." Captain Freeley was tasked to set this up for Colonel Bigwood.[ix]

The new secondary school on Upper Holland Road remained unfinished and empty at the beginning of World War II, earmarked for possible military use. America entered the war at the end of 1941, and the build-up of American forces in Britain began soon after. The troops wanted to send letters home, and the people at home wanted to send mail and parcels, so a US postal system was urgently needed. All the mail went through a 'first base sorting office', and Sutton Coldfield was selected as its location. Men moved into the new school buildings (now Plantsbrook School), and the post office took over Sutton Park Railway Station. By July 1st 1942, the sorting office had been set up by the thirty-two trained men, who were joined by more ex-postmen the next month. More and more American troops came across the Atlantic, and the scale of operations at the first base post office grew. More soldiers came to work there, but still more help was needed, and at the end of October, 51 local women had been recruited to work alongside the 140 Americans. In August 1943, rather than construct more camps (there were already American camps in Penns Lane and at Streetly Gate in Sutton Park), the hundreds of G.I.s based in Sutton were billeted on local people - everyone with a spare room had to give it up to a soldier if required.

The sorting office used existing railway property at first, while huge purpose-built premises were under construction. This utilitarian building of 52,000 square feet was ready by October 1942 German prisoners-of-war providing some of the labour force for its construction. Late in 1943, there were hundreds of soldiers and hundreds of civilian women working there, despatching two train-loads of mail every day, and even so falling behind with the work; at one time there was a backlog of over 100 trucks of mail in the sidings. The sorting office had been built to the specifications of the United States Army, with its own sidings and a loading dock which could accommodate fifteen trucks. At the end of the war it was taken over by the General Post Office and is still used for postal services today. It is one of the few American buildings of the Second World War still standing, and its local, national and international historical significance is now recognised, being grade II listed by English Heritage.[x]

Howard Butler was born in 1890 in Sutton Coldfield. During the First World War he missed out on joining the forces as he was sick. Howard was an egg merchant, who inspected the quality of eggs in a factory in Moor Street in Birmingham. He was one of three brothers who lived on Jockey Road, but once married, Howard moved to 32 Emmanuel Road. With the outbreak of the Second World War, Howard applied to join the Home Guard, and with no limits on medical standard he was signed up to 11 Platoon C Company, a member of H Section. Howard's platoon commander was Lieutenant Lewis and his section commander Corporal Lewis. The Platoon was based at the antiques shop on the Driffold, at the key junction leading into the town.

Howard's son Philip was born in 1940 and has some memories of the later days of the war. They had a United States soldier, Andy Hatzan who was lodged with them, and they kept in contact after the war. Most United States soldiers in the town were based at the United States Post Office (the site of the current Royal Mail building in Sutton). He remembers being put in the pram under the stairs when air raids occurred, with this being the safest place in the house. Philip also remembers being evacuated with his mother and brothers to Stratford upon Avon initially and later to Llandudno. They were based in a holiday camp at the end of the Severn Valley railway line. He has fond memories of being chased by a bull!

Philip's grandfather was a manager of M Myers Engineering in Birmingham. The Myers family were interned during the war, but his grandfather looked after the company which made bull dog clips, and after the war was awarded by being made a share holder of the company. Howard's mother did some nursing during the war when they were at home, and his father was busy being either at work or in the Home Guard, which he described as 'fun'. One of the abiding memories of the war was the visit of King George to Sutton in 1943.

The situation had fundamentally changed over the winter of 1942, with the German defeat at Stalingrad and the British victory at El-Alamain. In addition in the Pacific, although the Japanese offensive continued in Burma, the counter attacks by the British Chindits were starting, and the defeat of the Japanese at Midway had halted there expansion eastwards. They had failed to take Port Moresby and had not succeeded in taking Guadalcanal. The battle of the Atlantic had continued throughout 1942 with some difficult periods, (in the first six months of 1942, 21 U-boats were lost, less than one for every 40 merchant ships sunk). However, in August and September, 60 were sunk, one for every 10 merchant ships, almost as many as in the previous two years. The tide was starting to turn.

Fundamentally the Germany army, air force and navy at the start of 1943 no longer had the combat power capable to invade the British Isles. It was very unlikely that an invasion would occur, and the only real offensive would be a disruptive attack which was localised. That said, the Germans were still a mighty foe and were not yet defeated. There was also a fundamental shortage of infantry soldiers for the British Army, which was sustaining losses constantly across the world. The Home Guard was needed to allow the release of fit men to fight overseas, and to man those facilities in the United Kingdom which were critical to security.

[i] Warwickshire Subarea 12th March 1942, Warwickshire Archive.
[ii] Birmingham Mail advert 11th January 1941.
[iii] Home Guard Regulations 1942. A copy which can be found in the National Archives.
[iv] Birmingham Mail 16th December 1940.
[v] Richards, S (2019) *The Luftwaffe over Brum*.
[vi] Annie Hooper in comments to author during online research.
[vii] Chris Gracey in comments to author during online research.
[viii] Evening Despatch 7th February 1942.
[ix] Evening Despatch 2nd March 1942.
[x] Based on research by Martin Collins found in open source social media.

Chapter 13
Mobile Units and Maturity

1943 brought real changes to the war, but nothing was decided at the turn of the year. It was not until the 31st January 1943 that the 6th German Army surrendered at Stalingrad and the Germans were still deep into Russia. Although Operation Torch had occurred in North Africa, the battle of the Kasserine Pass on the 19th February 1943 led to the US army retreating in disarray and combined with the halting of Montgomery's 8th Army at Tripoli due to logistical issues, the campaign in North Africa was far from certain at this point. The battle of the Atlantic was still in full swing, but it would not be until 'Black May' in 1943 that the German U-Boats would receive their decisive defeat. Therefore although 1943 was a decisive year in the Second World War, at the turn of the year there was a considerable threat of a shift in circumstances, and therefore the defence of Britain was still a priority.

The role of the Home Guard in taking on thousands of guard and patrols duties in Britain was still hugely important, especially because of the lack of manpower available to the British Army at this point. By the summer of 1943, Britain had reached its limits in terms of mobilisation of fit young men to fight, as demands of service during 1943 was 912,000 men, but the supply of young men turning of age was only 429,000. Throughout this year, the size of the army was starting to shrink, and by 1944 the size of the army was reduced by 100,000 men. This shortage was particularly acute in terms of the infantry and combat arms where the majority of casualties fell. The merger of some units were occurring, and would lead to the merger and disbandment of whole divisions in 1944. The impact on the Home Front was that many units for home defence were frequently relying on the Home Guard, particularly in terms of the anti-aircraft defences.

In April 1943, Councillor W. Bigwood MC of Sutton Coldfield, who had commanded the 6th Warwickshire (Sutton) Battalion of the Home Guard since its inauguration, was promoted from the rank of lieutenant colonel to colonel and also appointed commander of 'E' Sector, Home Guard, which comprised the Sutton Coldfield and Nuneaton battalions. Colonel Bigwood retained command of the Sutton Battalion, whose area embraced Sutton Coldfield, Coleshill and Wilnecote. [i] To reflect these changes in 1943 the structure of the 6th battalion changed. Numbers were reduced, but also it became clear their role would be more likely to be counter parachute operations, and preventing commando attacks. The structure of both the sector and battalion had changed, with Colonel Bigwood now in command of all of E Sector, which had 2nd and 6th battalions in static roles, but also a mobile reserve of three 'Mobile Companies' held centrally at the battle HQ in Coleshill. This was a new structure and had to be formed from an administrative company structure which was not reflective of this. 24 Mobile Company came from Birmingham, and was attached for operations, however 44 Mobility was formed from soldiers of what was formerly A Company, with a platoon from D Company. 45 Mobility company was a force of 160 soldiers from C Company, with the surplus of this company being moved to the new M Company as a static unit. The company would be based at the Odeon Cinema as a reserve location.

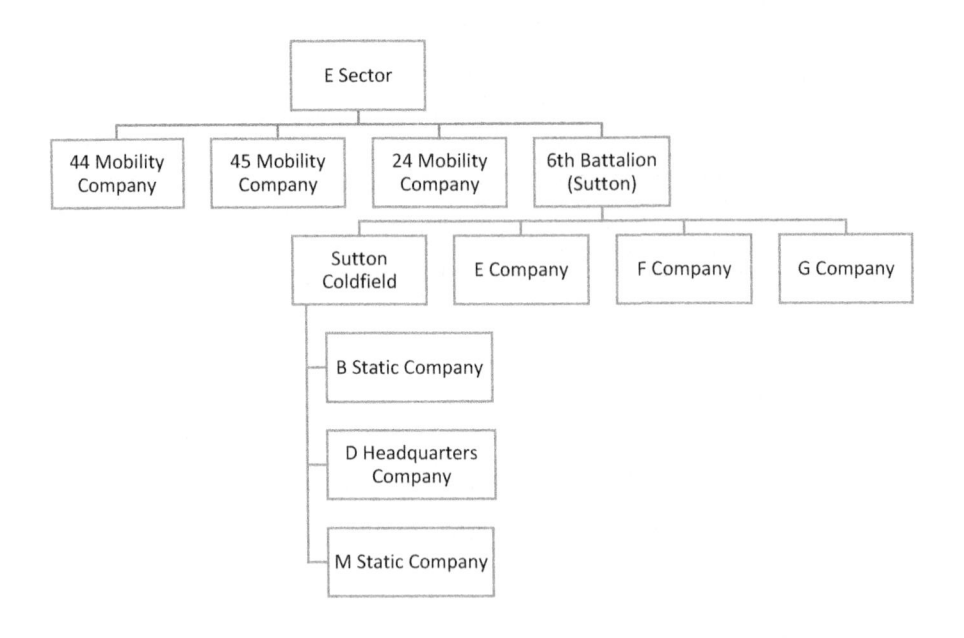

```
                           E Sector
    ┌──────────┬──────────────┼──────────────┐
44 Mobility  45 Mobility  24 Mobility   6th Battalion
 Company      Company      Company       (Sutton)
                              ┌──────────┬──────────┬──────────┐
                          Sutton      E Company  F Company  G Company
                         Coldfield
                             ├── B Static Company
                             ├── D Headquarters Company
                             └── M Static Company
```

Table 13: 6th Battalion Structure 1943

By the late summer of 1942, the organisation and armament of a 'battle platoon' had considerably improved. The vast economy of the United States of America was bringing in huge stores of equipment. Each platoon was now established as follows:[ii]

- Battle platoon headquarters:
    - Platoon commander with pistol, sten gun or rifle
    - Platoon Serjeant [sic] with rifle or shotgun and No. 36 grenades (rifle)
    - Runner with rifle or shotgun
    - Rifleman-Bomber with Enfield E.Y. Rifle Grenade Launcher, cup discharger and No. 36 grenades (rifle)
    - Sniper with sniper rifle.
- Three squads each consisting of:
    - Rifle group made up of:
        - Squad commander with sten
        - No. 1 Rifleman with rifle
        - No. 1 Bomber with grenades, shotgun, rifle or sten
        - No. 2 Rifleman with sten or rifle
        - No. 2 Bomber with grenades, shotgun, rifle or Sten Gun
    - BAR Group made up with:
        - Squad second-in-command with rifle or shotgun
        - No. 1 on the BAR, with the BAR
        - No. 2 on the BAR with rifle or shotgun.

B Company, although static, had a task to support 216 Mobile Unit and the Royal Airforce base at St Georges Barracks, so was in a much more offensive role than previously. They were also tasked to move to landing areas to the north and northeast of Sutton Coldfield. The company had 172 men in 1943. D Company had a number of standing guard duties at battalion headquarters, including eight men at battalion headquarters itself, four men on patrol in the park as part of the mounted patrol, and one non-commissioned officer and six men at Four Oaks Station. Captain Slater would command the company, and man both the sector staff as well as the battalion. The role of headquarters company became one of command and administration rather than combat, although one platoon was detached to 44 Mobility company as part of the reserve.

M Company was a new formation, with 94 soldiers, but 50 of these were new recruits. They conducted a nightly guard on Penns Lane where the 'SMS Wireless Station' was based. Major Trencham, who commanded this force, would muster them as a static company at Holly Cottage on Birmingham Road. Captain Gordon Young's E Company was now at 235 men, but retained their role on the River Tame as a static guard force. However, both this company as well as F Company (of 544 men under Major Mitcheson) would now muster each a 150 man reserve unit to act as a mobile strike force if needed. Coleshill Company, now 695 men, also had wider roles in addition to their static guard duties. One officer and 25 other ranks would move to Castle Bromwich on alert to defend their aircraft factory and its airfield, another 25 other ranks would form the basis of a second company which would be based in Coleshill for mobility. These response companies were based on the Vitguard Scheme, and were known as Red Warning Companies.[iii] The Vitguard Scheme gave operational order to defend factories in Birmingham Garrison from sabotage by enemy units. Three battle platoons were to be formed into a company and on the codeword 'Bugbear', each battle platoon would assemble at their own factory and mobilise. This new response gave new utility to the Home Guard at a time when the chances of invasion were reducing.

With this diminished threat, Colonel Bigwood was keen to utilise the local invasion committees which coordinated the civilian and military efforts, to ensure that the threat of invasion, but also sabotage and commando raids, were still being considered. Even in early 1943, despite the reduced likelihood of any invasion, the utility of invasion committees were still valued, especially due to expected assaults by German commandos and parachute forces. The Home Guard companies were encouraged to re-vitalise the committees by being given forms to go through with the local committees to test against their plans. Company commanders went to the local committees armed with a number of questions, such as 'Have invasion committees Headquarters and alternate Headquarters? Are contacts established with all local experts? Have they a clear conception of the plans already in existence?'[iv] For a population who had suffered huge amounts of restrictions and were entering the fifth year of the war, there was a general apathy to revitalise these defences.

Restrictions for the civilian population had become a way of life in Sutton Coldfield, with both Defence Regulation and other parliamentary legislation having an impact on everyday life. The two key acts of parliament were the Emergency Powers (Defence) Act 1939, which was passed prior to war being declared, and the Emergency Powers (Defence) Act 1940, which was passed after the fall of France. Many different measures were introduced such as identity cards under the National

Registration Act 1939. From 29th September 1939, everyone had to carry the paper National Registration Identity Card. A registration form took place of every household in 1939, updating the information from the census of 1931 to ensure the government had information about the population. The original identity card was yellow for adults and brown for children and in 1943 this changed to blue for adults. The requirement to carry the card did not change until 1952, despite them being largely ineffective as they did not have a photograph on them.

Further restriction came in the form of rationing introduced by the ministry of food, but other rationing occurred with items such as petrol. In 1939 the United Kingdom imported 70 percent of its cereals, cheese, sugar and fats and 80 percent of its fruit. Half of the United Kingdom's meat was imported, and imported feed was needed to sustain domestic meat production. To feed the country of 50 million, imports were critical and the battle of the Atlantic was fundamentally an attempt by the Germans to starve Britain into submission. Rationing meant that to buy most rationed items, each person had to register at chosen shops and was provided with a ration book containing coupons. The shopkeeper was provided with enough food for registered customers. Purchasers had to present ration books when shopping so that the coupon or coupons could be cancelled as these pertained to rationed items.

Rationed items had to be purchased and paid for as usual; rationing restricted what items and what amount could be purchased. Items that were not rationed could be scarce. Prices of some unrationed items were controlled; prices for items not controlled could be unaffordable high for many. A large number of people followed guidance to 'dig for victory' in order to supplement their diets. During the war, numerous publications were issued to encourage home cooking, and the reduction in the usage of foods which were difficult to import. 'War time cookery to save fuel, food and value' was issued by the National Food Campaign in 1940. Advice such as never throwing away the stock pot as it contains precious vitamins, and cooking on one unit of heat (such as a stew) was given. The Ministry of Food in their war cookery leaflets, gave advice such as adding mash to steamed puddings to fatten them out, and the use of stale bread too. Leaflets were also issued by the Ministry of Agriculture and Fisheries to encourage chicken ownership and turning waste into eggs. On the 11th February 1941 special authority was granted to go rabbiting in the park to enhanced food supplies. Additional war time allotments were also allocated across the borough from the town council. Including on Chester Road near banners gate, Birmingham road, near the Wylde green hotel and Park Road, near Clifton road. In 1941 80,000 ration books for the 40,000 residents of Sutton were issued by the ladies and pupils of Sutton High School for Girls, under the Food Executive Officer Mr Peter Conon.[v]

Wartime propaganda was used a lot to encourage the eating of products which had better supplies. Such was the case with carrots, where campaigns such as 'Carrots help you see in the dark!' were used. A campaign put out by the Air Ministry, that our Air Force had excellent eyesight due to eating carrots, was to deflect the enemy from knowing the Royal Airforce were using airborne interception radar to detect aircraft before they reached Britain. Even newspaper articles put forward by British intelligence announced that some staff had outstanding night vision that enabled them to see the enemy in the dark by eating carrots. This rumour spread and other posters were made for the blackout; the propaganda was so persuasive that the general public took to eating carrots to help them find their way during the blackouts. With sugar rationed and carrots being easily grown, this helped the Ministry of Food also, with carrot cake becoming a firm favourite for many. On 1st July 1942, the basic civilian petrol ration, announced on 13 March 1942, was abolished. Thenceforth, vehicle fuel was only available to official users, such as the emergency services, bus companies and farmers. The priority users of fuel were always the armed forces. Many rations continued up to 1954, almost ten years after the war, key shortages were in soap, petrol and paper.

Many other social issues were exacerbated by the war. Hospital waiting lists had been growing due to growth of population and progress of medicine and surgery. The Cottage Hospital had been working at capacity as the war continued. On Rectory Road, a house known as 'Good Hope' had been turned into an auxiliary hospital. The house was originally used as a convalescent home for patients from Sutton Cottage Hospital, High Street, which was struggling to meet the capacity demands of an expanding population in Sutton Coldfield and north Birmingham. The 17 acre site which had started life as a large Victorian house was put up for sale for £15,000 and the Mayor of Sutton William Moss led a campaign to raise contributions from residents to purchase it, this eventually would become Good Hope Hospital.

The manpower issues were also being exacerbated by the routine of Home Guard duties, with volunteers not compelled to attend; if training was not to a high standard, then often numbers would rapidly drop off. A letter from the Company Commander of E Company to Wilnecote Detachment Commander talked about attendance at Lieutenant Matthews' Platoon being only the old faithful which was very disappointing in June 1943. The focus of the note from Captain Gordon Young, the company commander talked about the relationship between Platoon Sergeant Major Smith and Platoon Sergeant Greenway, and the impact on promotions in the platoon, and therefore their happiness. The Detachment Commander makes it clear that he is unimpressed by this lack of leadership and notes that Captain Gordon Young had been in the Officer Training Corps and never the army, therefore he was dealing with things that should not matter rather than training. He also notes he was evacuated from London to Wilnecote to work and did not know his men as well.

The focus on effective training in most cases produced some excellent training programmes, and a high standard of soldiering. However, this had to be balanced with other war priorities. Notes from Headquarters Western Command Instructions No. 101 laid down that "Loss of time and wages" should not take place at this stage in the war and therefore the only way to make both the Home Guard practicable was to earmark volunteers whose work is not vital for enhanced training.[vi] By 1943 the training documents were very much comprehensive and during this year the document 'Qualifications for, and conditions governing the award of the Home Guard proficiency badges and certificates', was issued. This document was a far cry from the improvisation of 1940 and led to a condition of formal training standards, much like those of the Territorial Army prior to the war. In many ways the Home Guard was become a professional force much like the Territorial Army.

Home Guard Instruction No. 56 'Summer Training for 1943' was issued on 20th February 1943 by General Headquarters Home Forces. It was issued down to section level and 6th Battalion received 52 copies, which allowed a scale of 10 per company. Although the situation was looking a lot more positive, it noted that the conditions for invasion could return, and therefore troops must remain motivated and interested. The possibility of airborne and seaborne raids remained real, and the risk was higher due to the state of readiness of the enemy being much higher with there elite parachute and commando units.[vii]

There were a number of issues with training which were highlighted by the General Headquarters reports including the poor quality of shooting, due to a lack of ranges, instructors and ammunition, as well as new weapons. There was also highlighted a poor use of fire control and poor use of cover by soldiers in exercises, resulting from a relaxed attitude to the threat.[viii] To counter these issues, ammunition to commanding officers had now increased to allow better quality of marksmanship. Bombing was highlighted as a particular issue due to lack of live throwing, therefore the qualifications for the use on ranges was expanded to include "any officer who attended a course where they were used, and any non-commissioned officers who qualified at a small arms school".[ix] This was a less risk averse approach and would allow a lot more use in training.

The focus of Home Guard training was the basics being done well, with a 'walk before run' approach to new soldiers. Wilnecote Detachment orders for training on the 31st May 1943 highlighted the large number of courses (many around leadership) available to the soldiers of the detachment. These courses included live grenade practise at Whittington Range E1, E2 and F7 on Sundays and spigot mortar team live training in the summer. It highlighted the need of officers to lead these activities, and to be inspirational in their approach. Training was not free; a note from the Lieutenant Quartermaster of C Company stated that for the 19 bookings of the Walmley Parish Hall from March to August 1942, a charge of £7 / 2S / 2D was paid.[x] Other key issues for training were Sten Gun ammunition and the fact that camouflage cream had to be purchased at their own expense. In the grand scheme of the war, these were relatively minor frustrations.

Sutton Park was a key location to enable training in both the Home Guard, but also for other military and civilian organisations. Within the park the Agricultural Committee cultivated 95 acres and timber was felled in Westwood Coppice, Upper and lower Nuthurst and Hollyhurst, so that 12,000 cubic feet of timber were removed. Powells Pool Camp (later known as Whitsuntide Camp) was used from 1940 as an internment camp for 8000 Germans and Austrians living in Britain. It was initially a tented camp with some very basic facilities for the 700 men transferred in from the racecourse at Kempton Park. The camp was owned by the Ministry of Home Security and there were considerable complaints in the media over the poor conditions that the interns were kept. Including talk in parliament for an inquiry, prompted by Mr Attlee.

By 1941, the interns had been moved to the Isle of Man and had been replaced by Czech communist soldiers who refused to fight in British army; at this point the camp had been improved to wooden huts. 539 mutineers from the Czech brigade were sent from their unit in Leamington Spa to Sutton Park to be held.[xi] They had mutinied whilst being based at Cholmondeley Castle in Cheshire over being communists and having served in the international Brigade. The mutineers were moved from camp to camp, to Oswestry, then York then Sutton Coldfield by August 1940.

They were offered to join different British units, most accepted but 180 refused. Most of the remainder then joined the pioneer corps, but 70 men refused and were discharged as civilians in early 1941.

In 1942 Whitsuntide Camp was repurposed as a training camp. It was first used in 1942 by 1000 members of the National Fire Service, who gathered to train from all over Midlands, and were inspected by the King George. Throughout 1943, the camp was used for courses and basic training by the Home Guard, it was able to be booked as a transit camp. Captain Gordon Young led training for 80 men from 11th to the 15th June 1943 in the area, as a company battle camp. The area was also used by the 6th Army Cadet Battalion, who were based in Sutton Coldfield. There are a number of argumentative statements between Birmingham City Council and the Home Guard over charging for use of the camp, as there were blurred lines over ownership. The training camp continued to be used after the war for the National Fire Service, and then later for eastern european potato pickers.

In 1944 a second camp, originally used as a tented camp for Italian Prisoner of War, was re-purposed at Longmoor Pool, beside Coppice Wood[xii]. After the surrender of the Italians, it became a holding camp for troops from the free Polish Army and then after D Day was used to hold German prisoners of war. In 1945, Mary Kennard of female mounted section remembers the prisoners having a huge bonfire on the hill to the east of Longmoor Pool to celebrate the end of the war. Another prisoner of war camp was at the junction of Jerrys Lane and Flackwell Road opposite the Leopard Public House. The Italian prisoners provided labour for harvesting the crops from the cornfields between Witton Lodge Road and Perry Common Road and were used on other things out of season.

Finally, there is evidence of some testing of armoured vehicles in Sutton Park, with tanks made in Willenhall by Wilkins and Mitchell, who normally serviced sewing machines. There is evidence of these vehicles being brought to the park by train on the Walsall to Sutton line, to be tested by American forces, possibly those who were headquartered at the Trees Pub and housed in the Pheasey Estate. Wilkins and Mitchell after the war became Version Wilkins or Version International and made power presses. It was cited in a newspaper[xiii] after the war that amphibious Sherman tanks were tested prior to D Day in a small pool off Deakin Road, called James' Pool. The tanks were stated to have been modified by Metro Camel in Washwood Health. It was even rumoured that Field Marshal Montgomery visited prior to D-Day the site (he did visit Birmingham at this time). However, much of their activity during the war is shrouded in secrecy and therefore the actual activity is largely unknown.

Some central training took place organised by battalion headquarters, as well as camps arranged out of area, such as the one run by Lieutenant Payne who took 40 men from No.5 Platoon to Drayton Bassett for a training camp.[xiv] A training course was held on the 20th December 1942 in the Royal Hotel assembly room. The training was organised by the Intelligence Officer Lieutenant Turner, but lessons were of various types. Sergeant Brown taught security, camouflage, and German Army organisation, Sergeant Palmer map marking and sketching, with Corporal Singer talking through compasses and bearings. There were also lectures on gas and ammunition. Sergeant Kemp talked through operations and patrols, Sergeant Powell enemy aircraft and tanks, and Sergeant Winnall talked through messages, logs and incidents. This centralised training was well attended by those who were keen to learn more in many different roles.

As well as improvements to training, there were considerable improvements to the weapons and equipment that the Home Guard had by 1943. The Home Guard was now armed with Sten guns and a wide variety of support equipment, including over 100,000 Boys anti-tank rifles. In addition, there were considerable improvements of the ammunition scales held by the units, as shown by this table from E Company, which shows the rounds per weapon system available.

Calibre	Weapon	Rounds per Weapons
.300 BDR	Rifle (HG)	170
.300 CTN	Lt Auto Rifle (HG)	1670
	LMG Ground (HG)	1450
	AA LMG (HG)	3100
	HMG (HG)	8500
.300 Tracer	AA LMG (HG)	1150
36 Gren Rifle		12
36 Hand Grenade		48
68 Grenade		68 per platoon
73 Grenade		50
74 Grenade		100
75 Grenade		72
Northover Mortar		100

Table 14: Ammunition Holdings 1943

In addition to the physical improvement, the 6th Battalion was now much better organised, with clear orders and direction delivered on a routine basis. By the end of the summer 1943, it was ordered that every platoon should have manned their action stations with all equipment and tested their administrative arrangements; this was not a small task considering the size of the force involved. It was highly encouraged to include night attacks during training as well as utilising gas and testing sentries and practising static points of defence.

To activate the Home Guard in case of emergency, a system of mustering had been divided which was conducted by groups, listed geographically. D Company had groups VII to XII and these were under the runners allocated by Lieutenant Ollis. Each group had a first, a 1st reserve and 2nd reserve, to then mobilise downwards the rest of their men. For example, Group IX 1st was Cpl Pemberton at 35 Coleshill Road (who had a car), the 1st Reserve if he was not contactable was Private S Spenser at 474 Walmley Road, then 2nd Reserve was Private W Hayward at 2 New Hall Drive. Most runners had bicycles and these were noted in the orders. The system was a simple method of quickly mustering large numbers of troops in an emergency or to an incident.

The above-mentioned Lieutenant John Alfred Ollis of Walmley was a Sergeant Major in the First World War in the Royal Scots. He served in Palestine, taking part in active fighting against the Turks in 1916 at Duweidar. He joined the 6th Warwickshire (Sutton) Battalion Home Guard and was appointed as the chief guide. His hard work and diligence meant that in 1944 he was appointed as the assistant adjutant. He was known as the officer that kept on going, when others had stopped.

An example of the detail contained in orders can be shown by Battalion Orders Number 163 (Part 1) on the 2nd April 1943. This was a mature document showing how far the battalion had come and started by reminding all officers of the battalion conference, at the Royal Hotel on the 9th April in 1830. It also mentioned that on the 12th April, there would be an ammunition and bombing instructors conference, under the battalion bombing officer. This showed that the staff under battalion headquarters and in the quartermasters department were now operating and functioning in an efficient was and coordinating across the companies.

The orders give insight into the routine of a battalion, for example it mentions that Private W G Wilkins of F Company was fined £2 at Wilnecote Petty Sessions (Court) on the 30th March 1943 for failing to perform a Home Guard duty on 25th January 1943. Then it mentions that 2nd Lieutenant M H Campbell had passed the Army Gas School. The routine of army life was found within the orders, which reminded officers that they were not insured if Defence Regulation 52[xv] approval had not been granted for the training area; a far cry from 1940. There were also reminders of the numbers of troops allowed in vehicles and that on courses over five days, civilian ration books must be taken. Such routine could be found in any home based British Army battalion from any time in the last hundred years. It is testament to the maturity of the administration of the battalion, that such a routine was in place. Finally, the orders ended with an interesting anecdote which shows that the amateur feel of the battalion was still there in some respects; it stated that "a recent case has occurred in which a member of the battalion endangered both his own and his childrens' lives through the constructing explosives in his own home.

Whilst the commanding officer realises that this man's action was purely one of enthusiasm, he directs that the practise must cease."

Such orders were also found at company level, such as those on the 31st May 1943, in this case Wilnecote (E and F Company) Detachment Orders. This mentioned a talk by adjutant on discipline on June 2nd to Wilnecote Detachment at 20:00 for all officers. Also, training was available for Spigot Mortar of No.2 Platoon E Company and No.5 and No.6 Platoon F Company, as well as live grenade training, at Wittington Ranges for 40 men on a Sunday. Finally, it mentioned that camouflage cream could be purchased by platoons at their own expense from G H F Manufacturing Company Limited, 65 South Molten Street, London. The routine of company life was reflected in these orders, and give a interesting insight on the priorities of the day.

A well as routine orders, operational orders were produced to ensure that the battalion and companies could react to incidents when they occurred. A series of codewords were developed to ensure that activity was correct for the required response: these were listed in Operational Order Number 1. Codeword 'Newton' stated that battalion and company headquarters move to battle stations, that observation posts must be manned in the daytime, with three men at important posts. In addition, night personnel doubled must be double with all Home Guard in uniform. Soldiers would be paid compensation for attendance on this operation. On escalating to 'Action Station', earmarked transport was taken over with transport personnel mobilised, guards at vital points established to full strength, 25 percent of the battalion was mustered and field work began at defensive locations.

Codeword Oliver would see 100 percent mustering of Home Guard (on pain of desertion), with key personnel (railway, public service) exempt for two days. During this alert, key war industry workers work remained at their factories at 75 percent, and men may be returned to industry for this purpose. This was expected to be called if there was an airborne attack on Birmingham to disrupt war works and would be alerted by the ringing of church bells.

Company operational orders went into much detail, such as Wilnecote Detachment Operational Orders Number 1 produced on the 14th October 1943. These included orders to deny enemy access through 'Two Gates' through four road blocks. And it stated that defence was to be continued to the last man if necessary. For 'Action Stations', F Company were to provide a garrison with all men and arms with their headquarters based at Dosthill Road air raid shelter by the warden's post with one section of F Company No.5 Platoon as guard. The company were to man four garrison locations, Park Farm (6 Platoon F Company), Railway (5 Platoon F Company), Tamworth Road (4 Platoon F Company) and Dosthill Road (7 Platoon F Company), each of around 40 men including one BAR. All positions were to have range cards, fire positions and obstacles camouflage. A counter attack force of two battle platoons (2 Platoon F Company) of a total of 80 men, based at Smith's Garage and Two Gates Club, as well as a counter attack force of three platoons of 105 men from 1 Platoon F Company Platoon and a mobile patrol of one battle platoon (3 Platoon F Company) made up of 30 men and a bomb disposal squad. Throughout, senior cadets from 6th battalion of the Army Cadet Force would provide cyclists, liaison officers and runners. The local invasion committee would use civilian labour for defence positions. This was an extremely comprehensive plan which was at a high level of maturity, and demonstrated the hard work of the staff in bringing it to this state.

1943 was also a year for parades and demonstrations, as the battalion found capacity to conduct these events amongst their training and operational schedule. On the 16th May 1943 in Sutton Park, the battalion conducted a series of demonstrations with a march-past the salute taken by Brigadier A. M. Ramsden and Air Vice Marshall J C Andrews.[xvi] This third anniversary parade took place over three hours and consisted of events across the town, including a display by the Air Training Corps at the Odeon Cinema, and a procession through the town by the local military units, including a heavy anti-aircraft mobile gun with tractor. Also, a travelling bomb kiosk to raise money was set up outside the Boldmere Hotel. A football match at Bishop Vesey School between Royal Airforce Sutton and Royal Airforce Stafford took place as well as a parachute display at Brampton Hall.

The battalion conducted a platoon attack on parachutists northwest of Rowton's Cottage. "Rifleman, snipers, machine gunners and bombers cooperated as a team and smoke grenades were used."[xvii] A dressing station was established and instructions brought by the mounted section (as runners). An enemy tank in target woods was captured in night ambush. The attack included live firing of Spigot Mortar and bombs and nearby displays of weapons, intelligence and signals. Throughout the event, money was raised for various good causes such as the programme sold in aid of the YMCA Canteens (Sutton Coldfield Division). "Suffice to say that the spirit which was as its foundation three years ago has continued and with that spirit has been a corresponding efficiency which has built a high reputation among its kind."[xviii]

This demonstration by the 6th Battalion and Colonel Bigwood was the peak of the reputation of the battalion and of the Home Guard in the eyes of the population of Sutton Coldfield. The reputation of the troops who had held out and been willing to fight when under-equipped against the greatest odds, was cemented in the minds of the whole town. The impressive nature of the highly trained soldiers was a far cry from the coveralls and arm bands of 1940, and the equipment was as good as many regular units. The war was far from over, but after this date, and the invasion of Italy, the war seemed to be turning into an unstoppable victory by the Allies. The reputation of the Home Guard in this context would start to dim, as the population focused on the end of the war and what would come next.

[i] Evening Despatch 16th April 1943
[ii] As quoted in Home Guard Instruction No. 51: Battlecraft and Battle Drill for the Home Guard, Part II Battle Drill, War Office, 1942, p.4. Available online.
[iii] Orders for Vitguard Scheme – Red Warning Company – 9th May 1944. Available in the Warwickshire Archive.
[iv] 943 Invasion Committees. Available in the Warwickshire Archive.
[v] Sutton Coldfield News 28th July 1941
[vi] Part 1 Orders 6th Battalion 16th February 1942. From my private collection, but I have now donated a copy to the archive in Sutton Coldfield Library.
[vii] Home Guard Instruction No.56 'Summer Training for 1943' – Available at the Warwickshire Archive.
[viii] *Ibid.*
[ix] *Ibid.*
[x] Part 1 Orders, 7th June 1943. From my private collection, but I have now donated a copy to the archive in Sutton Coldfield Library.
[xi] From article by Richard Gaskell 2004
[xii] There is much discussion around where things were in Sutton Park, and this is likely to continue, with currently the lack of evidence to identify military and civil defence locations, as well as war industry. I hope in a further addition of this book I may have more. A good source of information is Roberts, S. (2021) Sutton Park A Social History 1900 – 1950.
[xiii] Quoted in Sutton Coldfield Observer 4th February 2005. There are a huge number of variations of this story including comments of tanks being in the Old Brickyard Pool in Barnard Road.
[xiv] Part 1 Orders, 7th June 1943. From my private collection, but I have now donated a copy to the archive in Sutton Coldfield Library.
[xv] Defence Regulation 52, was the military authority to train on public land. Such regulations were largely ignored in many cases, and only really applied when higher priorities that military training appeared from 1943.
[xvi] Birmingham Daily Post 17th May 1943. In addition, a video the exercise is available (unknown source), but I have now donated a copy to the archive in Sutton Coldfield Library.
[xvii] *Ibid.*
[xviii] *Ibid.*

Chapter 14

1944 and Standdown

The tide had turned by 1944 and in international terms, the war in Europe was in a period of calm before the storm. The major actions of Operation Overlord by the Allies in the west, and Operation Bagration by the Soviets in the east, would mean the beginning of the end for the Germans. Fighting continued in Italy, and would be difficult throughout spring and summer, but the build up ready for these major offensives became inexorable and even the most pessimistic realised that an invasion of Britain was now impossible for the Germans to achieve.

So why keep the Home Guard under such circumstances? Firstly, there was a fear of raids by commando forces, *Fallschirmjeger* and the constant threat of spies and saboteurs. These activities meant that thousands of vulnerable points and key infrastructure needed to be guarded and patrolled. It was in this area that the Home Guard provided a huge amount of manpower, and gave real utility to the war effort. However, in addition to this static and mobile defence required, the Home Guard tried to generate additional tasks to prove their worth, in a sense to justify their continued existence.

The final change in the Regional Command structure came on the 17th February 1944, when the threat of invasion had lapsed and therefore a much more simplified command structure was needed. Southern Command took over both Eastern and South Eastern Command, allowing a large scale defensive area to hold the invasion troops preparing for D-Day. The remainder of England was divided between Northern and Western Command. Western Command was broken down into three Districts: Mid Western District, North Western District and Northern District. This was a much simpler structure, with less administration of defensive areas. Warwickshire found itself in Mid Western District with Worcestershire, Herefordshire, Shropshire and Staffordshire. Therefore, the existing structure which had built administration and unity for defence were broken down, and led to their requirement to build new relationships, most of which were not given the top priority for defence.

Other Home Guard units found utility in the role of supporting the Air Raid Precaution forces and civil defence with the attacks by the V Weapons causing a new fear across Britain. No V weapons fell on

Birmingham or were aimed at it and the accepted wisdom was that the city was out of range. However, this doesn't alone explain things, principally because Manchester was attacked. Ground-launched V weapons from Europe were aimed at Southern England initially (fired from parts of liberated Europe later), and therefore the V1 (Doodlebug) couldn't reach Birmingham. However, Manchester was attacked by Heinkel 111 planes firing V1's, therefore if Manchester was in range, so was Birmingham. One big raid took place on Manchester consisting of 60 planes on the 24th December 1944. It was assumed by the Germans there wouldn't be many defences in the path of Manchester if the Heinkel fired off the Skegness coast (such was Allied air-superiority over British skies in late 1944 they couldn't risk going too far in). Many went off course once fired, landing in towns such as Oldham. Some were shot down one reached Manchester's outskirts. In fact, the attack was so scattered it was only when the Nazis later broadcast that Manchester was the target did the Allies know. The heavy anti-aircraft coastal defences, there mainly to protect southern and eastern England, also blocked the path to Birmingham, therefore the Germans did not pick it as an "experiment" for this aeroplane method of firing V1's, which was abandoned after the Manchester raid due to lack of Heinkel fuel. No V2's were plane-launched, and like the ground based V1 they couldn't reach Birmingham when launched from Europe.

The V1 did have one impact on Sutton Coldfield with the flow of refugees again coming to the town. In May 1944, Chief Billeting officer and town clerk Mr R Walsh organised the reception for mothers and children who evacuated from London due to the V1 Bomb threat. They were received in the British Restaurant in the south parade and found billets around the town. Medical Officer of Health D J H Wright examined them.

On the 1st April 1944, the final reorganisation took place of the 6th Battalion, in order to give it greater mobility to counter enemy spoiling attacks prior to D Day.[i] All of the companies were now allocated as either 'mobile companies' or 'town defence companies' There was also an allocated 'Recruit Training Company'. By 1943 there were 49 Home Guard transport units in Western Command, from 127 across the United Kingdom; they were numbered 2200 Home Guard to 2249 Home Guard. These units provided the truck mobility to Home Guard units for both strategic supply, but also for movement to areas where they may be needed. The battalion mobile company was '44 Mobile Company' under Major Hollands, with B and M Companies designated as town defence. Wilnecote Detachment provided troops for 43 and 45 Mobile Companies and also retained some static defences under E and F Companies.

The links between the Home Guard and the youth organisations within the town grew over 1945, with much training now being conducted by the 6th Cadet Battalion of the Royal Warwickshire Regiment. In addition, the band of this cadet unit were used for many ceremonial events. The 1st Sutton Coldfield Sea Scouts were also used to in support of some of the training exercises, especially to play enemy agents and runners. A tragic incident occurred with the Sea Scouts when Arthur Donald Pocock of 23 Clifton Road, a rifle instructor in the Home Guard and a gun demonstrator at Vickers Armstrong and B.S.A. factories was manning the shooting range at the amusement park. Two sea cadets paid for a round at the shooting gallery, took their rifles (which were already loaded) from the attendant, and, while their four pals looked on, began shooting. Sadly, they shot the attendant and he later died. "There is no suggestion of any ill-feeling, horse play, or negligence. This was a simple accident which occurred in the hands of a youngster handling a rifle, who failed to appreciate that in handling these rifles loaded with ammunition they have to be treated with the greatest respect."[ii] This did not spoil the relationship between the unit, and on the 7th August 1944 a Regatta was held by the 1st Sutton Coldfield Sea Scouts on Powells Pool, which was supported by men of the 6th Battalion.

As the Allies advanced towards Germany and the war in Europe coming to an end, the decision was made to stand down the Home Guard with effect from the 3rd December 1944. The Battalion would not be disbanded formerly until the 31st December 1945, but no operational activity took place after December 1944. On announcement of stand down, the administration of organising the closing down of logistics occurred. Each company was tasked to reduce the equipment holding of soldiers, and to complete final administration. Major Slater, who commanded D Company, wrote a letter to all soldiers on the 7th November addressing the return of clothing on stand down, stating that the soldiers could retain battledress, cap with badge, anklets, boots, greatcoat, anti-gas cape, chevrons and titles and respirator (until civilian use of this item had finished). It made clear that at this point any outstanding travel expenses and subsistence will be paid, but no Home Guard items were able to be purchased. The retention of this uniform was in order to theoretically allow the 'standing too' of the Home Guard if needed.

However, the majority of the battalion effort went into the planning of the final parade of the 6th Battalion, to cement their legacy in the history of Sutton Coldfield. A letter from the adjutant to all officers on 13th

November 1944 talked about a gift from the officers to the commanding officer. The battalion second-in-command, Major Witt, called a meeting and decided on purchasing a silver salver, engraved with the Warwickshire Regiment crest and suitable wording. The fun raising for the gift was oversubscribed so a presentation was made to the Cottage Hospital from the Colonel. It was presented on December the 3rd at the Odeon Cinema, on the occasion of the final parade. The over-subscription showed the respect that the men had for their commanding officer, who had let them through this incredible period of history.

What followed were a series of company parades and dinners to say thank you to the troops, followed by a large scale send off of the whole battalion in the town. One of these company parades was in Walmley on the 10th December 1944, and had the mayor and the commanding officer in attendance at the parish church. A parade then took place by the Home Guard, Civil Defence Services and Girl Guides in support. These parades took place across the many sub-units of Wilnecote Detachment, the specialist companies of D Company and in each of the rifle companies. The goodbye and thank you was done well locally, with the population turning out to cheer and say thank you to the Home Guard for their service.

The final battalion parade took place on Sunday the 3rd December 1944. The battalion paraded at 10:20 at the Odeon Cinema for a series of addresses, firstly by Lieutenant General Sir John Brown, then Colonel C H V Cox and then Sir John Mellor. The mayor then spoke, followed by an address by the Commanding Officer and the presentation to the commanding officer by the second-in-command of the silver salver. The battalion then marched around the town from Hollands Road, through

Birmingham Road, along the Parade, Mill Street and finally onto the High Street. The parade order was the civilian police, the commanding officer (mounted) and orderly, Lieutenant Fisher and Mounted Section, the West Bromwich Silver Prize Band, the second-in-command, adjutant and regimental sergeant major. Then followed the marching troops with the sector and battalion Headquarters Officers led by Major McCrae, followed by 44 Mobile Company led by Major Hollands, then B Company led by Major Cozens, M Company led by Major Trenchman and then D Company led by Major Slater. The band of the Women's Auxiliary Air Force led the second column which consisted of Coleshill Detachment led by Major Griffiths, the band of Polesworth Company Home Guard and Wilnecote Detachment (E and F Companies). To the rear of the column were the band of 6th Cadet Battalion Royal Warwickshire Regiment, the cadets of the 6th Battalion Army Cadet Force, the Joint Training Corps and finally all Home Guard soldiers who had left the battalion in civilian clothing, led by the senior officer. On the parade, all officers were in battledress with greatcoats and other ranks in battledress. No weapons were carried.

After the parade, a final dinner was held attended by Lieutenant Colonel P N Dingley and Lieutenant General Sir John Brown, hosted by Colonel Bigwood and Major Witt. The food was potage royal to start, roast goose and pork for main with sprouts and potatoes. Trifle was for desert and cheese biscuits with celery after. The final dinner was a splendid affair, with many fine speeches made, and anecdotes of the last five years under arms together. The war was not yet over, but Britain was safe and these men and woman had played their part in this. At new year, Colonel Bigwood wrote in the Birmingham Post a note to "thank all Officers, Warrant Officers, N.C.O.s and men the 6th Warwickshire (Sutton) Bn.

Home Guard for their loyal and devoted service since May, 1940. He wishes all of you very prosperous New Year, with, the hope of an early peace, which you have striven so hard achieve."[iii]

As the new year came, the former members of the Home Guard went back to their normal lives, with the uniform they held often being left in the loft to gather dust. The soldiers of G (Coleshill) Company dusted off their uniform again on the 18th February for a sad occasion, the death of Captain Manning. Captain Manning was buried at Coleshill will full military honours. He had the unusual distinction of jumping in promotion from sergeant to captain. He started in the ranks, and his keenness so impressed his senior officers that when a vacancy occurred in the command of the company charged with the defence of Hams Hall Power Station, Sergeant Manning, as he then was, was given the command with three pips.[iv]

On the 7th April 1945, the order was received for the withdrawal of AF B 2606 ID Card, which would be held in Warwick until disbandment; request letters were sent out from battalion to each soldier to return them. Further administration occurred on the 25th May 1945 with the request that all secret documents would be returned to the Territorial Army Association for storage. Such low level administration continued in the spring, with documents, files and equipment slowing being returned to archives and storage. After the war a number of associations were started for the old boys of the Home Guard to come together. Each Company had its own Home Guard, which were active for some years after the war. The objectives of the association were 'To maintain old associations and friendships, promote recreations and amusements of all kinds and help fellow members who may temporarily be in difficulties.'

The news received on Monday May 7th 1945 of the German High Command's unconditional surrender put the people of Sutton Coldfield "in a joyous mood". The following morning, newspapers announced that Tuesday May 8th was Victory in Europe Day, and a national holiday. A thanksgiving service was held in King Edward's Square in front of the Town Hall, where flags of the United Nations flew from 22 masts.[v] Many houses were decorated with flags, bunting and victory posters. At night the Council House, Town Hall and Fire Station Tower were outlined with hundreds of coloured lamps. All over town, bonfires were lit and fireworks let off, and there was dancing in King Edward's Square until late. Quantities of beer were consumed in the pubs that night. Street parties were organised; a large one in Station Road, Wylde Green near the railway bridge included a stage with music: "the atmosphere and group singing was joyous and noisy with all of us just surfacing from six years of war, blackouts, rationing and bombing." [vi]

The war was finally over, and the history of the largest mass volunteer army in the history of Britain had come to an end. The formal disbandment occurred after the war, with some parades taking place in London to celebrate the achievements during the war. But for the majority, the Home Guard moved into their past.

The utility of the Home Guard has been debated hotly by historians. Post-war there was a view that the activities against so called fifth columnist was an overreaction and unnecessary. Peter Flemming argued[vii] that the reaction to lights by Home Guard at night was unrealistic. It would have required the fifth columnist to knew what unit he was signalling to, and which attack target and direction, as well as two way communications to get this by wireless and an air force that could identify the light at such a distance. Such a link in circumstances was probably unrealistic. Guy Liddel Head of Counter Espionage in MI5 recorded on 9th June 1940, "The fighting services are becoming more and more restive about a fifth column. In some cases they are taking matter into their own hands, but generally the wrong cases." The argument of the failure of the German's to infiltrate Britain in the way expected does not mean that there was no utility in the guard and patrol functions. This is particularly true in the context of these roles been taken over by Home Guard from regular forces and therefore allowing the regulars to be in reserve to defend from invasion, and later to be able to be deployed to operations overseas. As early as the 16th September 1940, Churchill was planning to move one quarter of his infantry to North Africa.

The Chiefs of Staff on 19th June 1940, warned the cabinet that invasion was imminent, and this was followed on the 25th June 1940 when Ironside presented a defence plan of the Britain known as Operational Instruction Number 3. This plan saw relatively week forces holding the coastline, but Leopard Brigades available in reserve to strike when able. The Local Defence Volunteers were at this point seen as expendable manpower. Ironside spoke on 5th June 1940 about meeting brutality with brutality and in the planned defence, the use of chemicals was arranged, and also holding out to the last man was the order of the day for the Local Defence Volunteers. Even though there was a shortage of weapons and ammunition, the situation was rapidly improving, and also a huge proportion of those initial members of the Local Defence Volunteers were veterans of the Great War and able to understand how to man a static defence. What's more, they were defending their homes, and there is no greater motivation.

Although there was initial opposition by the Vice Chiefs to the concept of giving over half the country to the Germans before a counter attack, even under Alan Brook (the new Commander in Chief Home Forces), the idea of maintaining a mobile reserve was maintained. When the main threat of invasion came on the 7th September, and Codeword 'Cromwell' was issued to tell soldiers to take up battle stations, the Home Guard were better equipped, and ready to fight. A million men with rifles would have caused huge disruption to any invasion, particularly as they were motivated enough to fight to the death.

The air defence of Great Britain was coordinated fighter command and Anti-Aircraft Command played a key role, especially when the Blitz started. The Home Guard took on the role of supporting the civil defence, even though it was not pre-planned, because these were their homes and families being bombed. As the Blitz continued and then eventually ended, the Home Guard found itself in 1942 at the peak of its capability and expanded to take on much of the nation's anti-aircraft capacity. 142,000 volunteer Home Guard soldiers were members of the anti-aircraft units, 7000 were in coastal artillery and 7000 were trained in bomb disposal. Of note, 32,000 women were members officially of the Home Guard by 1943, although many had been members in an unofficial capacity since the early days.

As early as November 1940, Sir Edward Grigg, the Under Secretary of State for War announced in the commons that the Home Guard, 'which has hitherto been largely provisional in character' was to be given a 'firmer and more permanent shape.'[viii] There was a new Director General of the Home Guard responsible to the Commander in Chief Home Force, and across the battalions the adjutant and quartermaster for the Home Guard were full time paid roles, much like in the Territorial Army. There were much better weapons and equipment, and although they had no powers of punishment, the Home Guard Officers were now commissioned, and appointed on merit with normal military ranks. In February 1941, the Home Guard manning was strong enough to justify the discharge of those over the age of 65.

As the war continued and the threat reduced, the requirement to conduct guard duties and patrols across vulnerable points never diminished, with the threat of German parachute and commando attacks to disrupt D Day plans and the expectation of the Brandenburg Regiment being used in such a role, ensuring that vigilance must be maintained. When in 1943 General Franklyn was appointed to be Commander in Chief Home Forces, the Home Guard well equipped, mainly young with advent of conscription and trained in static point defence. Conscription maintained the strength of the Home Guard to over one and a half million men, and although there was a threat of a fine or jail for non-attendance, it rarely had to be used. Of the 180,000 men who left in 1941, 60 percent transferred to the regular forces, 20 percent were expelled (mainly due to age) and 20 percent resigned. The cost to nation of a Home Guard volunteer was one fortieth of regular soldier in peacetime.

Those who served in general had positive experiences of their time in the Home Guard. Major Mitcheson, who commanded the Wilnecote detachment, reflected that he lived a "full life" during the war. He was never at home in the evening or weekend from the 18th May 1940 until September 1940. "No pay at all, no rations or privilege. Many were working minors who were in the pits all day." Those who served only a short time and then went into the regular forces, felt it was a good stepping stone into the life they would join. Those who fought in the previous war felt it was a role they could do well, despite their advancing years. There was some disappointment that no Home Guard medal was issued, but those who served for three years were entitled to the Defence Medal, which many felt happy to wear.

The 6th Warwickshire (Sutton) Home Guard were one of over a thousand Home Guard battalions. It was larger than most, with the geography of the Midlands allowing a large force to be built up in defence of the north east of the city. But it was also a battalion that saw active duty in the Blitz, and was recognised as having a high level of competence during its training. On stand down, it walked around the town with drums beating and their heads held high. Those who served remembered a happy battalion and were proud to have played a part. It is over 80 years since the events in this book took place, and the few who remain are getting fewer still. I hope in some small part the memory of those who served is remembered by this book, and those who live in our town remember the actions of the many in our time of need.

Chapter 15
Bibliography

Atkin, M. (2015) *Fighting Nazi Occupation (British Resistance 1939 – 1945)*. Pen and Sword.

Bigwood, W. (1940) *Handbook of the 6th Warwickshire (Sutton) Battalion Home Guard*.

Brancker, M. (1972) *All Creatures Great and Small: Veterinary Surgery as a Career (My Life & My Work)*. Education Explorers.

Brazier, C. & Rice, S. (2018) *Condition Red*. West Midlands Police.

Brown, P. (1944). *1940-44 Being a diary of D Company 20th Battalion (Kent) Home Guard*. Published by Kent Home Guard.

Cambridgeshire and Isle of Ely Territorial Association (1944) *We Also Served*. Local Publishing.

Churchill, W. (1955) *Finest Hour*. Houghton Mifflin Harcourt.

Clarke D. M. (2011) *Arming The British Home Guard 1940 – 1944*. Cranfield University.

Danchev A. and Todman, D (eds.) (2001) *Field Marshall Lord Alan Brooke. War Diaries 1939- 1945*. Weidenfeld & Nicholson, London.

Flemming, P. (1958) *Invasion 1940*. Hamish Hamilton.

French, D (2008) *Military Identities: The Regimental System, the British Army and the British People 1870 – 2000*. Oxford.

Gardiner, J. (2004). *Wartime Britain 1939 – 1945*. Review

Longmate, Norman. (1974) The Real Dad's Army: The Story of the Home Guard. Arrow Books, London.

MacKenzie, S. P. (1996) *The Home Guard A Military and Political History*. Oxford Uni Press.

McKay, S. (2021) *Secret Britain*. Headline.

Osbourne, K. (2000) *A History of Bishop Vesey's Grammar School - The Twentieth Century*.

Richards, S (2019) *The Luftwaffe over Brum*.

Roberts, S. (2021) Sutton Park A Social History 1900 – 1950.

Robinson, D. (2006) *Invasion 1940: Did the Battle of Britain Alone Stop Hitler*. Robinson Publishing

Skennerton, I. D. (1988) *British Small Arms of World War 2*. Greenhill Books, London.

Skennerton, I. D. (1993) The Lee-Enfield Story: The Lee-Metford, Lee-Enfield S.M.L.E. and No. 4 Series Rifles and Carbines, 1880 to the Present. Greenhill Books, London.

Archive References

Archive	File Name	File Reference
Warwickshire Archive	A Company Logbook	CR 301/21
Warwickshire Archive	A Company Logbook	CR 301/22
Warwickshire Archive	B Company Logbook	CR 301/23
Warwickshire Archive	C Company Logbook	CR 301/24
Warwickshire Archive	45 Mobile Company	CR 301/25
Warwickshire Archive	D Company Logbook	CR 301/26
Warwickshire Archive	D Company List	CR 301/27
Warwickshire Archive	44 Mobile Company	CR 301/29
Warwickshire Archive	M Company Logbook	CR 301/30
Warwickshire Archive	Coleshill Company Logbook	CR 301/31
Warwickshire Archive	Wilnecote Company	CR 301/32
Warwickshire Archive	Officers Roll	CR 301/33
Warwickshire Archive	List of Volunteers 22 May 1940	CR 301/34
Warwickshire Archive	Birmingham Home Guard Record	CR 4367/2/1
Warwickshire Archive	Coleshill Company Records	CR 1380
Warwickshire Archive	Clothing and Equipment Book E Coy	CR 4763/1/1
Warwickshire Archive	Stores and Equipment list (Damaged)	CR 4763/1/3
Warwickshire Archive	4th Battalion Clothing and equipment list	CR 4763/1/2
Warwickshire Archive	Photos	CR 4763/2
The National Archies	Home Guard List 1941	Western Command
The National Archies	Home Guard List 1942	Western Command
The National Archies	Home Guard List 1943	Western Command
The National Archies	Home Guard List 1944	Western Command
The National Archies	1st Battalion Warwickshire Home Guard	WO 199 / 3454
The National Archies	3rd Battalion Warwickshire Home Guard	WO 199 / 3456
The National Archies	6th Battalion	WO 199 / 3457

The National Archies	Warwickshire Home Guard Solihull Garrison Maps	WO 199 / 3462
The National Archies	C Sector Exercise Eastgate 1943	WO 199 / 3463
The National Archies	Coventry Garrison Operational Orders	WO 199 / 3481
The National Archies	Coventry Garrison Maps	WO 199 / 3484
The National Archies	GHQ Home Forces	WO 199/665
The National Archies	GHQ Home Forces	WO 199/669
The National Archies	G.H.Q. Standing Operating Instructions	WO 199/249
The National Archies	Home defence against invasion: "Julius Caesar" plan	IIH/246
The National Archies	Regional Commissioners	HO 199/15
Sutton Coldfield Archive	ARP Records	WW2 File
Sutton Coldfield Archive	Demonstration	16-May-43
Sutton Coldfield Archive	Final parade	03-Dec-44

---

[i] Available at the National Archives under AP/46/1535/23.
[ii] Evening Despatch 17th November 1944
[iii] Birmingham Daily Post. 20th December 1944.
[iv] Evening Despatch 19th February 1945.
[v] Sutton Coldfield Historical Society.
[vi] Quote from John Wilson, who was 14 at the time.
[vii] Flemming, P. (1958) *Invasion 1940*. Hamish Hamilton.
[viii] Longmate, Norman. (1974) The Real Dad's Army: The Story of the Home Guard. Arrow Books, London.

Annex A – Battalion Strength over time

Table 15

Numbers of soldiers who served in each company throughout the conflict.

Company	Soldiers Served
A Company	713
B Company	528
C Company	369
D Company	808
E Company HQ	134
F Company HQ	138
E/F Detachment	1236
G Company	1489
Unknown	1126
Total	**6541**

Table 16

Company strength by year.

Organisation	1941	1942*	1942	1943	1944	Oct 44
6th Battalion	2651	1781	*2345*	*2590*	*2521*	*2234*
A Company	320					
B Company	252	220			172	145
C Company	314	240				
D Company	364	400			297	
E and F Company	812	600			779	
G Company	589	211			695	
M Company		110			94	
43 Mobility Company						
44 Mobility Company					138	
45 Mobility Company					241	

*Establishment

Annex B – List of unit locations

Table 17

Unit and Subunit locations.

Unit	Subunit	Locations	Remarks
6th Battalion	Battalion HQ	The Royal Hotel, 25 Highstreet, Sutton Coldfield.	
A Company	Company HQ	Moorlands Cottage, Snowhill Road. Streetly, Sutton Coldfield	
A Company	No. 1 Platoon	The Crown Public House, Walsall Road, Four Oaks	Sections A - D
A Company	No. 2 Platoon		Sections A - D
A Company	No. 3 Platoon		Sections A - D
A Company	No. 4 Platoon	Lone E, Hillwood Common Road, Four Oaks, Sutton Coldfield	Sections A - D
B Company	Company HQ	The White House, 183 Whitehouse Common Road, Sutton Coldfield	
B Company	No. 5 Platoon	Moor Hall, Sutton Coldfield	
B Company	No. 6 Platoon	Moor Hall Golf Club, Sutton Coldfield	
B Company	No. 7 Platoon	Mayfield, Lichfield Road, Four Oaks	
B Company	No. 8 Platoon		

Company	Platoon	Location	Notes
B Company	Wishaw Platoon	White Lion Pub in Hill Village Road, Wishaw	
C Company	Company HQ	The Priory, Maney, 62 Birmingham Road, Sutton Coldfield	1st May 44 - 45 Mobility Company
C Company	No. 9 Platoon	Sutton Coldfield Football Ground, Coles Lane, Sutton Coldfield	
C Company	No. 10 Platoon	Lind Vista Garage, Sutton Coldfield	
C Company	No. 11 Platoon	Colbourne Antiques, The Priory, Maney, 62 Birmingham Road, Sutton Coldfield	
C Company	No. 12 Platoon	Reddicap House, Reddicap Hill, Sutton Coldfield	
D Company	Company HQ	Sutton Police Station, 9-11 Station Street, Sutton Coldfield	
D Company	No. 13 Platoon	Five factory units in Sutton town centre	
D Company	No. 14 Platoon		
D Company	No. 15 Platoon	Mounted Platoon, Riding School, Town Gate	Included woman's Axillary Section
D Company	Electricity Department Section	Electricity Department, corner of Riland Road and Coleshill Road	
D Company	South Staffs Water Section	South Staffs Water Building, Sutton	

		Coldfield	
D Company	British Legion Section	British Legion, 16 Rectory Road, Sutton Coldfield	
D Company	Boldmere Garage Section	Boldmere Garage, Boldmere, Sutton Coldfield	
D Company	Southaltons Section	Southaltons Factory	
D Company	Railway Section	Railway Station, Sutton Coldfield	
D Company	Signals Platoon	The Royal Hotel, 25 Highstreet, Sutton Coldfield.	
D Company	Regimental Police Section	The Royal Hotel, 25 Highstreet, Sutton Coldfield.	
D Company	BHQ Guard Platoon	The Royal Hotel, 25 Highstreet, Sutton Coldfield.	
Wilnecote Detachment	Detachment HQ	Action Station: Morris and Shaw Ltd Old quarry, Glascote Lane, Wilnecote Office: Wilnecote Police Station	7 village strong points
E Company	Company HQ	E Company HQ – Kingsbury Hall Kingsbury / Personnel Office, Doultons Works, Wilnecote	

		Office: Wilnecote Police Station (40) Action Station Morris and Shaw Ltd	
E Company	No. 1 Wilnecote Platoon - A Patrol	1 Platoon E Company – Congregational Chapel, Glascote Lane, Wilnecote Wilnecote Police Station (40)	
E Company	No. 1 Wilnecote Platoon - B Patrol		
E Company	No. 1 Wilnecote Platoon - C Patrol		
E Company	No. 1 Wilnecote Platoon - D (HQ) Patrol		
E Company	No. 2 Dosthill Platoon	Old Sunday School, Church Lane, Dosthill	
E Company	No. 3 Kingsbury Platoon	Kingsbury Hall, Near Tamworth Office: Hathernware, Cliff Action Station: Oakleigh, Kingsbury	
E Company	No. 4 Hurley Platoon	Police House, Wood End, Near Atherstone (40) Tib Hall Hurley	
E Company	No. 5 Platoon		
E Company	No. 6 Platoon	Congregational Chapel	

F Company	Company HQ	Police Station, Glascote Office Tamworth Colliery Company Action Station Alvecote Grange, Nr Tamworth	
F Company	No. 1 Glascote Platoon	The Dolphin Pub, Glascote Glascote Police Station (40)	
F Company	No. 2 Amington and Alvecote Platoon	Amington Working Men's Club Alvecote Post Office	
F Company	No. 3 Shuttington Platoon	Shuttington ARP Post, Manor Farm, Shuttington	
F Company	No. 4 Glascte and Amington Colliery Platoon	G&A Colliery	
F Company	No. 5 Platoon	Hurley	
F Company	No. 6 Platoon	Queen's Head, Newton Regis	
F Company	No. 7 Platoon		
F Company	No. 8 Platoon		
G Company Coleshill Company	Company HQ	Old Police Station 47 High Street, Coleshill 113 High Street Alternate HQ	7 village strong points
G Company Coleshill Company	No. 1 Platoon		
G Company Coleshill	No. 2 Platoon		

Company			
G Company Coleshill Company	No. 3 Platoon		
G Company Coleshill Company	No. 4 Platoon		
G Company Coleshill Company	No. 5 Platoon		
G Company Coleshill Company	No. 6 Platoon		
G Company Coleshill Company	No.7 Platoon		
M Company	Company HQ	Holly Cottage, Sutton Coldfield	Static unit from 1943
43 Mobile Company	Company HQ	Moorlands Cottage, Snowhill Road. Streetly, Sutton Coldfield	3 Platoons and Tactical HQ -24 May 1942 order of battle
44th Mobile Company	Company HQ	Newlyn, The Driffold, Sutton Coldfield	3 Platoons and Tactical HQ -24 May 1942 ORBAT
45th Mobile Company	Company HQ	Holly Cottage, 58 Birmingham Road Sutton Coldfield	3 Platoons and Tactical HQ -24 May 1942 ORBAT
BA Company	Response Unit	Whitacre Waterworks,	

		Shustoke	
HG Company	Response Unit	Elmdon Airdrome - 1 x Platoon	
RW Company	Response Unit	Castle Bromwich and Coleshill RW Companies (Pl Size as part of G Coy)	

Annex C - OKW Directive No.16
On preparations for a landing operation against England

16th July 1940

Directive No. 16 On preparations for a landing operation against England

Since England, in spite of her hopeless military situation, shows no signs of being ready to come to an understanding, I have decided to prepare a landing operation against England and, if necessary, to carry it out.

The aim of this operation will be to eliminate the English homeland as a base for the prosecution of the war against Germany and, if necessary, to occupy it completely.

I therefore order as follows:

1. The landing will be in the form of a surprise crossing on a wide front from about Ramsgate to the area west of the Isle of Wight. Units of the Air Force will act as artillery, and units of the Navy as engineers. The possible advantages of limited operations before the general crossing (e.g. the occupation of the Isle of Wight or of the county of Cornwall) are to be considered from the point of view of each branch of the Armed Forces and the results reported to me. I reserve the decision to myself. Preparations for the entire operation must be completed by the middle of August.

2. These preparations must also create such conditions as will make a landing in England possible:

a. The English Air Force must be so reduced morally and physically that it is unable to deliver any significant attack against the German crossing.
b. Mine-free channels must be cleared.
c. The Straits of Dover must be closely sealed off with minefields on both flanks; also, the Western entrance to the Channel approximately on the line *Alderney-Poitland*.
d. Strong forces of coastal artillery must command and protect the forward coastal area.
e. It is desirable that the English Navy be tied down shortly before the crossing, both in the North Sea and in the Mediterranean (by the Italians)1. For this purpose, we must attempt even now to damage English home-based naval forces by air and torpedo attack as far as possible.

3. Command organisation and preparations. Under my overriding command and according to my general instructions, the Commanders-in-Chief will command the branches of the Armed Forces for which they are responsible. From 1st August the operations staffs of Commander-in-Chief Army, Commander-in-Chief Navy, and Commander-in-Chief Air Force are to be located at a distance of not more than 50 kilometres from my Headquarters (*Ziegenberg*). It seems to me useful that the inner operations staffs of Commander-in-Chief Army and Commander-in-Chief Navy should be placed together at Giessen. Commander-in-Chief Army will detail one Army Group to carry out the invasion. The invasion will bear the cover name *'Seelöwe'*. In the preparation and execution of this operation the following tasks are allotted to each Service:

a. Army: The Army will draw up the operational and crossing plans for all formations of the first wave of the invasion. The anti-aircraft artillery which is to cross with the first wave will remain subordinate to the Army (to individual crossing units) until it is possible to allocate its responsibilities between the support and protection of troops on the ground, the protection of disembarkation points, and the protection of the airfields which are to be occupied. The Army will, moreover, lay down the methods by which the invasion is to be carried out and the individual forces to be employed, and will determine points of embarkation and disembarkation in conjunction with the Navy.

b. Navy: The Navy will procure the means for invasion and will take them, in accordance with the wishes of the Army, but with due regard to navigational considerations, to the various embarkation points. Use will be made, as far as possible, of the shipping of defeated enemy countries. The Navy will furnish each embarkation point with the staff necessary to give nautical advice, with escort vessels and guards. In conjunction with air forces assigned for protection, it will defend the crossing of the Channel on both flanks. Further orders will lay down the chain of command during the crossing. It is also the task of the Navy to co-ordinate the setting up of coastal artillery - i.e. all artillery, both naval and military, intended to engage targets at sea-and generally to direct its fire. The largest possible number of extra-heavy guns will be brought into position as soon as possible in order to cover the crossing and to shield the flanks against enemy action at sea. For this purpose, railway guns will also be used (reinforced by all available captured weapons) and will be sited on railway turntables. Those batteries intended only to deal with targets on the English mainland (K5 and K12) will not be included. Apart from this the existing extra-heavy platform-gun batteries are to be enclosed in concrete opposite the Straits of Dover in such a manner that they can withstand the heaviest air attacks and will permanently, in all conditions, command the

Straits of Dover within the limits of their range. The technical work will be the responsibility of the Organization Todt.

    c. The task of the Air Force will be: To prevent interference by the enemy Air Force. To destroy coastal fortresses which might operate against our disembarkation points, to break the first resistance of enemy land forces, and to disperse reserves on their way to the front. In carrying out this task the closest liaison is necessary between individual Air Force units and the Army invasion forces. Also, to destroy important transport highways by which enemy reserves might be brought up, and to attack approaching enemy naval forces as far as possible from our disembarkation points. I request that suggestions be made to me regarding the employment of parachute and airborne troops. In this connection it should be considered, in conjunction with the Army, whether it would be useful at the beginning to hold parachute and airborne troops in readiness as a reserve, to be thrown in quickly in case of need.

4. Preparations to ensure the necessary communications between France and the English mainland will be handled by the Chief, Armed Forces Signals. The use of the remaining eighty kilometres of the East Prussia cable is to be examined in co-operation with the Navy.

5. I request Commanders-in-Chief to submit to me as soon as possible

    a. The plans of the Navy and Air Force to establish the necessary conditions for crossing the Channel (see paragraph 2).
    b. Details of the building of coastal batteries (Navy).
    c. A general survey of the shipping required and the methods by which it is proposed to prepare and procure it. Should civil authorities be involved? (Navy).

- d. The organisation of Air Defence in the assembly areas for invasion troops and ships (Air Force).
- e. The crossing and operation plan of the Army, the composition and equipment of the first wave of invasion.
- f. The organisation and plans of the Navy and Air Force for the execution of the actual crossing, for its protection, and for the support of the landing.
- g. Proposals for the use of parachute and airborne troops and also for the organisation and command of antiaircraft artillery as soon as sufficient English territory has been captured.
- h. Proposal for the location of Naval and Air Headquarters.
- i. Views of the Navy and Air Force whether limited operations are regarded as useful before a general landing and, if so, of what kind.
- j. Proposal from Army and Navy regarding command during the crossing.

[signed] ADOLF HITLER

Annex D – Raids on Sutton Coldfield

HE – High Explosive

ICD – Incendiary

UKN – Unknown Munition

K – Killed in Raid

I – Injured in Raid

ARP Raid Number	Scale of Raid	Date	HE	ICD	UKN	K	I
1	Major	8/9 Aug 1940	6		3		
2	Major	13/14 Aug 1940	21		29	1	2
3	Major	15/16 Aug 1940		500	23		
Not Listed by ARP	Minor	16/17 Aug 1940	23				
4	Major	17/18 Aug 1940	12	600			
5	Major	18/19 Aug 1940			30		
6	Major	19/20 Aug 1940	3		17		
7	Major	23/24 Aug 1940	23	300	7		
8	Major	24/25 Aug 1940	23			1	1
9	Major	25/26 Aug 1940	2	Large Number			
10	Major	26/27 Aug 1940	25	80			
Not Listed by ARP	Minor	28 Aug 1940	6				
11	Major	2/3 Sep 1940	9				

12	Major	12 Sep 1940	4				
13	Major	15/16 Sep 1940	10				
14	Major	16/17 Sep 1940	21				
Not Listed by ARP	Minor	17 Oct 1940	1				
Not Listed by ARP	Minor	25 Oct 1940	1				
15	Major	28 Oct 1940	6	200			1
16	Major	29/30 Oct 1940		100	11		
Not Listed by ARP	Minor	1 Nov 1940	2				
17	Major	2 Nov 1940	2	1			
18	Major	6 Nov 1940	11	100			
19	Major	8 Nov 1940	2				
Not Listed by ARP	Minor	9 Nov 1940	3	1			
20	Major	19 Nov 1940	8				
Not Listed by ARP	Minor	20 Nov 1940	1	100			
Not Listed by ARP	Minor	21 Nov 1940	9				
21	Major	22/23 Nov 1940	4		2		
22	Major	3 Dec 40		1	17		
23	Major	21/22 Dec 1940	1	200			
24	Major	12 Mar 41	8	900			2
25	Major	09/10 Apr 1940		100			

26	Major	10/11 Apr 1941	31	250			
27	Major	17 May 41	11	100	6		
28	Major	5 Jun 41	3	100	10	4	6
29	Major	9 Jul 41	9				1
30	Major	25 Jul 42	2				
Not Listed by ARP	Minor	28 Jul 42				1	4
31	Major	30 Jul 42	27	240		1	11

Printed in Great Britain
by Amazon